THE FIRST TIME
INVESTOR

THE FIRST TIME INVESTOR

How to Start Safe, Invest Smart, and Sleep Well

Larry Chambers

Second Edition

McGraw-Hill

New York   San Francisco   Washington, D.C.   Auckland   Bogotá
Caracas   Lisbon   London   Madrid   Mexico City   Milan
Montreal   New Delhi   San Juan   Singapore
Sydney   Tokyo   Toronto

Library of Congress Cataloging-in-Publication Data

Chambers, Larry.
   The first time investor : how to start safe, invest smart & sleep well / by
Larry Chambers.—2nd ed.
    p. cm.
   Includes bibliographical references.
   ISBN 0-07-013070-1
   1. Investments.   2. Finance, Personal.   I. Title.
HG4521.C4513   1998
332.67'8—dc21   98-30381
                              CIP

McGraw-Hill

A Division of The McGraw·Hill Companies

4 5 6 7 8 9 0 DOC/DOC   0 3 2 1 0

ISBN 0-07-013070-1

The sponsoring editor for this book was Kelli Christiansen, the editing supervisor was Donna Muscatello, and the production supervisor was Suzanne W. B.
Rapcavage. It was set in Times by Hendrickson Creative Communications.

Printed and bound by R. R. Donnelley & Sons Company.

This publication is designed to provide accurate and authoritative information in
regard to the subject matter covered. It is sold with the understanding that neither
the author nor the publisher is engaged in rendering legal, accounting, or other professional service. If legal advice or other expert assistance is required, the services of a competent professional person should be sought.

          —From a Declaration of Principles jointly adopted by a Committee
              of the American Bar Association and a Committee of Publishers.

McGraw-Hill books are available at special quantity discounts to use as premiums and sales promotions, or for use in corporate training programs. For more
information, please write to the Director of Special Sales, McGraw-Hill,
Professional Publishing, Two Penn Plaza, New York, NY 10121-2298. Or contact your local bookstore.

Contents

16.98

Introduction

*The problem with learning from experience
is that we get the test before the lesson.*

Alfred E. Neuman

WHY DID YOU PICK UP THIS BOOK ANYWAY? Did the words
strike a chord when you read the title? Are you looking for
information that will make you a better investor, or help get
you started? Do you want to hear about ways to save enough
to send your kids to college, or build that dream cabin in the
mountains, or get that advanced degree you keep saying you're going to get
someday? Do you want to have extra money socked away for your kid's
wedding, or for your own comfortable retirement? Do you want to be in
charge of your own financial future? After all, if you don't have a good plan
for your future, you may not like what's waiting for you when you get there.

What if—in a period of 3 months, 6 months, or 1 year—you could see
a marked growth in your invested money? This book is designed to not only
encourage you but also give you a strategic way of organizing your own
resources for taking confident steps on the path to a secure financial future.
That is the promise of this book—it will give you a systematic investing
plan based on academic research, to get you started investing the right way—
safely and smartly.

I have spent 25 years taking intentional actions to become financially
independent. I sought out the best of the best. I spent 15 years working for
some of Wall Street's most prestigious stock brokerage firms. Today I help
some of the top investment advisors and money managers organize, write,
and publish their knowledge and expertise in articles and books. This gives
me access to a fountainhead of current knowledge about what works in

investing and what doesn't. I'm now on track to having over a million dollars in my own retirement plan—and I'm just a regular guy.

What kind of investor are you? Experienced? A do-it-yourselfer? Do you simply seek validation of your own investment ideas? Or do you prefer to delegate responsibility to someone with more experience and investment skills? You can and should have it your way when investing. You simply need to match your investment preference with a process that will give you the confidence to get started—or keep you going. We're going to take investing apart—dissecting, explaining, and analyzing it—so you won't be dependent on luck or hype.

At first glance, this doesn't look like a book for the first time investor. Being an investor today is much more difficult than it was just 10 years ago. The size and complexities of today's financial marketplace equal confusion. The Dow Jones industrial average has doubled in the past 2 1/2 years, and 10,000 on the Dow seems less of a fantasy everyday. Money keeps flooding into the market, and the New York Stock Exchange daily trading volume is 4 times that of 1990. The economy is zipping along, inflation has all but disappeared, and unemployment rates have dropped to a postwar lows. There are infinitely more choices and investments to sort through and be concerned about. Today, there are more mutual fund choices than stocks listed on the New Your Stock Exchange, over 1500 of which were created in just the past 3 years.

Technology has given ordinary people complex tools, without good advice on how to use them. Never have so many people in the United States experienced such control over their financial futures, yet felt such a need for help. Often the most conservative advice nestles right up against market predictions and stock touting, without giving investors a way of evaluating their choices. To try to apply lessons learned from mistakes made along the way is a hard and discouraging road. The problem is that most people become investors without having the wisdom of experience. They get the tests without first getting the lessons.

Right now, more than ever, you've got to know what you're doing. You don't get a second chance at building a retirement fund. And you can't depend on messages the media experts deliver. The financial media tell their audience, "Just about anyone can retire rich with shrewd stock picking and up-to-the-minute information. Just read this magazine, or watch my show." But you can't believe it just because it's in print or on television. For example, in August 1997, *Money* magazine proclaimed to its 1.9 million readers, "Don't Just Sit There . . . Sell Stock Now!" and went on to claim that the magazine never advocated market timing. I'm sure the editors patted themselves on the back when the market suffered its biggest one-day percentage decline in a decade only 2 months after the article was publishcd. But what happened next? The market gained much of that loss back in the following trading session. The Dow moved into the 9,000 territory, nearly 10 percent above the 8,200 level when the magazine told its reders to sell. Ouch!

SmartMoney, one of the hottest new magazines to come along in years, touts long-term growth investing yet pumps out new stock picks every month. And remember the Beardstown Ladies? Those homespun grandmother investors had so much publicized success that they created a mini-industry. What they didn't tell us was that the club counted dues as part of total return, adding these to stock dividends and apppreciation. Their adjusted 10-year declared annual return of 23.4 percent came in *far* below at 9.1 percent— and even that doesn't reflect the ladies' execution costs.

Then there is the on-line crowd, and some of the advice is good: *Motley Fool, Armchair Millionaire, Bloomberg Personal Finance,* and *Kiplinger's Personal Finance.* The *Motley Fool* on-line site generates 20 million impressions each month. *Microsoft Investors* boasts 110 million impressions for its Web site. The not-so-subtle message often is, "Fire your broker and listen to us." But who is watching over these guys? If brokers told their clients what journalists so boldly tell their readers, the Securities and Exchange Commission would pull their licenses—but financial journalists are not subject to the same licensing or registration. They are not held accountable and are generally narrowly focused on short-term performance. They loosely hand out investment advice that professional advisors and brokers must be registered to give. Remember this truth: The media are not held accountable for advice given to the public.

Back in 1995, on-line journalist James Cramer, regularly seen on ABC's *Good Morning America* and CNBC, wrote a *SmartMoney* column recommending four stocks. There was only one problem—he did not disclose that he had a large stake in those stocks. Luckily for him, the Securities and Exchange Commission cleared him of any wrongdoing because he didn't sell his shares after the prices jumped. Today Cramer no longer recommends stocks. Smart guy. But this opens up some tough questions. How do you know when someone has a hidden agenda, is overstating his or her stock-picking prowess, or is selling you down the under-performance road? What does that person stand to gain? You can't know. Good and bad advisors all go by the same title.

This book was written for the first time investor who wants to approach investing with eyes fully open. I'll show you how to think and take action as a seasoned investor would. I'll help you organize, operate, and understand the risks of investing, and I'll provide you with a long-term plan based on modern portfolio management—a plan you can effectively implement and measure for yourself.

Are you skeptical? That's okay. In fact, I invite you to be. I don't sell securities for any firms, and I'm not going to be writing for *Money* magazine after the editor reads this introduction. Since writing the first version of *First Time Investor,* my own personal quest has led me away from Wall Street and to the top academics in the field of financial economics, whose wisdom is backed by a mountain of research and proof, including breakthrough academic theories that won three Nobel Prizes in economics in 1990. This is unbiased research, not aimed at backing up sales hype. My goal is to communicate this knowledge in an easily understandable format so that as many people as possible can apply it. When you understand how stock markets work, you can put the odds on your side and you are more likely to take that plunge into investing.

Hey, don't worry, you can still buy that hot stock that you just can't pass up, or go after those 100 percent returns promised in stock option trading. Once you have a solid investment strategy in place and understand the risks, you can still make well-considered speculative investments. The difference is, you will know how to weigh the risks you are taking.

First Time Investor includes model portfolios demonstrating how ordinary *savers* can become extraordinary *investors,* simply by following logical steps. It also presents revealing and useful dialogue with some of the nation's top financial advisors and economists. The reader will learn how the best and the brightest do it and come out ahead. See Fig. I–1.

YOU WILL LEARN

- What actions to take to get started investing *today.*
- How the economy works and why *this* is the best time to begin.
- How to expand your core saving strategy into an investment program.
- How to formulate a program that has the greatest probability of success.
- What the concept known as *modern investment theory* really means.
- How to build a low-cost passive investment program that outperforms all other strategies.
- How to use dissimilar asset classes to lower your risk and increase your returns.
- How to begin to globally diversify.
- How to manage your own retirement fund.

FIGURE I–1 Operating States of Investing

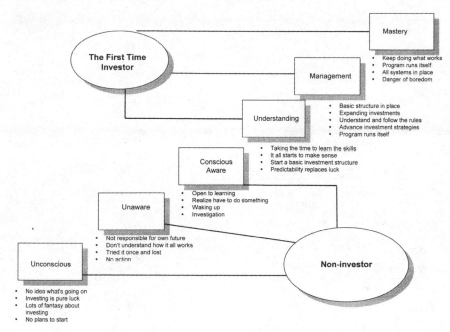

- How to defer taxes.
- How to finance your kids' education.
- And how to put all this together in one comprehensive, worry-free plan.

Yes, this book was written for *you*. I've learned how the game is best played. I know what's reasonable and what can be expected. I want to help you get started, just as I would help a relative or friend. I will tell you everything that's worked for me, plus the things that haven't.

Let's get started.

Acknowledgments

My staff, Karen Johnson, Charlene Koonce Broudy, and Mayo Morley.

John J. Bowen, Jr., at Reinhardt Werba Bowen Advisory Services for his generosity in making this book happen, along with Ben Bingaman, Sandra Baseman, Rich Boone, and Marlene Bass for their help.

The staff at Lockwood Finanical Group: Len Reinhart, Jim Seuffert, and Kate Monaghan.

Michael Lane, president, Advisor Resources of Aegon Financial Services Group Inc. Jeff Saccacio, managing partner with PriceWaterhouseCoopers LLP. *Armchair Millionaire* Web site's Lewis Schiff and Doug Gerlach.

I would also like to thank three leading members of the financial economic community—Harry Markowitz, Merton Miller, and William Sharpe—whose research was rewarded with the Nobel Prize in Economics, and which provides the foundation for the investment section of this book. In addition, I would like to thank Eugene Fama, Ken French, and Meir Statman, for their academic research in applying these principles.

No one deserves more credit for the application of this research than the principals at Dimensional Fund Advisors. David Booth and Rex Sinquefield. They were early pioneers in the development and application of investment strategies for the institutional investor.

I would like to also thank Russ Prince, Kenneth Boone, John Burroughs, John Byrd, Max DeZemplen, Michael Dixon, Lucinda Fairfield, Gerald Gasber, Dan Goldie, Gary Pia, Charles Putney, and Michael Ritchie.

I'm deeply grateful to Evan Simonoff, editor-in-chief at *Financial Planning* magazine, Marcia Vickers at *On Wall Street,* and Dan Jamieson and Cheryl Cooper at *Registered Representative,* and Jeff Rattiner and Andrew Popper at *Financial Advisory Practice* magazine.

A special thanks to Bob Clark, editor in chief *Dow Jones Investment Advisor.*

I would like to also acknowledge The International Association for Financial Planning and Bill Mullen, Drew Washburn and James Suellentrop at the Institute for Investment Management Consultants, for their assistance.

Also, my editors at McGraw-Hill, Jeff Krames, Kelli Christiansen, and Stephen Isaacs.

And a special note of thanks to the staff at the Ojai Post Office, Mary Ellen, Reba Seba, Denise Carroll, and Leslie Haugan.

THE FIRST TIME INVESTOR

KNOW YOUR OUTCOME, TAKE ACTION

1

THE TIME TO START IS NOW

Y OU SHOULDN'T WAIT TO HEAR SILVER TRUMPETS BLOW before you decide to get started. Investing shouldn't wait for that large windfall, winning the lotto, or an inheritance from Aunt Louise. Getting started and making a profit don't require luck, an advanced degree, or special intelligence. It's more a matter of "behavior" than of making the right investment choices.[1]

What are some of those correct investor behaviors?

1. Start saving money now.
2. Turn your debt into equity.
3. Evaluate future needs.
4. Have a strategy.
5. Maintain investing focus and discipline.
6. Seek professional help when appropriate.
7. Teach children about investing.

Let's examine what these behaviors look like:

---

[1] Dalbar, Inc., studied 4200 investors and ascertained that the profits investors made were 8 times more dependent on behavior than on investment choices.

BEHAVIOR 1: BUILD A CORE "SAVINGS" PROGRAM

The first step to creating a sound financial future is to develop a positive savings *mentality*. This might require changing your internal "conversation" about money. Many of us feel we don't have enough money to set aside a portion of it for savings. We complain that it's too late to begin, or we postpone getting started until some future event comes to pass. And if we do have some savings, we don't want to risk it by investing.

Begin to identify good personal motivators for changing your own internal conversation, and practice statements that reflect a positive, empowered attitude.

Overcome the hurdle of getting started. Start small, but be consistent. Put money into a savings vehicle where you virtually *can't* spend it. You'll be encouraged by how quickly your weekly or monthly contributions add up. Challenge yourself to increase the amount frequently. From time to time, add a lump sum to your savings as if you were paying yourself a bonus or a reward.

Saving that is automatic is a far more successful method than just hoping to have some money left over at the end of every month. Set up a plan with your bank or employer for an amount to be deducted from your account monthly and sent to your savings account automatically. Consider this as paying yourself first. You'll soon forget that it's even being deducted. Would giving up 5 percent of your monthly income really cramp your life-style? Whether you want to save for higher education for a child, a new home, or a comfortable retirement, *paying yourself first* is a prudent layaway plan for your future.

Utilize liquid or short-term interest or dividend-producing savings vehicles, such as savings accounts, money market funds, and certificates of deposit (CDs). Even after you've begun investing, retain a core savings vehicle for emergency funds.

A core savings vehicle will be the base upon which you build overall financial security. The point is to first have a safe place to start saving, then to build outward. Think of this core vehicle as the mothership as you explore the infinite space of investing. It's your energy source.

Saving is not the same as investing. A *saver* is someone who saves money regularly but who does *not* assume the risks of ownership. An *investor* is someone who is rewarded for assuming the risks of ownership and who has an expectation of return through appreciation in the capital value of the securities owned. I see again and again people using investment products with a saving mentality who end up disappointed when returns aren't regular or don't match advertised performance, and savers who end up disappointed because they never get ahead. The secret is to build your resources in a core saving vehicle and then to move into investing from this base.

BEHAVIOR 2: TURN CONSUMER DEBT INTO EQUITY

Use the same muscles you've been using for years. You have regularly made payments on a car, or a mortgage or rent, or credit cards, or all these and still survived. As you pay off consumer items, take the previous outgoing monthly amount and send that same amount to a mutual fund company or an investment fund. We've all built up this muscle; don't lose it.

If you still buy consumer goods on credit and are reading this book, you are a fantasy investor. Let's change that together now. Debt is the reverse of savings and investing, and it acts as a drag on future income. Debt breeds urgency which leads to unwise decision making and undermines investment strategy. It's why even smart people fall prey to scams. Too much debt creates fear. A decision made from fear is often a wrong decision.

Other than a home mortgage if you have consumer debt, you should not begin investing. First eliminate the debt. Why? Because you are paying off an interest rate that is difficult to match by conventional investing.

A Formula for Success

You need to focus like a laser beam to bust through your debt problems. If all you're doing is making minimum monthly payments on every debt you have, you will never make a dent in them. Instead, get absolutely focused on destroying your debt. Target 10 percent of your income to reduce debt. Almost anybody who does this can be totally debt-free within 7 years.

It's an easy formula: just prioritize your monthly debts based on how long it would take to pay them off only paying the minimum payment due each month. Beginning with the debt with the shortest payoff time, add some nominal amount, such as $200, to each monthly payment. Don't add a little bit to each of your debts—dump it all on just this one and continue paying only the minimum on the balance of your debts. You'll be amazed at how fast that first debt will disappear. Now, take the total monthly amount you paid to the first debt and add it to the monthly payment of the debt with the next shortest payoff time. When that one is paid off, apply the new total to the next debt, and son on. Continue with each debt until you're free and clear. Now take that cumulative sum of monthly payments and build a savings account with no interruption of your lifestyle!

Okay, you say, that's a great plan but it's all you can do right now just to make the minimum monthly payment on your debts. Where are you going to come up with any extra money to add to a payment? This is where your determination and commitment come into play. First, look at your daily spending patterns. Ever notice that no matter how much cash you start with, it disappears at the same rate? Give yourself an allowance and then, stick to it! Do some obvious things like cut down or eliminate buying from vending machines and carry snack items with you, buy a regular coffee rather than the more expensive cappucino, and buy bulk groceries and plan meals ahead. Another sure-fire way to regularly generate a healthy lump sum by the end of the month is to dump any coin change you receive into a jar or baggie *throughout* every day. If you don't raid that "piggy bank", you'll be surprised at your month's total.

Next do some *plastic surgery*—cut up the credit cards! If you feel you really need to, keep only one credit card, preferably American Express or a similar credit plan that you have to pay off every month. Don't inadvertently accumulate more debt!

Okay then, the next step from here is investing.

BEHAVIOR 3: EVALUATE FUTURE FINANCIAL NEEDS

Why are you saving anyway? Do you have a clear vision of what you want to achieve and how much money you will need to achieve it, or are you shooting in the dark? Charles Greenwald, past chairman of the board for General Motors, estimated that every hour of planning returns three hours of execution.

What are your chances of accumulating a million dollars? This is the conceptual point of no return where most people feel so overwhelmed or defeated that they lose the motivation to even begin. But if you saw that *you* could realistically have that much accumulated at a certain future date— and the math when double-checked actually added up—wouldn't you be highly motivated to begin? I was.

This is where the difference between saving and investing begins to make sense. You can *invest* your savings at a return rate that will accelerate accumulation and put your financial goal within your reach—without risking your base savings. The methodologies in this book will show you how.

Once you see that you can reach your goal, you can start on that road by comparing what you *have* now with what you *need* to accumulate to achieve that goal. The difference is called a *shortfall*. A shortfall is the amount of money needed to fill the chasm between the reality and the fantasy of reaching your goal. Then you can begin to make your dream a reality. What better motivation is there in life than that?

BEHAVIOR 4: ESTABLISH A CORE INVESTMENT STRATEGY

When I first signed up for algebra, it made no sense at all to me, and there seemed to be no real purpose to it. The process called algebra was like reaching into the unknown and coming up with something equally unknown. Everyday there seemed to be a new unfathomable formula that I had to accept on faith, and if I missed one day of class, I was really lost.

The problem is most investment strategies are full of $2 words that most people don't understand, as unfathomable as an algebraic equation to the uninitiated. Investment people have their own complete language, as do lawyers, doctors, and other specialists. I'm going to simplify investment language into concepts that make sense and that you can apply.

On Strategy: Three Main Points

1.   Find a simple strategy that builds on what you already know.
2.   Find a strategy that organizes your resources—money and time—in order to consistently achieve a specific result. A good approach that builds confidence is to start small and watch to see if a certain result is repeated. The brain craves certainty and is always trying to distill the predictable from the uncertain.
3.   If you can benefit from reading a book that took somebody 10 years to research and write, then you should do that.

In 1952, Professor Harry Markowitz started to build an investment strategy that took more than 30 years to develop and be recognized as *modern portfolio theory*; he won the Nobel Prize for his work in 1990. You can benefit from the fruits of that man's focused labor. All you need to do is to apply the proven and celebrated strategy he presented to the world. Use the same ingredients—index funds and asset class mutual funds—and follow his tested recipe.

The next chapter describes the best ingredients and the order and sequence in which they should be utilized. As in baking, don't put the yeast in after you've already got the bread in the oven.

The first action in the sequence is to establish a place for your money that you feel confident about and where your money will grow without your having to constantly check up on it. When you watch your money grow, your confidence grows with it. Start by making small investments—$100 or $200 or $1000—and watching the result. An index mutual fund or a favorite growth mutual fund is your best bet at this point. These reduce investment risk through diversification and offer professional money management.

According to Lipper Analytical, 91 percent of managed mutual funds underperformed the average performance of the Standard & Poor's (S&P) 500 index over the past 5 years.[2]

The point is not to get only a 1-percent higher rate than in your savings account or to find the mutual fund with the highest return. The idea is to start to use an investment vehicle that you understand and that builds your confidence. You can expand that vehicle in stages. If you can't sleep at night, back off.

Get started *now* in order to give your investment program as much *time* as you possibly can. Every year that you put off investing, accomplishment of future financial goals becomes more difficult. For every year you wait, you need to increase both your monthly investing amount and the risk you take to achieve the same result. See Table 1–1.

Go step by step, noting all the details. When you establish systems that work, a high degree of trust will accrue. Constantly make improvements.

BEHAVIOR 5: DEVELOP YOUR INVESTMENT FOCUS AND DISCIPLINE

Put time into developing your own personalized *investment policy statement*. This document should reflect your return objectives and constraints, such as time horizon, liquidity needs, and available funds. This will serve as the blueprint to measure the effectiveness of your investments.

Eliminate investment *noise*. Look past all the hype and maintain realistic expectations. Upgrade your knowledge about investing. Education is the

TABLE 1–1   How to Have a Million

Amount You Have to Invest Per Month

Starting Age	8% return	10% return	15% return
25	$310	$180	$45
30	$470	$300	$90
35	$710	$490	$180
40	$1,100	$810	$370
45	$1,760	$1,390	$760
50	$2,960	$2,500	$1,640
55	$5,550	$5,000	$3,850
60	$13,700	$13,050	$11,600

[2] *Dalbar Mutual Fund Market News,* May 11, 1998, p. 10.

key to simplifying all the investment advice and products available and knowing how to apply proven principles to your own situation. Don't let someone tell you that he or she can achieve a 100 percent return for you without offering proof—lots of proof.

Set investment boundaries. If something doesn't fit your plan, don't do it. Your personal investment policy statement can be a gauge to keep you from making emotional decisions about your investments that are inappropriate.

BEHAVIOR 6: FIND A FINANCIAL COACH

Most people need some help with their investment decisions. Most of us are busy making money to invest and don't have the time or expertise to research every vehicle. Even top athletes have a coach. True, you can get started investing on your own, but you will reach a point where a knowledgeable financial coach is your best guide to achieving the next level. A financial coach can be a tax or financial planner, an investment consultant, a broker, or an investment adviser.

Collaborate with your business associates or friends to create an informal investment advisory board. By having influential people on your advisory board, you will gain insight into areas of investing that you may not otherwise become aware of.

Look for ways of investing that are fun. Join an investment club or visit an Internet site. The more good, clean fun you have in your life, the more productive you'll be and the better you'll become at time management.

BEHAVIOR 7: TEACH YOUR FAMILY ABOUT INVESTING

Providing for family is at the heart of everyone's financial concerns. But who said it was up to you alone? Don't operate in a vacuum, leaving those you care about in the dark. There is no better way to provide for the future of your loved ones than to teach them to help themselves. Not only does this empower them as participants, but also it gives them a better appreciation of your efforts. Once you know your savings and investment strategy, and you can do it again and again, you are ready to teach it to your family.

2

THE STOCK MARKET— NOTHING IS BEING HIDDEN FROM YOU!

M Y MOTHER TOLD ME, "DON'T BELIEVE EVERYTHING YOU HEAR." Well, when it comes to investing, that's good advice. Have you ever heard a little voice in the back of your head telling you to do something, such as buy a stock or invest with a certain advisor, only to be disappointed later? Well, the problem with conversations in your head is that you are talking to someone who agrees with you.

I don't believe everything I hear about investing. In fact, I disagree with just about every investment strategy—except one so simple you will be amazed that no one has ever told you about it before. The best way to illustrate this simple strategy is by telling you this true story.

Let me take you back to around the year 100, when the top scientist of the day, Claudius Ptolemy, mistakenly placed Earth at the center of the universe. Based on this belief, he developed a comprehensive system for tracing the motion of the planets and calculated the orbits for each. Soon he had an extensive 13-volume work that was the accepted authoritative source throughout Europe.

About 1,200 years later, Nicholas Copernicus questioned Ptolemy's work and developed his own theory, postulating that the sun is at the center of the universe and Earth is just one planet rotating around it.

No one wanted to believe the sun theory. Then another academic by the name of Galileo used his new invention, the telescope, to show Pope Paul V that Copernicus' theory was indeed accurate. The Pope didn't like what he saw and demanded that Galileo abandon the Copernican theory. Galileo stood his ground, and the Pope tossed him in prison. The moral of the story: Let someone else present new politically incorrect theories, even if they are factually correct.

No, that's not what I meant to point out! Here's the real rub. There are thousands of people who have built careers and businesses around current-ly accepted Wall Street investment theories. But the truth is, there is no proven basis for many of the most touted investment beliefs, including that value can be added to an investor's portfolio through individual stock selec-tion and market timing. Many of our most cherished investment beliefs are based on a collection of false assumptions. When the truth is finally sifted from the faulty paradigms, what you've got is a lot of "experts" in the invest-ment community with egg on their faces.

We cannot begin to accept any really new body of knowledge until the chains of our old false beliefs are broken. So let's start breaking those chains and getting investment-related facts straight. We have a wealth of data at our fingertips now on almost any investment out there; advances in tech-nology plus the availability of personal computers have made it easy to col-lect, manipulate, and study mounds of data. It's hard to believe now how little information there was to study 30 years ago. For instance, time series data were virtually unavailable on most asset categories; even the S&P 500 index time series was hard to find.

There is a long tradition of an unbiased academic community examining the workings of financial markets. In the early 1900s, a French mathemati-cian named Louis Bachelier set out to study market statistics, specifically the French future markets and French government bonds which traded at the Bourse. He examined a series of future market price changes in an attempt to determine the mathematical properties of these futures. He wanted to find out if there was a way to determine future market movements using past trends—in other words, whether the next event or next time period could be foretold. This is what any investor would love to be able to do. If an investor could accomplish this task, untold riches would await her or him.

What Bachelier found, however, was that there was no information, no statistical pattern, whatsoever uncovered by any of the time series infor-mation. There was, in fact, no way to mathematically or statistically predict the future movements of the market. He found that the historical sequence of price changes provides no usable information for predicting the next price change outcome.

Bachelier's study was lost to the world for some time and never looked at in depth again until after World War II. Eventually, however, that work set the stage for the next investigation by academics.

Forty years later, in the 1950s, universities and research institutions had new access to computers and set about using these tools to analyze data. Some of the first computer applications, in fact, focused on the returns of stock market indices and individual stocks and bonds. The academic community began analyzing these data with no particular theory or outcome in mind except the desire to learn from whatever might be discovered. It turned out that a number of academics working in different places—Holbrook Working[1] and Harry Roberts[2] at the University of Chicago, Neil Osborne[3] at IBM Research, and others—started noting similar events.

These academics independently found rates of returns and price changes to be serially uncorrelated. Again, that unanimous finding was that there was no predictability discernible from previous time series information in relationship to the next future outcome event. The sequence of rates of returns for weekly outcomes, several years of daily outcomes, or long series of monthly outcomes all appeared random. Prior price data uncovered no knowledge of what the following price might be. It was as if the numbers were taken from a table of random numbers; a computer generating a series of random and unrelated numbers would produce the same result. Independent studies, in other words, showed the inability to forecast stock market movements.

Then in 1959, Harry Roberts, professor emeritus of statistics at the University of Chicago Business School, reversed the method of study.[4] He instructed a computer to generate a series of 50 random numbers with a certain mean and standard deviation showing a normal distribution. The result was that famous bell-shaped curve we all love.

The resulting 50 numbers corresponded roughly to the typical weekly price change of the typical stock; that is, in fact, why Roberts chose those parameters. Now, remember, there's no predicted value for these numbers; by their very construction, this series of numbers is empty of content. Roberts

[1] Holbrook Working, "A Random Difference Series for Use in the Analysis of Time Series," *Journal of the American Statistical Association,* vol. 29, March 1934, pp. 11–24.

[2] Harry V. Roberts, "Stock Market Patterns and Financial Analysis: Methodological Suggestions," *Journal of Finance,* vol. 14, no. 1, March 1959, pp. 1–10.

[3] M. F. M. Osborne, "Brownian Motion in the Stock Market," *Operational Research,* vol. 7, March–April 1959, pp. 145–173.

[4] Roberts, "Stock Market Patterns and Financial Analysis," pp. 1–10.

then arbitrarily started off with a price of $40 and used random patterns to develop graphs that looked like stock returns.

Roberts next made up stock names, assigning a name to each chart, and took these to LaSalle Street in Chicago—at that time, the hotbed of technical analysis. He introduced himself and asked for advice from the leading technicians of the day as to how to play the stock market based on the random data assembled in these charts. Every one of the technicians had a very strong opinion about what Roberts ought to do with each of these securities.

The patterns that the chartists were observing and speculating about were generated by a computer and were simply the combination of a random series of numbers. There was, by construction, *no* actual pattern, *no* information. When random numbers are accumulated, patterns seem to emerge. The patterns in the mind of the viewer, not in the data.

Roberts wrote up this story in a famous article published in 1959 entitled "Stock Market Patterns and Financial Analysts."[5] The technical "experts" were not amused. Even today, as you flip through the financial channels on television, you will still see technical experts predicting what the market is going to do next based on the shape and pattern of a chart. They obviously still haven't gotten Roberts' message.

MODERN PORTFOLIO THEORY

Harry Markowitz is credited with the investment concept known as Modern Portfolio Theory.[6] This revolutionary concept involved a 180-degree change in viewpoint from what was considered *the* way to design and manage a stock and bond portfolio. Before Markowitz's work, investment portfolio design was centered on superior stock selection. Analysts would research the particular industries and companies. They'd take balance sheets and internal company analysis, combine these with earnings projections and future expectations, and come up with predictions for the future. Even now, most Wall Street stock brokerage firms and money managers continue to follow this approach, believing they can somehow discover the one nugget of value and opportunity which no one else has uncovered.

In attempting to find a truly valid investment approach, Markowitz and other financial academics in subsequent years hit upon the concept of considering risk first and returns second. To do this, Markowitz determined that the entire portfolio's risk or volatility should be the central issue.

[5] Ibid.

[6] Harry Markowitz, "Portfolio Selections," *The Journal of Finance,* March 1952, pp. 77–91.

It was Markowitz who created a concept of blending investments together in a manner that lowered the overall volatility of the total portfolio. Markowitz found that if two investments were blended together that went up and down in value at opposite times—even if these investments were both so-called risky or volatile investments—the overall portfolio's risk or volatility could be reduced.

The impact upon the total portfolio was a canceling out, or reduction, of the total portfolio's volatility. Again, this valuable information was ignored by the financial professionals of the time. These scientifically proven concepts were dismissed as the musings of out-of-touch academic eggheads who knew little about the "real world" of investing. It wasn't until 30 years later that Markowitz was awarded the Nobel Prize for his work.

Next, William Sharpe expanded Markowitz's work and designed a method to measure volatility. Sharpe called the concept the *capital asset pricing model* (CAPM). In his mathematical formulations, Sharpe established the market as having a beta measurement of 1.0. For example, if the beta of a particular investment were 1.10, then the expectation was that it would outperform the market by 10 percent when the markets went up and underperform by 10 percent when the markets went down.

Sharpe was able to evaluate a specific portfolio against the market itself, which allowed him to mathematically determine whether the portfolio was getting what the market was offering. To investment professionals, this meant they could, for the first time, determine an expectation for future performance based upon the beta measurement of the portfolio. The result of this knowledge is a greater certainty about unknown future expectations, at least in theory.

Like Markowitz's new thinking before him, Sharpe's concept was slow to be accepted, but eventually the CAPM approach became a centerpiece for portfolio design. His work and refinements over the next 20 years spawned a large variety of changes and improvements in the investment field, from valuable measurements of portfolio performance, to creation of index-based funds, to applications in the field of corporate finance. These concepts were major theoretical innovations in the study of market behavior and asset valuation.

Throughout the 1960s and early 1970s, the focus of most academic work was to determine how efficient markets are. In 1965, Professor Eugene Fama of the University of Chicago wrote his authoritative thesis[7] entitled "The

[7] Eugene F. Fama, "The Behavior of Stock Market Prices," *Journal of Business,* vol. 37, no. 1, January 1965, pp. 34–105.

Behavior of Stock Market Prices" (which the *Journal of Business* published in its entirety), coining the phrase *efficient markets* and explaining how markets appear to be able to fully absorb new information coming in, so that all prices of all securities reflect all known information. This theory is based on the simple truth that, due to the rapid assimilation by the market of any new information, expectations of future price changes are revised randomly and accurately reflected in the value of the stock.

For example, if a stock has an initial price of $10, the next change in price has an equal chance of being an increase or a decrease in value. If it goes up to, say, $11, the next change in price still has an equal chance of going up or down. The implication is that stock market prices follow a random walk and that price changes are independent of one another.

In Fama's empirical testing, he established that:

1. Past stock prices are of no value in predicting future prices.
2. Publicly available information cannot be used to earn excess returns consistently.
3. Mutual fund managers, as a group, cannot *beat* the market.[8]

The most popular test of Fama's proposition was the examination of mutual fund performance in a classic study by Michael Jensen.[9] He looked at the performance of mutual fund portfolios from 1945 to 1964. The managers of the funds he studied were the best and brightest in the investment community. If anyone possessed special insight into the inefficiencies in the market that could be capitalized upon, these experts would. They would also be able to use these insights to advantage before the rest of the population. If, on the other hand, markets are efficient and stocks are basically correctly priced at any time, experts wouldn't be able to beat the naive strategy of buying a sampling of all the securities in the market.

Jensen found that the proportion of managers who underperformed the market was significant. Of the "real experts" who had exceptional performance on the positive side, the percentage was much lower than one would expect. Experts were, in effect, trying to figure what a stock price was worth when the market had already efficiently determined the price.

THE SHOCKER!

Then an article published in *American Economic Review* in 1964 by Richard Ipolitto shocked the academic community. Ipolitto claimed that managers as

[8] Ibid.

[9] Michael C. Jensen, "The Performance of Mutual Funds in the Period 1945–1964," *Financial Analysts Journal,* November 1989, pp. 587–616.

a group could beat markets and that markets were inefficient. Mutual fund managers not only could take advantage of this inefficiency, but also could beat a market portfolio's performance even after expenses. This was an amazing result with widespread implications. Ipolitto had conducted his study using the same single-factor model as Jensen had, yet presented opposite results.

Edwin Elton and Martin Gruber[10] set out to replicate Ipolitto's study, using exactly the same ingredients. They quickly found out they could not duplicate his results. Why? It turned out that Ipolitto's finding that mutual fund managers had significantly outperformed the market was largely due to his own data entry errors. Ipolitto had entered negative returns as positive returns, but had never entered a positive return as a negative return. All his mistakes were in the favor of mutual fund managers. When Elton and Gruber corrected these errors, much of the excess performance was eliminated. Then they looked at other factors, small stocks and fixed income holdings, to find out if these factors were important. If they were not important, then the sensitivity of these various factors to mutual funds would show up as zero.

They found that not only did mutual fund managers on average *not* add value, but that performance was reduced by significantly more than their fees! They even found that the higher the manager's fees on average, the lower the performance. Paying more for mediocre performance is nobody's idea of good value.

The popular press back then gave a lot of attention to the Ipolitto study, publishing numerous articles stating that markets don't work. The Elton and Gruber study, on the other hand, received little publicity in the popular press; but luckily for academics, the study received a lot of attention in their world. It is the most comprehensive mutual fund study and by far the best study available on mutual fund managers to date. If anyone is a fan of the idea that markets don't work efficiently, he or she is not going to enjoy the results of this study.

The Elton and Gruber study came to the same basic conclusion that Jensen's had many years earlier. Even though the time periods and mutual funds were very different, the results are strikingly in the same direction. Mutual fund managers who use what's called *active management* do not just underperform markets, they do so significantly. An investor should not pay fees for something that has been proved not to work!

---

[10] Edwin J. Elton, Martin J. Gruber, Sanjiv Das, and Matthew Hlavka, "Efficiency with Costly Information: A Reinterpretation of Evidence from Managed Portfolios," *The Society for Financial Studies,* 1993.

THE BREAKTHROUGH

It was not until 1992 that Professors Eugene Fama and Kenneth French, both from the University of Chicago, caused the next major breakthrough. Their landmark research was published in the article "The Cross-Section of Expected Stock Returns," which explained profit determination in investment portfolios[11] and illustrated why it was not necessary to buy a sampling of the whole market, or individual securities that had higher risk, in an effort to outperform the market as a whole. Rather, Fama and French developed new asset classes that segmented the market and allowed for superior performance at the same risk as for the market as a whole.

It is ironic that the most competitive industry in the world, the financial services industry, still gives advice based on the erroneous belief that markets do not work. The truth is that no other pricing system in use in the world today appears better able to allocate resources than the free market system.

All an investor needs to do to participate in the free market system's creation of wealth is to own a broadly diversified portfolio of equity securities. The individual companies owned will attempt to maximize shareholder value to the investor's benefit.

What does this all mean that is significant to the first time investor? That nothing is hidden from you. No one out there knows if a stock is undervalued or overvalued. There is no secret information that gives someone else an advantage not available to you.

[11] Eugene F. Fama and Kenneth F. French, "The Cross-Section of Expected Stock Returns," *Journal of Finance,* June 1992, pp. 427–465.

3

INVESTMENT STRATEGIES

"If it's stupid and it works, it ain't stupid."

A STRATEGY IS A SPECIFIC WAY OF ORGANIZING YOUR RESOURCES— money, time, and knowledge—in order to consistently get a specific result, a result that can be duplicated. The problem is that most investment strategies can't duplicate the results they produce. If they could, you'd be able to duplicate what Peter Lynch did, or anybody else for that matter.

Think of a master baker with 30 years of experience. He has a repeatable strategy for making an award-winning cake, which he has written out in a recipe. He knows just which ingredients to use and the exact quantities of each. He has mastered the quality, order, sequence, temperature, and duration needed to achieve a repeatable result. Once you've learned the baker's strategy, you can do it the same way yourself, and you can teach that strategy to somebody else. Let's see how close we can get to such a strategy in investing.

We'll start by examining various investment strategies to see which ones are truly effective, and we will weed out those that have been proven to be ineffective.

About 97 percent of all mutual funds use an investment management strategy called *active management*. As the words accurately describe, active

managers move a lot of things around. Think of the last time you moved—
it cost you both money and time. It's the same principle in investing. Although
there are many active management techniques, they basically involve market timing, security selection, or a combination of the two.

MARKET TIMING
Market timing is the attempt to be in the market when it goes up and out of
the market when it goes down. Market timers have to be right twice. First,
they must get out of a particular market before it declines. Then they must
get back in early enough to catch the next market rise. See Fig. 3–1.

STOCK PICKING
Stock picking involves trying to identify securities that are undervalued and
will deliver market-beating returns. Stock pickers attempt to select the best
individual stocks through research and analysis.

A fellow by the name of Terrance Odean, Associate Professor at the
University of California at Davis, studied 10,000 individual accounts at a
major discount brokerage house over a 7-year period. He discovered that, on
average, the stocks that the investors sold performed better than the stocks
that they bought. In reality, stock trading actually reduces performance rather
than improves it.

FIGURE 3–1   Market Timing Chart

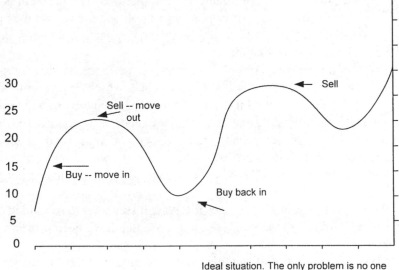

Ideal situation. The only problem is no one
can do this consistently.

The common link with these strategies is that they involve subjective forecasting and the likelihood of human error that accompanies it. The pickers and timers think prices adjust slowly enough that the investors can systematically uncover incorrectly priced securities and add value beyond the added management and trading costs.

In a 1953 study, Maurice Kendall concluded that stock prices follow a *random walk* and are thus unpredictable as long as investors have access to all relevant information on the stock in question.[1]

FLIPPING A COIN

If you flip a coin, about one-half the time it's going to come up heads, and one-half the time it's going to come up tails. But consistently flipping heads for a period of time doesn't tell you anything about the next flip. You are just as likely to flip heads again as tails.

In Fig. 3–2, we utilized a random number generator in our computer to simulate what might happen with 10,000 coin tosses. (I couldn't find any volunteers to do it.) The graph illustrates clearly how a coin toss is a random walk, in which future directions cannot be predicted on the basis of past information. There is no information to perceive in the sequence. The randomness can be likened to a drunken soldier; he is just as likely to show up in one place as another—in a general vicinity—and there is no way to predict where he's going to end up in the morning. At least that's been my experience.

In the financial market, a random walk means that you cannot determine by price movement what's going to happen next. The coin has as great a chance of landing heads up as tails up. The drunken soldier cannot predict himself where he's going to end up, so how can anyone else? The markets have the same randomness in the short run.

Ever since the results of Kendall's study were released, controversy has surrounded his random walk hypothesis. A strict interpretation of Kendall's results would imply that no technique of stock portfolio selection can consistently outperform a simple buy-and-hold strategy that utilizes a broadly diversified group of securities. In other words, the most popular market indices which represent broad segments of the marketplace will outperform the majority of professional money managers on a consistent basis.

According to former Princeton University Professor Burton Malkiel, "a blindfolded chimpanzee throwing darts at the stock pages of *The Wall Street Journal* could select a portfolio that performs as well as one carefully cho-

[1] Maurice G. Kendall, "The Analysis of Time Series, Part I: Prices," *Journal of the Royal Statistical Society,* 1953. vol. 96, pp. 11–25.

FIGURE 3–2   Results of 6,666 Coin-Tosses

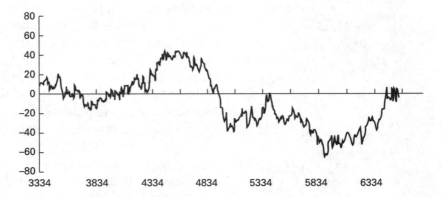

Reprinted with permission from RWB Advisory Services, Inc.

sen by the experts.[2] (See Fig. 3–3.) Today, a mind-boggling amount of information is available to professional investors and traders. Reuters alone delivers the equivalent of 27,000 pages of information each second to traders around the globe. Each market participant acts on his or her own, with significant capital and information resources, causing prices to reflect all known information.

The result of all this competitive activity is that today's price is the best indicator of the value of a stock. The truth is, however, that as good as Wall Street is at valuing stock given today's information, it can't tell you when the market is going to go up or down.

[2] Burton G. Malkiel, "A Random Walk Down Wall Street," Norton & Company, New York, 1973.

FIGURE 3–3   Active Managers' Success Outperforming S&P 500 Versus Dart Throwing

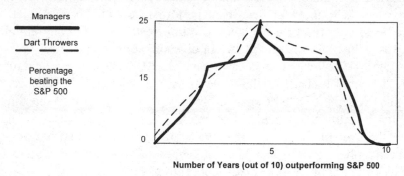

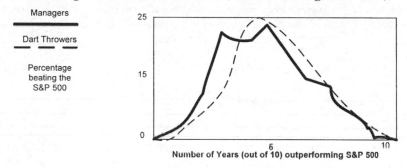

Research shows throwing darts works as well as an active management style.

Reprinted with permission from RWB Advisory Services, Inc.

Don't waste time scanning the stock pages to try to find the next Microsoft. You are as likely to pick a loser as you are to pick a winner. All you need to do to be a successful information investor is to participate in the free market system and its creation of wealth. You can accomplish this by owning a broadly diversified portfolio of equity securities. With this approach, you will outperform the majority of those who engage in costly buying and selling.

So let's now take a closer look at diversification.

DIVERSIFICATION

The term *diversification* is used so often by so many people that it has lost its meaning. In the financial world, diversification means not having all your

money in any one type of investment. Mutual funds, by design, are diversified. Investing in mutual funds is the first step you can take to reduce your
investment risk. Your overall investment performance should be less volatile
with a broad variety of investments than in investments of a single type.
Figure 3–4 illustrates the importance of diversification.

Figure 3–4 illustrates a single investment of $10,000 at an 8 percent return
during 25 years. The chart also illustrates diversifying the same $10,000 invest-
ment into five separate $2000 amounts producing various returns. While three
of the five investments showed a lower return than the single investment, the
total for the diversified side was substantially higher. While it's true you would
have been further ahead by being invested in just the "hot" fund, that's a matter of luck and not likely to be predictable beforehand.

FIGURE 3–4 Diversification

These graphs illustrate the compounding growth on two $10,000 investments over a 25-year period.
The $10,000 on the left assumes a single investment at an 8% return. The graph on the right assumes
diversification of $10,000 into five $2,000 investments at different returns.

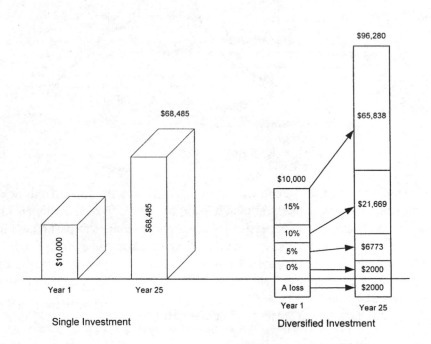

While three of the five investments
were a lower return than the single
investment, the total for the diversified
side was substantially higher.

Each asset responds differently to changes in the economy and invest-ment marketplace. As we discussed earlier, when interest rates drop, stocks take off. If you look back at the 1970s and 1980s, the market was down while interest rates and real estate soared. The trick is to own a variety of assets because a short-term decline in one can be balanced by others that are stable or going up in value.

The stock markets may go up one year and down the next, while other investments such as CDs might remain unchanged. Investors who own both shares of a stock fund and bond funds are usually better off in such a situa-tion than those who limit themselves to stocks only.

The higher volatility of stocks and bonds means higher risk. Suppose all your money is invested in stocks and you need to sell some of your holdings to meet an emergency. If the stocks in your mutual funds are depressed when you need to sell, you could be forced to take a loss on your investment. (Forget the tax deferral for now; that's only one part of the equation.) Owning other investments would give you flexibility in raising needed cash while allowing you to hold your stocks until those prices improved. A diversified portfolio provides both liquidity and comparative stability.

During the long run, to own a wide variety of investments has been the best strategy. Money market funds or cash can provide a foundation of stabil-ity and liquidity that is ideal for cash reserve. Bonds are good for steady high income, and stocks have the greatest potential for superior long-term returns.

EFFECTIVE AND INEFFECTIVE DIVERSIFICATION

Diversification is a prudent method for managing certain types of investment risk. For example, unsystematic risks, those risks associated with individual securities, can be reduced through diversification. However, it doesn't work to invest all your assets in the same market segment, or in segments that tend to move in tandem. The risk is that all your investments could decrease in value at the same time. For instance, investing in the Standard & Poor's 500 stock index and the Dow Jones Industrial Average would be ineffec-tive diversification since both tend to move in the same direction at the same time. Both are indexes composed of large capitalized companies in the United States.

Effective diversification means having a portfolio of investments that tend to move dissimilarly. This is the premise of Harry Markowitz's Nobel Prize–winning theory. He showed that, to the extent that securities in a port-folio do not move in concert with one another, their individual risks can be effectively diversified away. The overall risk of a portfolio is *not* the aver-age risk of each of the investments. In fact, you can have a low-risk portfolio that is actually made up of high-risk assets. When investments are combined in this way, you have achieved effective diversification.

This is a profound academic investment discovery that represents a dramatic breakthrough in investment methodology and the way many professional investors manage money. Many investment professionals now recognize that effective diversification reduces portfolio price changes in mutual funds and smoothes out returns when coupled with investments such as bank CDs and fixed-income-type investments.

COMBINING DISSIMILAR INVESTMENTS

Combining dissimilar investments can significantly enhance returns: If you have two investment portfolios with the same average or arithmetic return, the portfolio with less volatility will have a greater compound or geometric rate of return. For example, let's assume that you are considering two mutual funds. Both have an average annual expected return of 10 percent. How would you determine which fund is better? If one fund is more volatile than the other, their compound return and ending values will be different. It is a mathematical fact that the one with less volatility will have a greater compound return. See Fig. 3–5.

Purchasing asset classes with a low correlation to one another is the Nobel Prize–winning secret for achieving better portfolio consistency. What do I mean by *low correlation?* Technically, correlation is a statistical measure of the degree to which the movement of two variables is related. I found

FIGURE 3–5   Efficient Diversification Chart

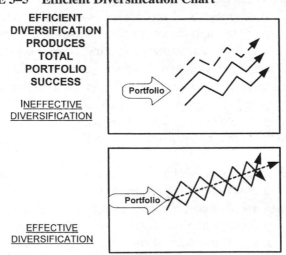

Reprinted with permission from RWB Advisory Services, Inc.

a simpler explanation in Burton Malkiel's book, *A Random Walk Down Wall Street*. He illustrated how broadly diversified securities can create effective diversification in a hypothetical story about an island economy.

Malkiel describes an island which is home to both a large resort and a manufacturing firm producing umbrellas. Weather affects the fortunes of both. During sunny seasons, the resort does a booming business, but umbrella sales plummet. During rainy seasons, the resort owner does very poorly, while the umbrella manufacturer enjoys high sales and large profits.

Figure 3–6 shows a hypothetical comparison of the two different businesses during different seasons. Suppose that, on average, one-half of the seasons are sunny and one-half are rainy (i.e., the probability of a sunny or rainy season is ½).

The first investor who bought stock in the umbrella manufacturer would find that one-half the time she earned a 50 percent return and one-half the time she lost 25 percent of her investment. On average, she would earn a return of 12½ percent. This is called the *investor's expected return.* Similarly, investment in the resort produces the same results.

Here's where the diversification angle comes into the story. A hypothetical investor invests one-half her money in the umbrella manufacturing business and one-half in the resort. During the sunny seasons, a $1 investment in the resort produces a 50-cent return, while a $1 investment in umbrella manufacturing loses 25 cents. The investor's total return as a result is 25 cents (50 cents minus 25 cents), which is 12½ percent of her total investment of $2.

FIGURE 3–6   Effective Diversification

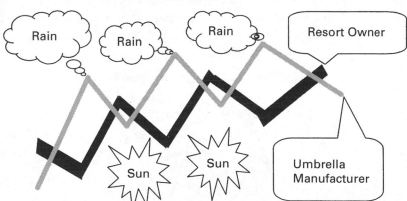

*1st year *2nd year *3rd year *4th year *5th year

The same thing happens during rainy seasons, except that the names are changed. Investment in the umbrella company produces a good 50 percent return, while investment in the resort loses 25 percent. The disadvantage or advantage of one investment over the other arises when there is a freak year—when it rains all year or is sunny all year. For instance, if an investor owns shares only in the resort and it rains all year, she might have a 100 percent loss. But in our diversified model, the investor makes a 12½ percent return on her total investment nonetheless.

This simple illustration points out the advantage of diversification. Whatever happens to the weather, and thus to the island economy, by diversifying investments between both firms, an investor is making a 12½ percent return each year. The trick that makes the game work is that while both companies are risky (returns are variable from season to season), the companies are affected differently by the same weather conditions; these two investments have a strong *negative covariance.*

Covariance measures the degree to which two risky assets move in tandem. A *positive* covariance indicates that asset returns move together whereas a *negative* covariance means they vary inversely. As long as there is some lack of parallelism in the fortunes of individual companies in an economy, diversification will always reduce risk.

If portfolios of volatile stocks are put together in a similar way, the portfolio as a whole will actually be less risky than any one of the individual stocks in it. It is this negative covariance that plays the critical role in successful management of stock portfolios. (See Fig. 3–7.)

20-20 HINDSIGHT

Consider the case of investing in Japanese stocks in recent times. At the beginning of 1998, the Nikkei Index plummeted to a 6-year low for the volatile Japanese stock market. Looking back at this period with the bene-

FIGURE 3–7   Portfolios That Have a Negative Covariance

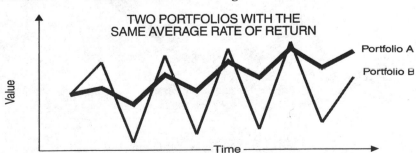

fit of "20-20 hindsight," one assumes that investment portfolios which stayed out of the Japanese market entirely would have performed better than those that diversified using Japanese stocks. Being invested entirely in U.S. stocks would have produced much higher returns—or would it? Is this one time that diversification failed to work? Before you answer too quickly, let's examine the data.

In Fig. 3–8, a portfolio mixture consisting of 75 percent in the U.S. market and 25 percent invested in the Japanese market is compared to both an all-U.S. and all-Japanese portfolio mixture—each consisting of 50 percent large company stocks and 50 percent small company stocks. Note that the 9.6 percent annualized rate of return from the combined 75/25 percent portfolio was higher than that of either of its components for the same 6-year period. In addition, the *standard deviation* of the blended portfolio dropped to 8.8 percent. (The standard deviation measurement helps explain what the distribution of returns will likely be. The higher the standard deviation, the greater the risk. A lower standard deviation usually means a lower return.)

Even though the Japanese market underperformed U.S. equities, diversifying with Japanese stocks enhanced the returns of the U.S. stocks while also lowering volatility. How is this phenomenon possible? *Because when one asset is falling, the other is likely to rise.* Thus, the combined portfolio will be less susceptible to volatility than the individual assets it contains.

FIGURE 3–8   Portfolio Mix Including the Japanese Market

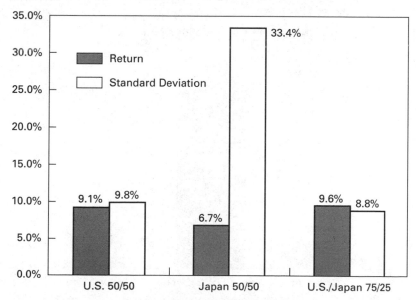

Reprinted with permission from RWB Advisory Services, Inc.

ASSET ALLOCATION

Only a few years ago, this term, asset allocation, did not exist. Modern Portfolio Theory added a third dimension to the process of diversification. The shorthand definition of asset allocation is to allocate your money among various asset categories.

Determining the right asset allocation is a big deal. It can be critical to your investment success. Although the terms are often used interchangeably, don't confuse asset allocation with diversification. They are not the same thing. Diversification is a result of *why*; asset allocation tells us *how much*.

As illustrated in Fig. 3–9, over 90 percent of total return variation is due to the asset allocation of your portfolio. In contrast, stock market timing and stock selection together account for less than 6 percent. (But you will not hear this fact from your stockbroker, no matter how friendly, even if your stockbroker is a relative.) No one wants to tell you that the service he or she is providing will amount to only 6 percent of your overall investment performance.

Tools for asset allocation range from a pen and notepad to sophisticated software programs. Software-assisted asset allocation has become common among professional financial advisors and eliminates much of the previous guesswork from the process. This is where an investment advisor or financial planner can really earn his/her fees. If you smooth out equity returns using proper asset allocation and diversification, generally speaking, you can outperform the major indexes over long periods.

FIGURE 3–9   Asset Allocation

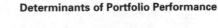

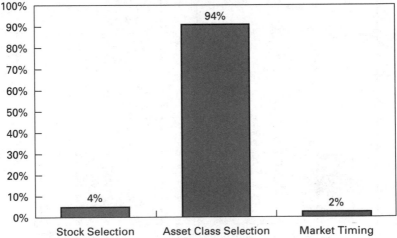

Reprinted with permission from RWB Advisory Services, Inc.

TIME

The last and critical ingredient to the whole investment mix is *time*. This one is my favorite because it is the one *known* element in our equation—it affects us all in the same way—nothing can speed it up or slow it down.

Given enough time, investments that might otherwise seem unattractive may become highly desirable. The longer the period over which investments are held, the closer actual returns in a portfolio will come to the expected average. This means short-term market fluctuations will smooth out.

The real challenge is to commit to a discipline of long-term investing and avoid compelling investment distractions. Commit to the strategy. With a long-term view, you can better choose investments that have the best chances for success. By adding the essential ingredient of time to your investment plans, you can almost be assured of success.

Beware of conventional approaches that measure rates of returns over 1-year periods. While this is the conventional and widely used approach, a 12-month time frame simply is not the best length of measure.

Do not listen to the news media because they also use an extremely short time frame—often limited to that particular day! The media play to the public's belief that gurus exist who can accurately predict when the market will turn up or down, and that a knowledgeable person can pick the *right* individual security or mutual fund. But every year, about one-half or more of the mutual funds don't outperform their benchmarks, and those in the upper half in 1 year have only about a 50 percent chance of repeating in any other year.

Uninformed investors believe that by regularly reading a financial publication, such as *The Wall Street Journal* or a financial magazine, they become insiders to information that gives them some advantage. When you look at long-term common stock investments, however, the ups and downs tend to straighten out. Wars and threats of wars merely become blips on the chart. Economic events are put in their proper long-term perspective.

The global equity portfolio in Fig. 3–10 presents another way of looking at how time affects risk. Notice that 1-year-at-a-time rates of return on common stocks over the years are almost incoherent, showing both large gains and large losses. Shifting to 5-year periods brings a considerable increase in coherence and regularity. The losses disappear, and the gains appear more consistently. Shifting to 10-year periods increases the consistency of returns significantly, showing positive average annual gains. Compounding over a decade overwhelms the single-year differences. *The gap between the lows and the highs narrows.*

Analysis shows over and over that the tradeoff between risk and reward is driven by one key factor—*time*.

FIGURE 3–10   Risk Over Time

Global Equity Portfolio Returns: January 1972–December 1997 Compound Annual Rates of Return

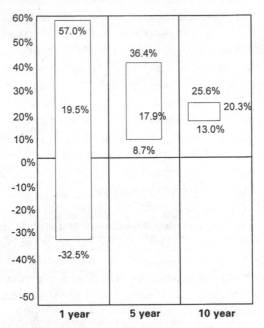

ROLLING PERIODS

Reprinted with permission from RWB Advisory Services, Inc.

No sensible investor would knowingly invest in a common stock for only 1 day, 1 month, or even 1 year. Such brief time periods are clearly too short for investment in common stocks, because the expected variation in returns is too large in comparison to the average expected return. Such short-term holdings in common stocks are not investments; they are speculations.

If we change measurement periods to longer time horizons, then expected rates of returns and variations in returns also change. If we measure an investment every 3 years, rather than every quarter, we can see satisfying progress that wouldn't be apparent on a quarterly measurement.

In most cases, the time horizon which investors use as the standard to measure results is far too short, causing dissatisfaction with investment performance. This dissatisfaction is perpetuated because stock brokerage firms reward their brokers according to the amount of trades or transactions per year, not how well clients have done.

Too often, people try to compress time. They have fantasies and dreams that can only be reached by getting rich quickly, but those attempts almost always end up on the losing side.

There is tried-and-true investment strategy that puts time on your side, avoids the mistaken activities of market timing and stock selection, and eliminates a lot of needless worry by making investing automatic: *dollar cost averaging.* With this strategy, an investor buys by the dollar's worth rather than by the number of shares.

THE PRINCIPLE OF SPACED REPETITION
This principle simply means investing equal dollar amounts at regular intervals: monthly, quarterly, semiannually, or annually. It's an effective method that can help you turn the characteristic fluctuations of common stock or mutual fund values into a benefit because you are investing over different time periods. See Fig. 3–11.

When prices are low, you'll be able to purchase more shares. When prices are high, you'll be purchasing fewer shares. Over time, you will purchase a greater number of shares at a lower price level, making your average cost per share generally lower than the normal average. For this strategy to be effective, you should consider beforehand if you will indeed be able to invest equal amounts at regular intervals over time. If prices are low, continue investing the same amount; you will be buying more shares at a lower price.

FIGURE 3–11   Dollar Cost Averaging or Spaced Repetition

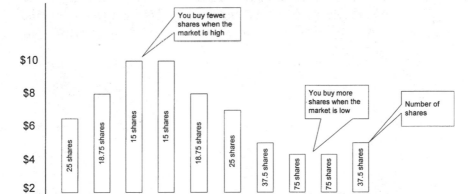

- Total amount invested: $1500 ($150/month)
- Average price of these 10 purchases: $6.00
- Average cost per share: $4.38
- Total shares: 342.50

When I first heard of spaced repetition years ago, it didn't make any sense to me. Then a shrewd old broker told me he liked the market being down because he could buy more shares. I instantly understood. With spaced repetition, the objective is to purchase shares at an average cost that is below the average price.

Figure 3–11 charts a $150 per month investment through a 10-month period. Share prices fluctuated during that time, but the investment amount held constant. When prices are at their low ($2.00), an investor is able to purchase more shares (75). When prices are higher ($10.00), an investor purchases fewer shares (15), for the same purchase price. Over time, that investor will purchase a greater number of shares (342.5) at a lower price level, thereby making his or her average cost per share ($4.38) lower than the general average price ($6.00) at which shares are purchased.

In effect, the investor is buying in quantity at bargain prices, and relatively little at exorbitantly high prices. This is just what a first time investor— or any investor—would want to do, right?

Investing becomes automatic with dollar cost averaging. It eliminates the worry of *Should I or shouldn't I?* Mutual fund investors using dollar cost averaging also have no reason to fear market declines. Indeed, an occasional decline becomes a benefit, permitting the investor to buy a greater-than-normal number of shares at lower-than-average prices. The dollar cost averaging investor begins to almost wait in anticipation of the next mini-crash, instead of dreading it. See Fig. 3–12.

But beware. Even armed with this valuable knowledge, you may be vulnerable to another ever-present danger lurking about in investment land. That danger is the temptation to lapse into being a "noise investor"—the subject of the next chapter.

FIGURE 3–12   The Investment Process

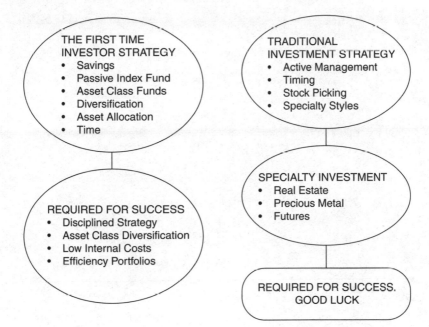

4

NOISE OR INFORMATION?

AS WE STAND ON THE THRESHOLD OF THE 21ST CENTURY, with the hindsight of what we have learned over the last two or three decades, we have an opportunity for unique clarity of thought regarding how the investment arena truly functions. For the very first time, in this evolutionary process of expanding knowledge about the capital markets, we can understand and explain the majority of a portfolio's behavior. We now have the ability to plan and design portfolios that take advantage of the scientifically proven information which has so recently become available. Through a combination of the efforts of academicians and real-world practitioners, we now have a "better way" to manage assets successfully.

Unfortunately, within this new clarity lies the confusion and misinformation which have grown out of an ever-expanding marketplace of investment products, companies, and solicitors of the same. Investors, both individual and institutional alike, are faced with a level of complexity that has grown exponentially over the last decade. It follows, then, that one of the most important issues affecting the investor today is how to make investment decisions, in other words, whether these decisions are based on investment *noise* or investment *information*.

An entire industry has developed and grown around one primary motivating factor. That factor is the absolute necessity to engage in transactions and trading. From brokers to advisors to investment newsletters, the message is to *buy and sell.* Without this commissioned activity, the industry, in its present form, simply could not exist.

Simultaneously with this development, there has been an explosion in the financial media that has its own compounding effect in the confusion factor which influences investors of every type. There are an almost limitless number of television shows, radio shows, magazines, and periodicals devoted completely to telling us how and where to invest, and there are countless others in which investing is featured prominently.

With all this "space" in either printed form or on the air which must be filled every single day, there is an absolute need to find—and sometimes even *create* information to talk and write about. The result of all these factors has been a proliferation of investment *noise.* One of my friends, John Bowen, CEO of Reinhardt Werba Bowen Advisory Services in San Jose, California, likes to call it investment *pornography,* because it presents a distorted view of reality and generally creates more problems than it solves. "This noise," says Bowen, "is the very lifeblood of today's investment industry. In order for the traditional investment system to function, you, the investor, must be motivated into action, and investment *noise* is the lubricant that makes the motivation machine move."

Unfortunately, these motivations to action (in other words, getting you to trade) have been proven to be the absolute opposite steps necessary to be successful as a long-term investor. There is a better way! And that better way involves becoming an *information investor,* instead of a *noise investor.*

What is a noise investor? Noise investors believe that by regularly reading a financial publication, they become insiders to information that gives them some advantage. Most noise investors significantly underperform the market. What noise investors don't realize is that chasing the hot stock and attempting to time the market swings are strategies that are costly to implement, have an extremely low probability of success, and are ineffective in adding value.

Information investors are the opposite of noise investors. Information investors understand how financial markets actually work, and they know how to use their financial market knowledge to consistently make money. Information investors focus on the overall investment strategy and portfolio, rather than view a specific investment in isolation, since academic studies tell us that each investment should be evaluated for its contribution to a portfolio's total return.

When you are able to take a step back, consider all the facts, and use your newly acquired knowledge of how markets work, the logical errors of "accepted" investment strategies will become clear to you. You will become an informed investor. The best part about being an informed investor is that you will be able to properly evaluate the investment advice you receive, and you will never again fall prey to the misguided recommendations of an uninformed advisor or investor or journalist.

Most first time investors have never heard of the academic theories of investing. They get their information from the news media, magazines, or TV. This "information" consists mostly of day-to-day noise and confusing distractions. Most is misguided and sensational and lacks any theoretical foundation. Many false ideas are so widespread that the public, for the most part, simply accepts them as fact.

Unfortunately, the investing public believes that a knowledgeable or gifted person can pick stocks or mutual funds by undertaking research to determine the *right* individual security or mutual fund. The point is that there are no gurus on Wall Street and that stock picking, timing, or option trading is a loser's game. What Wall Street calls an investment is actually speculation. The forecast of top research is nothing more than guesses, and analysis is nothing more than opinion.

Noise seldom translates to the highest returns for you. Although you're up 30 percent in one year, you are likely to lose that much or more the next year.

WHY NOT JUST BUY A PLAIN VANILLA MUTUAL FUND?
What do you think of Fig. 4-1? Look at the number-one manager in 1995—he's almost at the dead bottom of the list in 1996. Wall Street wants you to believe that there's a black box and that somebody is actually in control. But as you'll soon discover, nobody on Wall Street is keeping any secrets from you. Nobody knows what earnings are going to push a stock up, or that a stock is worth more or less than the price shows.

No matter how many times a mutual fund beats the market in the past, it has only a 50 percent chance of beating the market in the future. These apparently random outcomes are consistent with market efficiency.

Edgar Barksdale and William Green examined the performance persistency of 144 institutional equity managers from January 1975 to December 1989. They ranked the managers based on their results over a 5-year period. They then tracked what percentage of these managers performed better than average for the subsequent 5 years. Their results showed that regardless of where a manager places in the first 5 years, she or he is about equally likely to be above average as below average during the next 5 years. Again, it's a random pattern that is consistent with the laws of pure chance.

FIGURE 4-1   Mutual Fund Selection

Top 20 Mutual Funds, 1995 to 1996
One Year Rank vs. the Next Year (1996)

1ˢᵗ Year	Next Year	1ˢᵗ Year	Next Year
1	2898	11	7261
2	7268	12	7297
3	45	13	1705
4	7283	14	6
5	262	15	2497
6	6290	16	2719
7	7233	17	7050
8	3473	18	3256
9	7256	19	5383
10	7061	20	7351

Average run of top 20 in subsequent year = 4388
Average number of funds = 7857

Reprinted with permission from RWB Advisory Services, Inc.

Ronald Kahn and Andrew Rudd studied the performance of equity mutual funds from January 1983 to December 1993, and fixed-income mutual funds from October 1986 to September 1993. They find no evidence of persistence in performance for equity funds and insufficient persistence in fixed-income funds to validate their use (because the fixed-income funds underperform their benchmarks by so much). Kahn and Rudd concluded that, given only past performance information, index funds look best for both equity and fixed-income investments. Studies of mutual fund performance now span more than 40 years' investigation. The message is clear: While an occasional mutual fund may beat the market, there is no indication to support the idea that performance may repeat or continue. There is actually more proof that it will *not*.

Your job is to avoid the noise out there—huge events are brought to us instantaneously everyday. When you listen to the nightly news, sit back and ask yourself, What does this really have to do with me? Worrying about the daily moves of the stock market is like watching another police car chase on the 6 o'clock news. It plays on the viewers' emotions.

Here's an investment story I will tell on myself. I was the typical noise investor back in the early 1980s. I read how pre-1964 silver coins were going to be the next hot investment. I was mildly excited, but, being *cautious,* I held back until the next issue of my financial journal hit the stands. I flipped through the pages to read how silver coins were doing and became convinced silver was moving up. My hope turned to real excitement. It made me feel as if I'd made a private discovery.

Greed hit me hard. So I called my brokers and purchased two bags of pre-1964 dimes. That's the way the experts said to hold it. You can guess what happened next. As soon as I had my hands on the bags, the price of silver started to drop. My new emotion was a combination of fear and hope. I started hoping my dimes would go back up. How far? I would have been happy if they just went up to the price at which I bought them. I'd break even and wouldn't have to tell my spouse anything about my venture. Then I vowed never to do that again! But instead, the whole silver market collapsed. My new emotion became panic, and I tried to sell; but no one would buy the coins. I had to drive to a coin dealer in Las Vegas, who gave me the face amount on the silver dimes. I was relieved until the next information came out and silver hit an all-time high. I call that the emotional roller coaster ride of investing. See Fig. 4-2.

Instead of fueling an emotional roller coaster, accurate information leads to understanding and reduces uncertainty. It leads to peace of mind.

BASIC FINANCIAL BLUNDERS TO AVOID

Aside from the investment noise, nothing can stop you from meeting your future financial objectives more than making dumb investment errors. These common mistakes are not limited to inexperienced investors or those with moderate incomes. In fact, they were provided by years of hands-on experience of seasoned, sophisticated investors. It is important for you to recognize these errors so you can avoid them.

FIGURE 4-2   The Emotional Curve of Investing

Reprinted with permission from RWB Advisory Services, Inc.

1. *Being embarrassed to invest your small savings.* Small amounts add up. Begin saving something each month.

2. *Listening to investment noise.* It is very hard to stay on track with the tremendous amount of noise present. Develop a strategic, long-term plan, and turn a deaf ear to the noise.

3. *Lack of follow-through on long-range goals.* Concentrate on those instruments designed to fulfill your financial plan instead of a hodgepodge of investments bought on tips, hearsay advice, or casual comments from friends. Customize your portfolio to reflect your objectives and your ability to assume risk. If you like to invest exclusively in one industry or sector, you may wish to consider abandoning this practice and instead diversify in several. This can help reduce vulnerability to certain cross-cutting variables, such as government policies or consumer preferences, and eliminate emotion-based actions.

4. *Riding the emotional roller coaster.* To take the emotion out of purchasing stocks, you could use a mechanical means such as dollar cost averaging that demands a specified contribution on a regular basis, regardless of market conditions.

5. *Lack of detailed records for investments, loans, and taxes.* Many first time investors fail to maintain accurate financial records. Make the effort; it can help you monitor your investments' performance as well as aid your heirs after you're gone.

6. *Going against all the odds.* Find out what is realistic, and set your personal investment expectations to match reality. Start looking at stocks as you look at life. Use guidelines to keep yourself from reacting to market fluctuations. The fact is, nobody knows what the market is going to do.

7. *Confusing income with appreciation.* Don't confuse saving with investing. Do not expect index funds to pay high dividends or income. Understand your investments. Some stocks that have a high percentage of earnings and dividends may be a poor investment in terms of growth. A lot of people believe that as stock dividends increase, so does the worth of their holdings.

8. *Procrastinating.* Becoming an investor is going to require some of your attention and time. How much time? Set time deadlines, and take small, easy investment steps, one at a time. But don't put off starting.

9. *Not having an emergency fund.* Investments that lack liquidity either prevent you from getting your money quickly or force you to sell at discount prices. I have always heard you should have about 6 months' living expenses in liquid or cash equivalence. I ignored that advice for years, but when I became a writer and changed careers, I needed the emergency fund. I now make a game out of saving to cover my living expenses, and I keep extending the time periods further.

10. *Not taking advantage of employer savings and/or tax-advantaged investments.* Tax-deferred stock option plans or 401(k) plans may have employer-matching features. Talk to your benefits officer. Some investments can be made with "before-tax" dollars or defer tax on interest and dividends that accrue on the investment. These advantages could be used to "grow" your investment wealth more rapidly.

11. *Failing to use professional advisors.* Unless you have broad experience and plenty of spare time, you may save more in the long run by obtaining professional help. Advisors such as stockbrokers, financial planners, accountants, and tax attorneys can help you build and implement a comprehensive financial plan.

The real message is to control everything you can control. Take actions consistent with your financial goals, guided by sound advice. How do you know where to get sound advice? The answer depends on whether you are a do-it-yourselfer, verifier, or delegator.

CHAPTER 5

GET A FINANCIAL COACH

"The easiest way is often hardest."

DO YOU WANT HELP WITH YOUR INVESTMENTS? Do you want to delegate some of the responsibility for investing to an advisor, or do you just want verification that your ideas make sense? You have come to the right chapter. See Fig. 5-1.

To me, it's a lot easier to find a reputable investment advisor who understands passive investing and how the markets work than to try to do it yourself.

I asked Len Reinhart, chairman at Lockwood Financial Services, Inc., located in Malvern, Pennsylvania, to help explain the advisory process. Lockwood is a manufacturer of the services for fee-based advisors. Specifically, the company generates research and packages different money managers and mutual funds for fee-based advisors. That means advisors who are paid a fee—not a commission. The fee-based advisor may use Lockwood for her or his back office support.

Reinhart suggests that first time investors get advice from fee-based advisors or investment consultants. They are brokers who specialize in consulting on the process of investment management. This group also charges

FIGURE 5-1   Verifiers

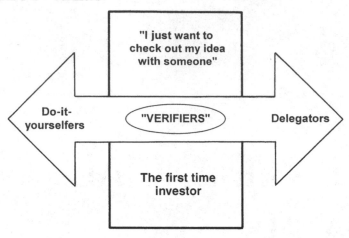

fees for services rather than commissions. In this way, they have no con-
flicts of interest in the investments they recommend.

Fee-based advisors and consultants and virtually almost any of the Wall
Street firm stockbrokers now have access to more than just their own mutual fund families. There are more than 8,000 registered mutual funds now
and 4,000 individual money managers. What these consultants do is to direct
you to the ones suited to your needs.

Brokers can provide you with free financial planning reports—which
can cost hundreds, or thousands, of dollars elsewhere. For a fee, broker-
based consultants in many large firms can help you establish your investment
objectives, do the research with the due diligence needed to find you an
appropriate money manager, and—most importantly—provide sophisticated monitoring and review of the money manager who is managing your
account. (If you're a trustee of a pension plan, this service may help you
comply with the Employment Income and Securities Act of 1974—but we
still recommend that you check with your legal counsel.)

One last note about brokers: You can't buy an individual issue of stocks,
bonds, or municipal bonds without the services of either a full-service or
discount brokerage firm. A full-service brokerage firm can help you research
the issues and can make recommendations. A discount house won't. That's
the distinction.

Some mutual funds are offered directly to the public at net asset value
without sales charges being added. A fund can do this because it does not
maintain a sales staff. It simply advertises and markets its shares by mail or
magazine.

How do you know how to find a good consultant? Spend some time, and ask some of the questions you might have from reading this book.

Len Reinhart gave me his list of questions used to locate a consultant:

1.   What is the consultant's education in investment consulting? *Answer:* Having a college degree doesn't qualify someone for investment consulting. They should have a certification designation from either Investment Management Consultants Association (IMCA) or the Institute For Investment Management Consultants (IIMC).

2.   What percentage of the consultant's clients are fee-based assets? *Answer:* You'd like it to be 60 or 70 percent or greater.

3.   What investment vehicles does the consultant offer? Mutual funds, individually managed accounts, annuities? *Answer:* You would like them to also have access to asset class mutual funds. Asset class funds and index funds are no-load, meaning you pay no commission to buy the investment, instead you pay only the advisor's or consultant's fee just as you would your attorney or accountant.

4.   Ask for three references to call. *Answer:* Most fee-based advisors generally don't mind if you ask for references of existing clients.

5.   Ask about the consultant's own investment history. *Answer:* They do what they are advising you to do.

6.   Have they ever lost money? *Answer:* They did, and they learned something from the experience.

The exact role that an advisor plays in your own investment arena is up to you. The more hands-on help you want, the more it will cost, but a solid foundation may be worth it. Include your family members in planning discussions, so their expectations will be in line with your strategies.

6

TEACHING YOUR CHILDREN TO INVEST

"Important things are always simple, simple things are always difficult."

HOW TO MANAGE MONEY is one of the most important lessons you can teach your children. Children who are excluded from open discussions of family financial affairs or sheltered from the financial realities of life can sometimes develop distorted ideas about money. They may make extravagant demands, often creating unnecessary squabbles about money, simply because they are uninformed about the family's financial resources.

When these children grow up, they may be ill-equipped to manage their own finances or unable to exercise good judgment in financial matters. The key is to teach your children to think about money and financial management from a positive point of view. Of course, introducing your children to money management is a very personal matter, and you as the parent must decide what is best for your child. Here are some tips you may find helpful:

• *Be open with your children about money matters.* Many families hold regular conferences, children included, to review finances. Every family member should be encouraged to speak out freely about her or his own priorities or goals. Thus, you can illustrate that priorities need to be set and that tradeoffs are sometimes necessary for effective use of money. Even a fairly young child should be able to understand, for instance, that paying for shelter and groceries takes a higher priority than buying a new bike or taking a trip to an amusement park. Attending these sessions can give your children a sense of involvement and a greater willingness to work toward meeting family financial goals.

- *Give your children regular allowances.* You can begin when they reach school age, and be sure to include at least some money that they are free to spend as they like without having to account to anyone. That way your children gain experience in deciding how to spend their own money.

  A recommended way to start is by giving a young child a small amount of money every day or two for little toys or treats. As the child gets older, you can spread out the payment periods and increase the size of the allowance and the purpose for which it is used. The child can have a greater voice as the years go by in determining what the allowance should be.

  A teenager, for example, might receive a monthly allowance that covers school lunches and supplies, hobbies and entertainment, and clothing. This can teach the child to plan, to save for necessities and special purchases, and to shop carefully for good buys. Giving an occasional advance against an upcoming allowance may be appropriate; but if your child overspends constantly, work with him or her to bring spending in line with available income.

- *Teach your children the value of working for extra money.* Children should learn at an early age that money must be earned. You do not want to pay your child for every routine household task, of course, but you might consider paying for special household chores, above and beyond the allowance.

- *Encourage your children to save for special goals.* You might begin with a piggy bank and advance to a passbook savings account so that each child can see firsthand how money deposited regularly can earn money through interest—and grow faster. A child can open a savings account at any age, but remember, banks generally require a social security number for all depositors. Once a child has a passbook account, she or he should have the freedom within reason to withdraw funds at will when necessary.

- *Introduce your children to checking accounts once they are old enough.* Opening checking accounts for your children when they are in their middle teens is one way for them to learn about simple banking transactions—how to make deposits, how to write checks, and how to balance checkbooks.
- *Teach your children the basics of investing.* Since money management is sometimes more than balancing your checkbook or opening a passbook savings account, you should also try to involve your children in a goal-oriented investment, such as for their college tuition. By actually owning a stock, a child can watch the stock market fluctuate, learn how investments help the growth of the U.S. economy, and gain an understanding of basic investment principles. And, as a stockholder, your child will periodically receive information on his or her investment, including an annual report, that may be interesting as well as educational.
- *Teach your children about credit once they are mature enough.* Credit has become such a substantial part of the U.S. way of life that teaching your children to use it properly is an important element of their financial education. Many stores permit teenagers to use family credit accounts with their parents' consent. You should supervise their use of credit closely, of course, to make sure they keep credit purchases modest and pay bills promptly.
- *Set a good example.* This is the best way to teach your children the principles of sound money management. No matter how much training you give them, many of their attitudes toward money will be influenced by the way *you* spend and save.

Now let's uncover some information about you in the next chapter.

7

HOW MUCH MONEY IS ENOUGH?

IF YOU KNEW YOU ULTIMATELY COULDN'T LOSE, that there were no secrets, that it could all be explained, wouldn't investing take on a whole new appearance? You wouldn't run out of patience, or feel overwhelmed and just give up and do nothing. You'd settle in and confidently wait for the inevitable gain to occur. The ability to be patient during difficult times requires an understanding of not only the stock markets but also your own reactions to uncertainty (risk).

And if you knew just how much money you needed at retirement, you could figure out how much risk you'll have to take to get there. You could stop focusing on trying to find the hot mutual fund and set about building your overall net worth. You'd have a plan. You could begin to manage your existing assets and future resources to meet your future needs.

Where do you start? You start not by looking at mutual fund returns, but rather by looking at how long you have before you retire and how much money you're going to need when you get there. If you first determine your projected monthly retirement expenses and income, then you can easily see any shortfall. A *shortfall* is the difference between what you will realistically need to have and what you will actually have. It's what happens when your anticipated income and other earnings do not cover all your expenses.

You can make these calculations on the back of a napkin or fill out a comprehensive financial planning form. I've provided you with tables to complete that are somewhere between both extremes. They'll help you determine the amounts needed to make up for any shortfall, the rate of return you will need to achieve, and the number of dollars you need to add annually to close the gap. Just knowing that should take some of the pressure off and should make the unknown less mysterious.

Most investors don't bother with this step, or they approach it backward. Total return based on historical performance has become the only financial gauge for most investors. But total return is nothing more than a visual display of the past, and only certain aspects of the past at that. It's not an indicator of the future. Historical performance tells only a fraction of what you need to know and can be very misleading.

Let's say you figure out that your shortfall is about $300,000 and you've got 20 years or so left before retirement. You have $50,000 from the sale of property to invest. What would most people do? They would jump at one of the advertisements in a money magazine, or they would seek out help from a traditional financial planner, stockbroker, or financial advisor. But if you take one of these approaches, you may still have a problem. Most investment sales organizations operate within the framework of pretax returns and relative performance. This gets you to focus on only the rate of return and how it compared in the past to others. You may be shown a dollar goal projection, illustrating the magic of compounding using the historical rate of return of 10 percent. That 10 percent figure sounds conservative. If the potential for the investment program would cover your shortfall at this 10 percent figure, you're impressed. At 10 percent, your $50,000 grows to $336,000 in 20 years and $872,000 in 30 years. You think, *I'm there!* And you invest in that fund.

But here's the *danger:* Total return drastically overstates the purchasing power that you will have because it ignores taxes, fees, and inflation. Together, these three asset eroders can bring your expected return down to as little as zero. Studies by Ibbotson and Associates show that historical after-tax, after-fee, after-inflation rates of returns on corporate bonds is about zero and the return on stocks, while higher, can be as low as 2 percent after all expenses are subtracted, including the advisor's fee. Sometimes experienced practitioners deduct for taxes and factor for inflation, but do not figure in the fees.

What a difference these oversights can make! With typical taxes of 2.5 percent plus fees, including the broker consultant's fee of 2.5 percent, your 10 percent return assumption is reduced to 5 percent. So after taxes and fees, your $50,000 in 20 years is worth not $336,000, but only $132,000. Subtract

3 percent for inflation, and real dollar projections drop to $74,000. *Whoops!* You will not hit your target!

You could be off by hundreds of thousands of dollars and not have the time needed to make it up. This creates frustrated investors who become, in effect, market timers—often selling an existing fund and buying a new one in hopes of gaining back lost ground. The classic buy-high, sell-low syndrome results. Investors who do this a few times become disillusioned with the never-ending process of picking new actively managed investments, and many quit investing altogether.

The point is, even if you are lucky and pick the best mutual funds, that still doesn't mean you will meet your actual objectives. Your goal should be to focus on the dollar amount you will need and on total after-tax return. Total *after*-tax return is after fees, after expenses, after any and everything that stands in your way of achieving that goal.

Advertisements for mutual fund companies are designed to show you total return, and most mutual funds are sold on that misleading criterion alone. Just look at the TV commercials and ads in the back of financial magazines. Even the tools that brokers and financial consultants have at their disposal, such as risk return graphs, style analyses, and Morningstar data, are ineffective because they are based on historical performance. All these strategies are based on predicting winners from past performance.

Why is this? Because Wall Street has been selling to huge pension plans for the last 50 years. The managers of pension plans need past performance to back up their investment decisions. If they buy a mutual fund or an individual stock and the next quarter the stock market drops, managers can pull out a Wall Street report documenting past performance, and they won't get chewed out. But a pension manager is subject to different motivations than you are. Unfortunately, selling past performance has become so hardwired into the investment profession's delivery system that most of us don't think twice about it. But we should.

The solution to this problem is to control what you can control: Understand what combinations of investments will give you the highest probability of making up any shortfalls, will lower your costs, and will operate your investment program fully aware of the tax consequences.

STEPS TO FOLLOW

When we plan for retirement, most of us quickly recognize that, indeed, our anticipated income and other earnings will not cover all our expenses, and we have a shortfall to cover. That's the beginning of putting an effective investment plan in place.

1.   Chart A: Calculate your monthly retirement expenses. Figure out
      how many dollars will be required to satisfactorily meet your
      monthly retirement expenses.

CHART A   Calculate Your Monthly Retirement Expenses

*First, estimate your current costs and those you expect to decrease when you retire, in columns A and
B. Then, in columns C and D, record your current costs and the projected costs that might increase
when you retire. The total represents your estimated annual retirement expenses.*

Costs that may be reduced at retirement	Current amount	Estimated amount	Costs that may be increased at retirement	Current amount	Estimated amount
Housing	$_____	$_____	Medical (Hospital insurance, supplemental insurance prescriptions, dentist	$_____	$_____
Life Insurance	$_____	$_____			
Transportation	$_____	$_____	Food	$_____	$_____
Clothing & personal care	$_____	$_____			
Taxes	$_____	$_____	Recreation and entertainment (Vacations, family travel, hobbies, etc.)	$_____	$_____
Business travel and entertainment	$_____	$_____			
Miscellaneous purchases	$_____	$_____	Auto insurance	$_____	$_____
Loan repayments and interest	$_____	$_____	Other	$_____	$_____
Education	$_____	$_____	Total costs	$_____ Column C	$_____ Column D
Total costs	$_____ Column A	$_____ Column B			

- You can expect total monthly retirement expenses to be approximately 75% of your current income.
- Think about how your expenses will change at retirement and then reallocate the dollars accordingly. For example,
  you may not spend as much on housing and auto but you may spend more on recreation, travel, and medical.

Total Current Monthly Expenses
(Add column A and column C)

Total Estimated Monthly Expenses at Retirement
(Add column B and column D

Estimated Annual Retirement Expense
[Multiply expenses (sum of columns B and D) by 12]

2.   Chart B: Calculate your retirement income. Primary sources of
      retirement income typically include employee-sponsored retirement
      plans, individual retirement accounts (IRAs), Keogh plans, SEP-
      IRAs, Social Security, and personal savings. Identify all the known
      variables that are under your control, such as time periods, tax rates,
      required cash flows, and fees. The focus should be on what's reli-
      ably predictable.

CHART B   Calculate Your Retirement Income Part 2

Your Projections   **Example I: My plans to retire in 20 years**

1. Annual retirement expenses
    (From Chart A, at the bottom of the page.)

    $ _____ $ 50,000   My estimated annual retirement
                                            expenses are $50,000

2. Retirement income

    a) Social Security income

    $ _____ $ 10,000

    b) Other income (defined benefit plans, post-
    retirement income, rents, royalties)   I estimate $10,000 from Social Security.
                                                           I estimate $10,000 to come from book
    $ _____ $ 10,000   royalties.

3. Total income
    (Add lines 2a and 2b)

    $ _____ $ 20,000   My total projected income is $20,000.

4. Income shortfall
    (Line 1 minus line 3)

    $ _____ $ 30,000   By subtracting my retirement income
                                            from my retirement expenses, I found a
5. Total assets needed at retirement   shortfall of $30,000.
    (From Table 1 on the next page)

    $ _____ $ 657,337   I plan on retiring in 20 years. Table 1
                                            shows that I'll need total $657,337 saved
6. Amount you have saved already for retirement   by the time I retire. Inflation is
                                                           considered in this amount.
    a) IRAs/Keoghs

    $ _____ $ 10,000   I also have saved $10,000 in my SEP
                                            IRA.
    b) Employer-sponsored retirement plans

    $ _____ $ 0

    c) Other investments/savings (stocks, bonds,
    CDs, mutual funds, money market funds, etc.)

    $ _____ $ 50,000   This is the value of my brokerage
                                            portfolio.
    d) Equity in home (optional)

    $ _____ $ 0   In my home. You've got to live some
                                            where.
7. Total amount saved
    (Add lines 6a through 6d)

    $ _____ $ 60,000   Combining the assets listed in line 6, I
                                            have saved this amount.
8. Value of current savings at retirement
    a) Portfolio Compounding Factor
    (From Table 2 on the next page)

    $ _____ $ 6.73
                                            In Table 2, I have determined the factor
    b) Multiply total from line 7 by line 8a   selecting 10% as my rate of return. 6.73
                                                           times $60,000 is $403,800.
    $ _____ $ 403,800

9. Asset shortfall at retirement
    (Line 5 minus line 8b)

    $ _____ $ 253,537   By subtracting $403,800 from $657,337.
                                            I estimated that is the amount I must have
10. Annual Savings needed   saved by the time I retire.
    (From Table 3 on the next page)

    $ _____ $ 4,000   In order to meet this goal, Table 3
                                            suggests that I save approximately
                                            $4,000 per year for the next 20
                                            years.

3. Use Tables 1, 2, and 3. Use these tables to help you calculate the amount of money you'll need to save for retirement. Keep adjusting the known variables. View financial goals as future liabilities that need to be met. This will help you to take the amount of risk needed—not too much or too little. You may think of yourself as a conservative investor; but if your shortfall is too large, you may have to become a more aggressive investor and take greater risks.

Table 1: Total Assets Requirement *(at retirement)*

If your income shortfall is	Years to retirement							
	5	10	15	20	25	30	35	40
$10,000	121,665	148,024	180,094	219,112	266,584	324,340	394,609	480,102
$20,000	243,331	296,049	360,189	438,225	533,167	648,680	789,218	960,204
$30,000	364,996	444,073	540,283	657,337	799,751	973,019	1,183,827	1,440,306
$50,000	608,326	740,122	900,472	1,095,562	1,332,918	1,621,699	1,973,044	2,400,510

Table 2. Portfolio Compounding Factor *(compounded annually)*

Years to your goal	Rate of return		
	8%	9%	10%
10	2.16	2.37	2.59
15	3.17	3.64	4.18
20	4.66	5.60	6.73
25	6.85	8.62	10.83
30	10.06	13.27	17.45

Assumptions:
Tax-deferred income
No depletion of principal
Annual return on assets: 8%
Annual inflation: 4%
Annual savings made at the end of each year (Table 3)

Table 3. Annual Savings Requirement *(needed to reach savings goal)*

If your income shortfall is	Years to Retirement					
	5	10	15	20	25	30
$50,000	8,190	3,137	1,574	873	508	304
$100,000	16,380	6,275	3,147	1,746	1,017	608
$150,000	24,570	9,412	4,721	2,619	1,525	912
$200,000	32,759	12,549	6,295	3,492	2,034	1,216
$300,000	49,139	18,824	9,442	5,238	3,050	1,824
$500,000	81,899	31,373	15,737	8,730	5,084	3,040

The balance of this book will show you how to apply the investment strategy that has the highest probability of achieving the absolute dollars you need within your time frame with the appropriate level of risk. Think of it this way. Your investment program should be designed to overcome any shortfalls, not to beat the stock market.

Before we actually put this knowledge to work, let's take a look at the different investment vehicles you should use in your investment program and why. Part Two will cover how mutual funds work.

HOW DOES
IT ALL WORK?

8

UNDERSTANDING HOW MUTUAL FUNDS WORK

FOOTBALL GREAT **R**AYMOND **B**ERRY *decided to study every great quarterback to discover the secrets of passing. His conclusion: The only thing they had in common was that they all threw the ball differently.*

This is not about which is the best mutual fund or the top mutual fund. This chapter will discuss the basic trading structure or vehicle you should use; it's called a *mutual fund.* Think of a mutual fund as a financial intermediary that makes investments on your behalf. The mutual fund pools all its investors' funds together and buys stocks, bonds, or other assets on behalf of the group as a whole. Each investor receives a certificate of ownership and a regular statement of his or her account indicating the value of the shares of the total investment pool.

A mutual fund, in other words, is an investment company that makes investments on behalf of its participants who share common financial goals.

Mutual funds continually issue new shares of the fund for sale to the public. The number of shares and the price are directly related to the value of the securities the mutual fund holds. A fund's share price can change from day to day, depending on the daily value of its underlying securities.

The main reasons why people invest in mutual funds are convenience, accessing professional knowledge, and the opportunity to earn higher returns through a combination of growth and reinvestment of dividends. See Fig. 8–1.

FIGURE 8–1   Households Investing in Mutual Funds, Millions
Source: FUNDAMENTALS, *December 1996, 1996 Securities Industry*

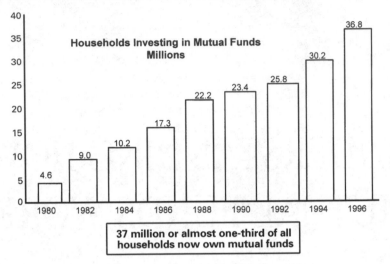

37 million or almost one-third of all
households now own mutual funds

To understand why mutual funds are so popular, let's examine just how mutual funds work.

HOW MUTUAL FUNDS WORK

The manager of the mutual fund uses the pool of capital to buy a variety of stocks, bonds, or money market instruments based on the advertised financial objectives of the fund. These objectives cover a wide range. Some funds follow aggressive policies, involving greater risk in search of higher returns. Others seek current income and no risk. Since each mutual fund has a specific investment objective, the investor has the ability to select a variety of funds to meet asset allocation and diversification needs.

When you purchase mutual fund shares, you pay the *net asset value*. This is the value of the fund's total investment, minus any debt, divided by the number of outstanding shares. For example, if the fund's investment value is $26,000, with no debt and 1,000 shares outstanding, then the net asset value (NAV) is $26 per share. The NAV is not a fixed figure because it must reflect the daily change in the price of the securities within the fund's portfolio.

In a regular mutual fund which includes thousands and often millions of shares, the NAV is calculated on a daily basis without commissions, in full and fractional units, with values moving up or down along with the stock and bond markets.

The biggest mistake that first time investors make when buying mutual funds is to look first (and sometimes only) at the prior performance of the fund or to pay too much attention to the current bond fund yield. Fund costs are an equally important factor in the return that you earn from a mutual fund. Fees are deducted from your investment. All other things being equal, high fees and other charges depress your returns.

Fees

Because of the large amounts of assets under management, investment companies are able to offer *economies of scale,* or competitive fee schedules, to their customers. The management fees charged depend on the complexity of the asset management demands. Foreign equity management requires substantially more research, specialized implementation, and greater transaction costs than the management of a U.S. government bond fund. Asset management fees reflect those differences. Equity mutual fund fees are higher than bond mutual fund fees.

Fee comparisons are particularly important. Remember to compare the proverbial apples to apples—in this case, similar equities to equity mutual funds; and similar bonds to bond mutual funds. See Fig. 8–2.

Keeping a Careful Eye on Costs

You can put more money to work for you in your investment by keeping a careful eye on costs. It's simply common sense—lower expenses translate to higher overall returns. The goal of the first time investor is to keep acquisition costs as low as possible. Let's look at costs.

FIGURE 8–2   Fee Comparisons of Various Mutual Funds

Mutual fund	Annual Performance	Management Fees	Net Performance
Foreign Equities	12.50%	1.25%	11.25%
US Large Cap	12.50	1.00	11.50
US Small Cap	13.00	1.20	11.8
Investment-Grade Bonds	7.80	0.65	7.15
High-Yield Bonds	9.25	0.75	8.50
Foreign Bonds	9.25	0.90	8.35

Sales Charges

Sales charges (or loads) are commissions paid on the sale of mutual funds. In the past, all commissions were simply charged up front, but that has changed. There are now several ways that mutual fund companies charge fees. See Fig. 8–3.

The sales charge is called a *load* and is subtracted from the initial mutual fund investment. A no-load fund does not have this charge, although other fees or service charges may be buried in its cost structure. Don't be misled: Nearly all mutual funds have a sales charge. Some are hidden, others are not. Let's talk about the ones that you can see. See Fig. 8–4. You can see about one-half of the $2.6 trillion invested in mutual funds is split evenly between load and no-load.

A *front-end load* mutual fund charges a fee when an investor buys it. Loaded mutual funds can also be *back-end load*—they have a deferred sales charge—and are sometimes known as *B shares*. This option has higher internal costs. If you decide to redeem your shares early, usually within the 5 years, you pay a surrender charge, as illustrated in Fig. 8–3.

FIGURE 8–3   (No-Load) Mutual Funds

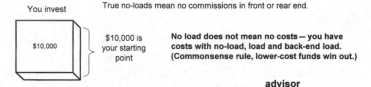

advisor

Sales loads are commissions paid to brokers and financial advisers who sell mutual funds. They typically range from 4 percent to as high as 8.5 percent of the amount you invest.

FRONT-END (LOAD) MUTUAL FUNDS

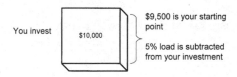

BACK-END (LOAD) MUTUAL FUNDS

Some no-load mutual funds have redemption fees that scale down the longer you hold them. The broker/advisor is paid a commission by the mutual fund company. If you leave the fund earlier than the scheduled commission that will be subtracted from your proceeds.

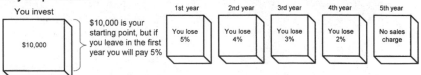

FIGURE 8–4   Growth of Long-Term Mutual Fund Assets

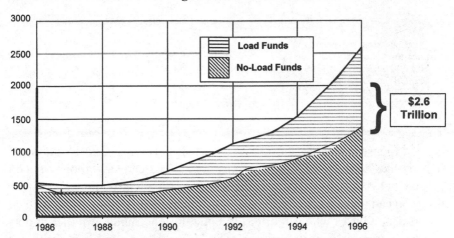

A customer who redeems shares in the first year of ownership would typically pay a 5 percent sales charge. The amount would drop by an equal amount each year. After 6 years, the shares could be redeemed without further charge. For large investments, you should never purchase B-share mutual funds. There are those brokers out there who will tell you it is better to invest in B shares, since you will not pay an up-front fee. If you invest a large amount, you will get a breakpoint inside an A-share mutual fund, and your annual costs will be lower.

- For A shares you pay the commission all at once.
- B shares have a contingent deferred sales charge. They are more popular with brokers because you don't pay any up-front load, but every year they take out 1 percent to pay the broker.
- C shares typically have even higher internal expenses and pay the selling broker up to 1 percent per year based on the amount of the assets. This fee comes directly from your investment performance. The C shares may have no up-front fee, but a possible 1 percent deferred sales charge in year 1 (sometimes longer), and higher annual expenses (up to 1 percent extra per year). I would avoid them.

See Fig. 8–5. You will notice that the public offering price is different from the net amount invested column. The offering price, known as the *ask price,* is greater than the fund's net asset value. The NAV is identified as the amount per share you would receive if you sold your shares.

No-load mutual funds do *not* mean *no cost.* Some no-load funds charge a redemption fee of 1 to 2 percent of the net asset value of the shares, to

FIGURE 8–5   Commission Schedule for Typical Mutual Fund

	Sales Commission as a percentage of:	
Purchase amount (A shares)	Public Offering	Real Cost
Less than $50,000	5.00%	5.26%
$50,000 but less than $100,000	4.00	4.17
$250,000 but less than $500,000	3.00	3.09
$500,000 but less than $1,000,000	1.00	1.01
$1,000,000 or more	0.00	0.00

cover expenses mainly incurred by advertising. Buying a no-load mutual fund is like doing your own plumbing work. You can save money if you know what you're doing; but if you don't have the required time and expertise, you can make a serious mistake. I highly recommend working with an investment advisor who can offer the same no-load funds. Another important fact to remember is that when you call the toll-free number of the mutual fund company with a question, you are serviced by an employee of the mutual fund company, and the advice you receive may be biased.

Investors who are truly devoted to learning about financial matters, and who follow financial news, reading enough to keep themselves well informed, may be able to do this for themselves. But most investors are not in this category and are well advised to seek professional guidance for their investments.

Operating Expenses
Fees pay for the operational costs of running a fund—employees' salaries, marketing, servicing the toll-free phone line, printing and mailing published materials, computers for tracking investments and account balances, accounting fees, and so on. A fund's operating expenses are quoted as a percentage of your investment; the percentage represents an annual fee or charge. You can find this number in a fund's prospectus in the fund expenses section, entitled something like "Total Fund Operating Expenses."

A mutual fund's operating expenses are normally invisible to investors because the expenses are deducted before any return is paid and are automatically charged on a daily basis.

Other Things You Should Know
Dividends
Dividends and capital gains (the profits from a sale of stock) are paid in proportion to the number of mutual fund shares you own. So even if you invest a few hundred dollars, you get the same investment return per dollar as those who invest millions. The problem is that you will have to pay taxes on this

amount even if it is reinvested. You can use a variable annuity to defer those taxes until you plan to spend the money.

Prospectus and Annual Reports

Mutual fund companies produce information that can help you make decisions about mutual fund investments. All funds are required to issue a prospectus. You can now get a lot of the mutual fund prospectus information from the Internet. You can take a look at the funds' past performance and see what asset class they really fall in. This legal document is reviewed and audited by the U.S. Securities and Exchange Commission.

Statements

Any mutual fund in which you participate will send you a year-end statement itemizing the income you've received. You should save this sheet along with other records of dividends, tax-exempt interest, and capital gains distributions, as well as records of the amounts received from the sale of shares for tax purposes.

Full-time Professionals

When you invest in a mutual fund, you are hiring a team of professional investment managers to make complex investment judgments and handle complicated trading, record-keeping, and safekeeping responsibilities for you. People whose full-time profession is money management will sift through the thousands of available investments in order to choose those that, in their judgment, are best suited to achieving the investment goals of a fund as spelled out in the fund's prospectus.

Full-time professionals select the portfolio's securities and then constantly monitor investments to determine if these continue to meet the fund's objectives. As economic conditions change, professionals may adjust the mix of the fund's investments to adopt a more aggressive or defensive posture. Having access to research analysis and computerized support, professional management can help identify opportunities in the markets that the average investor may not have the expertise or access to identify.

Diversification

Diversification is one important characteristic that attracts many investors to mutual funds. By owning a diverse portfolio of many stocks and/or bonds, investors can reduce the risk associated with owning any individual security.

To go it alone, you would need to invest money in at least 8 to 12 different securities in different industries to ensure that your portfolio could withstand a downturn in one or more of the investments. A mutual fund is typically invested in 25 to 100 or more securities. Proper diversification ensures that the fund receives the highest possible return at the lowest possible risk, given the objectives of the fund.

Mutual funds do not escape share price declines during major market downturns. For example, mutual funds that invested in stocks certainly declined during the October 27, 1997, market crash when the Dow Jones plunged 554.26 points. However, the most unlucky investors that month were individuals who had all their money riding in Asian mutual funds. Some fund shares plunged in price by as much as 30 to 40 percent that month. Widely diversified mutual funds were least affected.

Low Initial Investment
Each mutual fund establishes the minimum amount required to make an initial investment, and then how much additional is required when investors want to add more. A majority of mutual funds have low initial minimums, some less than $1,000.

Liquidity
One of the key advantages of mutual funds stems from the liquidity provided by this investment. You can sell your shares at any time, and mutual funds have a "ready market" for their shares. Additionally, shareholders directly receive any dividend or interest payments earned by the fund. Payments are usually made on a quarterly basis. When the fund manager sells some of the investments at a profit, the net gain is also distributed, but net losses are retained by the fund. Inside the mutual fund, when the dividends or capital gains are disbursed, the NAV is reduced by the disbursement.

Audited Performance
All mutual funds are required to disclose historical data about the fund through their prospectus—returns earned by the fund, operating expenses and other fees, and the fund's rate of trading turnover. The Securities and Exchange Commission (SEC) audits these disclosures for accuracy. Having the SEC on your side is like having a vigilant guard dog focused on the guy who's responsible for your money. Remember, all mutual funds are registered investments. This does not mean that the SEC recommends them, but it does mean the SEC has reviewed them for abuse and fraud.

Automatic Reinvestment
One of the major benefits of mutual funds is that dividends can be reinvested automatically and converted to more shares.

Switching

Switching, or an exchange privilege, is offered by most mutual funds through so-called family or umbrella plans. Switching from one mutual fund to another accommodates changes in investment goals as well as changes in the market and the economy. Again, this switching between mutual funds creates taxable implications. For instance, when you redeem a Franklin Growth and Income Fund and buy a Franklin NY Municipal Bond Fund, you have to pay taxes on the gains you earned.

Low Transaction Costs

When an individual investor places an order to buy 300 shares of a $30 stock ($9,000 investment), he or she is likely to get a commission bill for about $204, or 2.3 percent of the value of the investment. Even at a discount broker, the commission is likely to cost between $82 (0.9 percent) and $107 (1.2 percent). A mutual fund, on the other hand, is more likely to be buying 30,000 to 300,000 shares at a time! Its commission costs often run in the vicinity of one-tenth of the commission you would pay at a discount broker. Where your commission might be $0.35 per share, the mutual fund would only pay $0.05 per share or even less. The commission savings can (and should) mean higher returns for you as a mutual fund shareholder.

Flexibility in Risk Level

An investor can select from a variety of different mutual funds, finding a risk level she or he is comfortable with and goals that match his or her own.

1. *Stock funds.* If you want your money to grow over a long time, funds that invest more heavily in stocks may be most appropriate.
2. *Bond funds.* If you need current income and don't want investments that fluctuate in value as widely as stocks, more conservative bond funds may be the best choice.
3. *Money market funds.* If you want to be sure that your invested principal does not drop in value, because you may need your money in the short term, a money market fund or a guaranteed fixed-interest investment may best fit your needs.

No Risk of Bankruptcy

A situation in which the demand for money back (liabilities) exceeds the value of a fund's investments (assets) cannot occur with a mutual fund. The value can fluctuate, but this variation doesn't lead to the failure or bankruptcy of a mutual fund company. In fact, since the Investment Company Act of 1940 was passed to regulate the mutual fund industry, no fund has ever gone under.

In contrast, hundreds of banks and dozens of insurance companies have failed in the past two decades alone. Banks and insurers can fail because their liabilities can exceed their assets. When a bank makes too many loans that go sour at the same time and depositors want their money back, the bank fails. Likewise, if an insurance company makes several poor investments or underestimates the number of claims that will be made by insurance policyholders, then it, too, can fail. But mutual funds are held in separate accounts and are not part of an insurance company's assets.

Custodian Bank

A *custodian* is a separate organization that holds the specific securities in which a mutual fund is invested independent of the mutual fund company. The employment of a custodian ensures that the fund management company can't embezzle your funds or use assets from a better-performing fund to subsidize a poor performer.

HOW DO THESE VARIOUS PARTIES WORK TOGETHER?

After you have written your check to the mutual fund, the mutual fund company sends that check on your behalf to an organization functioning as a *transfer agent*. Here your investment is recorded and processed, and the real safeguards come into play. The agent transfers the money, not to the mutual fund's portfolio manager (the individual or firm that makes the investment decisions, technically known as the *investment advisor*), but to a *custodian bank*. See Fig. 8–6.

Once that custodian bank receives the money, it notifies the mutual fund that new money is available for investment. The fund manager checks a daily account balance sheet, and "new" monies are invested according to the mutual funds' investment policy.

The Investment Company Act of 1940's requirement of independent custody for each mutual fund's assets has turned out to be the key provision that has sheltered the industry from potential trouble for half a century. Separate custody means a mutual fund's parent company can go belly-up without any loss to the fund's shareholders, because their assets are held apart from other funds and apart from the parent fund.

Contrast this business structure with the far less restrictive setup between, say, individual investors and a real estate promoter, or investors and a stockbroker who may have direct access to her or his clients' accounts. In any number of notorious incidents, individuals in such a position have taken the money and run.

FIGURE 8–6   Relationship of Various Parties of Mutual Fund

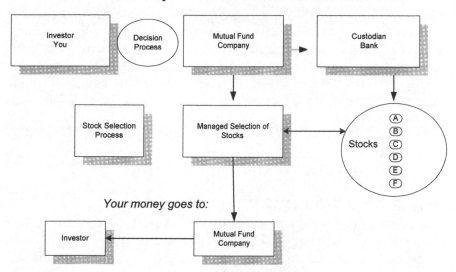

The limited partnership of the 1970s and 1980s was an excellent example of a poor business structure. During those years, many unregulated and
unregistered limited partnerships were formed, and investors sent their money
directly to the limited partnership company. An unscrupulous promoter could
simply write himself or herself a check. Financial scandals were numerous.

A money manager of a mutual fund has no direct access to the investors'
cash. The fund manager only decides how to invest shareholders' money. The
custodian who controls the underlying securities allows them to be traded or
exchanged with other institutional investors only after getting proper docu-
mentation from the manager. The upshot of independent custody is that it's very
difficult for a fund manager to use the money for personal purposes.

The Investment Company Act adds other layers of investor protection
as well. Independent accountants must regularly audit every fund. A fund's
board of directors, who serve as modern-day trustees, negotiate prudent contract terms with the fund's service providers and generally oversee the operation. The SEC has the power to inspect funds and bring enforcement action
against those who break the rules.

In addition, mutual fund firms have legions of compliance lawyers—
essentially in-house cops—paid to make sure that portfolio managers, traders,
and others follow the rules.

A Code of Conduct

Under SEC rules, fund managers are required to abide by strict codes of conduct. The codes require advance reporting of personal securities transactions so that there can be no conflict of interest between a manager's personal trades and what she or he does with the fund's securities. Otherwise, managers could "front-run" their own funds, personally buying or selling securities before the fund traded them in, to the managers' gain and possibly the fund's loss. To avoid such potential for self-dealing—that is, favoring one fund at the expense of another—the SEC has set down strict guidelines for when funds in the same company trade a security between each other rather than on the open market.

MAJOR TYPES OF MUTUAL FUNDS

The number of mutual funds has nearly tripled since 1980. In the current universe of approximately 8,000 funds, there are portfolios that suit most investment risk objectives. Likewise, the number of options has skyrocketed. There are funds that invest in high-quality growth stocks, or smaller aggressive growth stocks, or stocks that pay high dividends. Mutual funds that invest in corporate and government bonds are also available.

Many fund management companies offer a number of different types of funds under one roof, often referred to as a *family of funds*. A fund might include a growth stock fund, an aggressive growth stock fund, a fund that invests in stocks and bonds, a tax-exempt bond fund, a money market fund, and perhaps many others. Most mutual funds permit their customers to exchange from one fund to another within the group for a small fee, should their personal investment objectives change.

Following is a description of how, roughly, the $2 trillion currently invested in mutual funds breaks down. Despite endless variations, there are basically three broad categories of mutual funds: those aimed at providing immediate income, those oriented toward long-term growth or appreciation, and those that stress tax-free returns. The fund's objectives will be stated at the opening of the prospectus, indicating whether the fund emphasizes high or low risk, stability or speculation. Funds generally fall into one of nine major types: growth, growth and income, income, bond, money market, tax-free, metals, foreign, and specialized.

Stock Funds

Stock mutual funds invest only in stocks (also called *equity funds*). Following are the various types of stock funds:

Growth Funds

These stock funds emphasize growth. Dividend payouts will typically be low. These funds stress capital appreciation rather than immediate income. A typical growth fund would be the Vanguard S&P 500 Index Fund. This is a fund that consists of U.S. large-cap stocks and has the primary objective to equal the return of that of the 500 largest U.S. stock companies.

According to Morningstar, as of June 30, 1996, the average-growth mutual fund had returned 12.0 percent over the last 10 years, but only 9.4 percent after tax (assuming maximum brackets). This reduction in return is due to dividend and capital gain distributions made by the funds, which are taxable to investors.

Aggressive Growth Funds

Aggressive growth funds invest in smaller, lesser-known companies, giving these companies time and room for enough upward movement to perform spectacularly during a bull market. As the name implies, these funds are invested for maximum capital gains, capital appreciation, and performance. This type of portfolio can be highly volatile and speculative. The old adage "high risk, high return" would fit. Historically, the more aggressive funds, or small-cap funds, have outperformed the larger blue-chip growth funds. You should be aware, though, that these returns also come with higher volatility, meaning the roller coaster ride has much bigger dips.

Balanced Funds

These portfolios stress three main goals: income, capital appreciation, and preservation of capital. This type of fund balances holdings such as bonds, convertible securities, and preferred stock as well as common stock. The mix varies depending on the manager's view of the economy and market conditions. The theory here is that the managers will have a better crystal ball than you at home, since they make big bucks and sit in front of a computer terminal all day looking at graphs. I generally do not believe in these funds unless they have a static ratio of stocks to bonds. I normally look for the manager to keep 60 percent in stock and 40 percent in bonds. Since they are diversified into both bond and stock markets, these funds are most appropriate for investors who can afford only one fund.

Growth and Income Funds

Combining stocks and bonds, this type of fund makes a serious effort at capturing both modest income and a long-term rise in the stock market. The manager is typically looking for blue-chip companies that pay high dividends. Another strategy is to place a large percentage of the portfolio in equities and a portion in fixed income to generate the dividends. The concept of these funds is that they will have lower volatility and a more predictable and consistent return.

Income Funds

Their advertised investment objectives are safety and income, rather than capital appreciation, but I'm skeptical. Income funds invest in corporate bonds or government-insured mortgages; if they own any stocks at all, these are usually preferred shares. The danger lies in chasing higher yields and not looking at the risks. I had sold income funds back in the mid-1980s. I was unaware that the fund managers had paid a premium for high-yielding bonds, so when interest rates dropped and the bonds were called, the investors lost principal.

Utility Funds

Utility funds invest in stocks in utility companies around the country. Like bonds, utility stocks generate high income. Utilities are defensive investments in services that are needed, no matter how bad things get. The concept here is that everyone needs electricity, gas, water, etc. The problem is that we may need them, but sometimes the amount of regulation on these companies and the cost of distributing energy can negate the benefit of constant demand. Utility funds need to be treated as risk-based investments as any stock mutual fund would. I'd feel better recommending you just buy your local utility company.

Specialty Funds

Specialty funds are also known as *sector funds* because they tend to invest in stocks in specific industries. Sector funds should be avoided for large percentages of a portfolio. Investing in stocks of a single industry defeats a major purpose of investing in mutual funds—you're giving up the benefits of diversification. A sector fund would be something like the India Fund or a gold fund. They can be used to build a portfolio, but only in small amounts. I would caution anyone not to place a large percentage of a portfolio in these types of funds.

Specialty funds tend to carry much higher expenses than other mutual funds. The only types of specialty funds that may make sense for a small portion (10 percent or less) of your investment portfolio are funds that invest in real estate or precious metals.

Gold Funds

A gold fund is a cost-effective way to participate in the possible increase in the price of gold. Some funds invest only in South African stocks owning shares of mining firms. The downside is that gold can be highly volatile. These types of funds can help diversify your portfolio because they can do better during times of higher inflation.

Global Equity Funds

U.S. international and global funds focus their investments outside of the United States. The term *international* typically means that a fund can invest anywhere in the world except the United States. The term *global* generally implies that a fund can invest anywhere in the world, including the United States.

Hybrid Funds

Hybrid funds invest in a mixture of different types of securities. Most commonly, they invest in bonds and stocks. These funds are usually less risky and volatile than funds investing exclusively in stocks. Hybrid mutual funds are typically known as *balanced* or *asset allocation funds*. Balanced funds generally try to maintain a fairly constant percentage of investment in stocks and bonds.

Asset Allocation Funds

Asset allocation funds tend to adjust the mix of different investments according to the portfolio manager's expectations. Depending on the manager, these could also be called *market timing funds*. The only problem is that no one can accurately predict the actions of the market.

Bond Funds

Bonds are essentially IOUs. When you buy a bond, you are lending your money to a corporation or government agency. A bond mutual fund is nothing more than a large group (pack) of bonds. Most bond funds invest in bonds of similar maturity (the number of years to elapse before the borrower must pay back the money you lend). The names of most bond funds include a word or two to provide clues about the average length of maturity of their bonds.

For example, a short-term bond fund concentrates its investments in bonds maturing in the next few years. An intermediate-term fund generally holds bonds that come due within 7 to 10 years. The bonds in a long-term fund usually mature in 20 years or so. In contrast to an individual bond that you buy and hold until it matures, a bond fund is always replacing bonds in its portfolio to maintain its average maturity objective.

Bond funds are useful when you want to live off dividend income or when you don't want to put all your money in riskier investments such as stocks and real estate (perhaps because you plan to use the money soon).

Global Bond Funds
Global bond funds invest in foreign as well as in U.S. bonds. Historically, global bond funds have outperformed domestic bond funds, but you do assume additional risk.

Money Market Funds
Money market funds are the safest type of mutual funds if you are worried about the risk of losing your principal. Money market funds are like bank savings accounts in that the value of your investment does not fluctuate. This type of fund could be used as your core saving strategy.

Index Funds
Think of these funds as whole baskets of stocks, representing the various stock market indexes. The S&P 500 Index Fund is by far the most common index fund for both institutional and individual investors. It tracks the performance of the Standard & Poor's 500 Index, a capitalization-weighted index of 500 large U.S. stocks. It is estimated that over 95 percent of all retail indexed monies are invested in S&P 500 Index funds.

Following is a list of the indexes:

- The *Wilshire 5000* includes all 5,000 stocks on the New York Stock Exchange Annex as well as over-the-counter (OTC) stocks. The Wilshire essentially takes the entire market as an index.

- The *NASDAQ 100,* the National Association of Securities Dealers index of stocks traded over the counter via its automatic quoting system NASDAQ. The NASDAQ 100 measures price changes in 100 of the largest OTC industrial stocks.

- The *S&P 500,* also known as *Standard & Poor's Composite Index* of 500 stocks, consists of the New York Stock Exchange–listed companies plus a few of the American Stock Exchange and over-the-counter stocks. Also 7 percent are non-U.S. companies and investment companies which can be affected by currency translations. One of the downsides of the S&P 500 is that the companies are chosen by committee, rather than by market efficiency.

- The *Schwab 1000 Index,* possibly a better index, makes it possible for you to invest in 1,000 U.S. companies with just one investment. It includes common stocks of the 100 largest publicly traded U.S. companies, measured by market capitalization. This represents 82 percent of the U.S. stock market value. It's a broader index, a broader diversification, not selected by a committee or Charles Schwab, but according to a formula of market capitalization. The fund invests in large and medium-sized growth companies and is designed to track the broad U.S. stock price in dividend performance in order to keep pace with the market.

- *Morgan Stanley EAFE* (Europe, Australia, and Far East) *Index* is actually two subindexes of 1,000 stocks traded in Europe and the Pacific Basin; it is the most commonly used index for mutual funds that invest in foreign stocks.

Other Types of Index Funds

Warning: Be cautious with these index hybrids. Recent news indicates that some brokers are using these strategies to combat index investing and are advising their clients that they can trade these as they would a stock (which you now know doesn't work in the long run). Anyway, this new strategy is called *SPDRs,* "spiders," for Standard & Poor's depository receipts, available on the American Stock Exchange. SPDRs combine the advantage of index funds with the superior trading and flexibility of common stocks.

SPDRs buy and sell shares only to adjust the changes in the composite of the S&P index without the need to meet investor redemptions as an index fund does. When individual investors want to take money out, they simply sell shares on the American Stock Exchange.

If you want an index other than the S&P 500, there's Standard & Poor's Midcap, 400 depository receipts; and globally, there are SPDRs called World Equity Benchmark Shares, (WEBS) at select major international equity markets. The ticker symbols are SPDRs (SPY); Midcap is SPDRs (MDY) and Diamonds (DIA).

For information on SPDRs, call 800-The-Amex or click on www.amex.com. On WEBS, call 800-810-WEBS or click on: //websontheweb.com.$.

Here is a list of companies who provide financial services:

- *Vanguard Group,* 1-800-962-5160, www.vanguard.com.
- *Merrill Lynch,* 1-800-MERRILL ext. 2896, www.plan.ml.com/zine/tax. You can order the book *You and Your Money, A Financial Handbook for Women Investors.*

- *Charles Schwab and Co.,* 1-800-806-8481, www.schwab.com.
- *Fidelity Investments, www.fidelity.com.* You can ask for a rollover individual retirement account (IRA) kit, kit for retirees, mutual fund kit, brokerage kit, and retirement planning for small business.
- *Microsoft Money '98 Financial Office,* www.pcmall.com/money98.
- *National Discount Brokers,* 1-800-888–3999, www.ndb.com.

Asset Class Mutual Funds

For a moment, think of mutual funds as being like a huge automotive mart that offers everything from everyday economical cars to sports cars that go fast, but soon need a mechanic. There are lemons among them. You have to be wary of the seductive luxury cars with lot of extras that drive up the price. When I think in terms of the automotive mart analogy, I consider asset class mutual funds to be like my uncle's old Buick. He died long before the car did.

Asset class mutual funds are composed of financial instruments with similar characteristics. Unlike managers of index funds, asset fund managers actively manage costs when buying and selling for funds.

The most important attributes of asset class mutual funds are low operating expenses, low turnover, and low trading costs.

Low Operating Expenses

An important study of retail equity mutual funds by Elton and Gruber[1] finds that the more expensive a fund is, the worse it performs on average. Low expense is one of the main reasons to use asset class mutual funds.

Low Turnover

Active mutual fund managers do a lot of trading—this is how they think they are adding value. As a result, the average retail mutual fund has an annual turnover rate of 86 percent. This represents $86,000 of traded securities for every $100,000 invested.

High turnover is costly to shareholders because each time a trade is made, there are transaction costs involved. These costs include commissions, spreads, and market impact costs. These hidden costs may amount to more than a fund's total operating expenses.

Retail mutual funds have high turnover because they're under tremendous pressure to perform. Good short-term performance leads to a bonus

[1] Edwin J. Elton, Martin J. Gruber, Sanjiv Das, and Matthew Hlavka, "Efficiency with Costly Information: A Reinterpretation of Evidence from Managed Portfolios," *The Society for Financial Studies,* 1993.

for the manager and a flood of new money for the fund. If they are performing poorly, retail mutual funds often try to make up ground by changing the composition of their holdings.

If mutual funds sell a security for a gain, they must make a capital gain distribution to shareholders. This is because mutual funds are required to distribute 98 percent of their taxable income each year, including realized capital gains, to stay tax-exempt at the corporate level. No mutual fund manager wants to have her or his performance reduced by paying corporate income taxes.

Low Trading Costs
These are composed of commissions, bid/ask spreads, and market impact costs.

The Four Major Equity Asset Classes

1.   U.S. large-company stocks
2.   U.S. small-company stocks
3.   International large-company stocks
4.   International small-company stocks

These four equity asset classes represent more than 5,000 different stock positions in 14 different countries. U.S. large stocks mean the domestic companies with capitalizations greater than $50 million; small means less than $50 million. Academic research shows that large- and small-company stocks have low correlation with one another.

When the equity markets decline, fixed-income securities will dampen the fall. The two major equity asset classes are:

1.   Fixed income
2.   International fixed income

U.S. Equity Asset Class Mutual Funds

U.S. equity asset class funds and pure index funds have portfolios that are market-capitalization-weighted. In other words, the fund manager allocates money to U.S. companies based on the size of their markets, measured by market capitalization.

International Equity Asset Classes

Global investing is a hot topic on Wall Street and among money managers, many of whom for various reasons would rather have U.S. investors park their funds at home. They therefore discourage international investing for their clients. These clever managers and advisors have even come up with ways that investors can seemingly play markets abroad by using domestic assets. This theory holds that the way to make a global play—without taking on true global securities exposure—is to buy the stocks of U.S. multinational firms doing a great deal of business abroad.

This idea seems clever at first glance, but there are difficulties. What undermines this concept most is that stocks of multinational firms tend to follow the movements of their local markets rather than the international market. This is true regardless of the degree to which their operations are globally diversified. For example, Colgate gets about 80 percent of its revenues from foreign operations, yet its stock price still closely follows the U.S. market. Because stocks of U.S. multinational firms are so highly correlated with the U.S. market, they lose their diversification power.

It has become conventional wisdom that you should put some of your money in international equities. The two reasons most often given for this recommendation are that (1) foreign stocks have historically outperformed U.S. stocks and (2) foreign stocks provide good diversification due to their low correlation with U.S. markets. While it is true that international stocks measured by Morgan Stanley Capital International's EAFE Index have outperformed the S&P 500 since 1970, this occurs only because foreign currencies have outperformed the U.S. dollar. In local-currency terms, the returns of foreign and domestic stocks are about equal.

Instead of investing in international equities for higher returns, you should include them in your portfolio to reduce risk. The international and U.S. equity markets have a low correlation; they do not tend to move together. Given the data, our desire is for true global diversification, and our belief is that U.S. and foreign stocks have equal expected returns.

Most international asset class funds and pure index funds have portfolios that are market-capitalization-weighted. In other words, the fund manager allocates money to countries based on the size of their markets, measured by market capitalization. Currently, Japan is the largest of any market outside the United States. Therefore, a market-capitalization-weighted international fund will allocate more money to Japan than to any other country. This approach probably puts too much money in Japanese stocks. The overweighting occurs because, in Japan, it is common for companies to invest in the stocks of other companies.

These cross-holdings are counted twice, which overstates the market capitalization of Japan relative to the rest of the world.

Fixed-Income Asset Class Mutual Funds

Fixed-income securities are an important part of a comprehensive portfolio because they provide stability to counterbalance the high volatility of equities. While these funds have lower expected returns than stocks do, the funds add value to the portfolio by reducing overall volatility. Bonds are the primary tools for pinpointing your portfolio to your target risk level. A higher allocation to bonds reduces portfolio risk, and a lower allocation to bonds increases portfolio risk.

A bond represents a loan to an issuer, such as the U.S. government or a major corporation, usually in return for periodic fixed interest payments. These payments continue until the bond is redeemed at maturity (or earlier if called by the issuer). At the time of maturity, the investor receives the face value of the bond.

Many investors buy long-term bonds because they normally have higher current yields than shorter-term bonds do. Investors consider them safe, but in reality long-term bonds have many different kinds of risk. These risks include reinvestment risk, call risk, purchasing power risk, liquidity risk, and interest rate risk.

The major risk you face with long-term bonds is interest rate risk. Because prices of bonds move in the opposite direction of interest rates, when rates rise, prices of bonds fall, and vice versa. For example, consider a newly issued 20-year Treasury bond with a 6 percent coupon. If over the next 12 months, interest rates increase by 2 percent, new 20-year Treasury bonds will be offered with 8 percent coupons. Therefore, the old 6 percent bonds will be worth less than the new bonds since the new bonds have higher coupons. This illustrates how falling interest rates force bond prices up. Alternatively, interest rates may rise and force bond prices down. This inverse relationship between interest rates and bond values is an important risk of fixed-income investments. It can create significant volatility, especially for long-term bonds.

To give you an idea of how volatility of long-term bonds, consider the historical rates of total return of 20-year Treasury bonds over the last six decades. During the 1980s, long-term bond investors enjoyed one of the best decades ever, with gains averaging 12.7 percent per year. Bond prices soared during this decade due to declining interest rates. Because of these high returns, long-term bonds became very popular in the late 1980s and early 1990s, since investors frequently place too much importance on their most recent experiences. Psychologists call this *cognitive bias*. We call it *rearview mirror investing*. It is like trying to drive a car while only looking where you have been through the rearview mirror. It is crucial to analyze all statistical evidence available when you make financial decisions.

In contrast, consider the decade of the 1950s. This was the worst decade for long-term bond investors because they experienced an average annual return of –0.1 percent including reinvested interest.

Most investors don't realize that the volatility of long-term bonds is close to the volatility of common stocks. The historical data show that long-term bonds don't actually provide the low risk that many fixed-income investors are seeking.

The higher risk of long-term bonds would be acceptable if investors were sufficiently rewarded with higher rates of return. Eugene Fama of the University of Chicago has studied the rates of return of long-term bonds from 1964 to 1996, and he found that the term premium for longer-term bonds is not reliable. His research shows that long-term bonds have wide variances in their rates of return and, most important, that bonds with maturities beyond 5 years don't offer sufficient reward for their higher risk.

The predominant investors in the long-term bond markets are institutions, such as corporate pension plans and life insurance companies. These investors are interested in funding long-term obligations, including fixed annuity payments or other fixed corporate responsibilities. In general, they are not concerned with the volatility of principal or with the effects of inflation, since their obligations are fixed in maturity date and amount. You, on the other hand, should be concerned with inflation as well as volatility. This is because you are an individual living in a variable-rate world. You have a limit to the amount of volatility with which you feel comfortable.

Given the data, you should own fixed-income investments to provide stability to your portfolio, not to generate high returns. High returns should come from equities. Fixed-income securities can help offset the risk of your equity holdings and, therefore, lower the risk of your overall portfolio. You can best do this by using short-term fixed-income securities rather than long-term bonds. Short-term bonds have less volatility and a lower correlation with stocks and are a better choice for your portfolio. They will allow you to invest a larger percentage of your money in stocks while maintaining low portfolio risk.

International Fixed-Income Asset Classes

This asset class includes foreign government bond markets—the markets of Japan, the United Kingdom, Switzerland, the Netherlands, Germany, and France. They have credit quality equal to that of the United States, according to debt ratings by Moody's and Standard & Poor's.

The Emerging Market Asset Classes

Many institutional investors now recognize emerging markets as a separate and distinct asset class. The term *emerging markets* refers to the stock markets of the world's developing countries whose economies are growing fast enough to deserve the label *emerging*.

It is also important to keep in mind that while these markets may be defined as emerging, the companies whose stocks are being purchased are well-established companies in these countries. The countries must have well-organized markets that provide ample liquidity and also have a developed legal system that protects property rights and upholds contractual obligations. Typical holdings are national banks, land developers, and phone companies of various countries. Our current country choices include Indonesia, Turkey, Argentina, Malaysia, Philippines, Portugal, Israel, Mexico, Brazil, Thailand, South Korea, and Chile.

These emerging countries are experiencing rapid growth and improvements in their political, social, and economic conditions. You might conclude that the higher rates of economic growth in these countries should lead to higher stock returns. This is a common message communicated by the financial press and investment professionals. While it is true that emerging market countries have higher economic growth rates than the developed world does, this alone does not mean their stock returns will be higher, because stock prices already reflect the market's expectations of high growth.

What is not so widely understood is that emerging market returns are *not* due to faster economic growth. Higher returns are a reward for accepting higher risk.

Emerging market investing involves substantial risks including political instability, extreme market volatility, lack of liquidity, dramatic currency devaluation, high transaction costs, and regulatory risk. And because of a lack of reliable information, low accounting standards, and very poor financial disclosure, the first time investor should avoid these funds unless they are a small part of an overall asset class portfolio. Look at the statistics in Fig. 8–7.

Even though investing in emerging markets seems risky, you may be surprised to see that the volatility of the emerging markets' asset class is actually less than that of U.S. small-company stocks. You might also be surprised to see that international small-company stocks and U.S. small-cap companies have approximately the same standard deviation or risk level. In the next chapter you will learn how to combine these asset classes to lower risk while enhancing returns.

FIGURE 8–7   Asset Classes: Expected Returns

Cash Equivalents	5.1%	1926–1997
Two-Year U.S. Government	7.1%	1926–1997
U.S. Large-Company Stocks	13.5%	1926–1997
U.S. Small-Company Stocks	19.4%	1926–1997
International Large-Company Stocks	13.5%	1926–1997
International Small-Company Stocks	19.4%	1926–1997
Emerging Market Stocks	16.5%	1926–1997

Asset Classes: Standard Deviation—Years

Cash Equivalents	3.3%	1926–1997
Two-Year U.S. Government	3.9%	1926–1997
U.S. Large-Company Stocks	20.3%	1926–1997
U.S. Small-Company Stocks	38.5%	1926–1997
International Large-Company Stocks	20.3%	1926–1997
International Small-Company Stocks	38.5%	1926–1997
Emerging Market Stocks	29.0%	1926–1997

Reprinted with permission from RWB Advisory Services, Inc.

HOW TO READ NEWSPAPER MUTUAL FUND TABLES

Okay, if you must, just remember the chapter on investment *noise* and don't use the publications as your main source of financial information.

The first column in Fig. 8–8 is the net asset value price per share. You'll recall, the NAV is identified as the amount per share you would receive if you sold your shares (less deferred sales charges, if any). So on any given day, you can determine the value of your holdings by multiplying the NAV by the number of shares you own.

The second column shows the net asset value change from the day before.

The third column is the abbreviated fund name. Several funds listed under the same heading indicate a family of funds.

The fourth column is the fund's investment objectives indicator. You can find a listing of investment objectives in the footnotes.

The last two columns tell you the percentage of sales commissions and annual expenses.

FIGURE 8–8   How to Read These Tables

Source: Reprinted by permission of The Wall Street Journal. © *1995 Dow Jones & Company, Inc. All Rights Reserved Worldwide.*

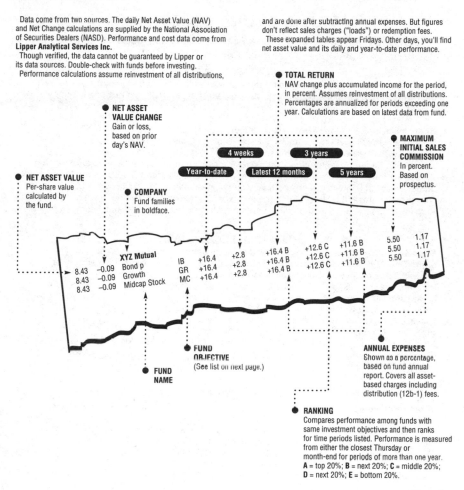

Data come from two sources. The daily Net Asset Value (NAV) and Net Change calculations are supplied by the National Association of Securities Dealers (NASD). Performance and cost data come from **Lipper Analytical Services Inc.**
Though verified, the data cannot be guaranteed by Lipper or its data sources. Double-check with funds before investing.
Performance calculations assume reinvestment of all distributions, and are done after subtracting annual expenses. But figures don't reflect sales charges ("loads") or redemption fees.
These expanded tables appear Fridays. Other days, you'll find net asset value and its daily and year-to-date performance.

● **TOTAL RETURN**
NAV change plus accumulated income for the period, in percent. Assumes reinvestment of all distributions. Percentages are annualized for periods exceeding one year. Calculations are based on latest data from fund.

● **NET ASSET VALUE CHANGE**
Gain or loss, based on prior day's NAV.

● **MAXIMUM INITIAL SALES COMMISSION**
In percent. Based on prospectus.

● **NET ASSET VALUE**
Per-share value calculated by the fund.

● **COMPANY**
Fund families in boldface.

4 weeks   3 years
Year-to-date   Latest 12 months   5 years

									5.50	1.17
XYZ Mutual					+16.4 B	+12.6 C	+11.6 B		5.50	1.17
8.43	−0.09	Bond p	IB	+16.4	+2.8	+16.4 B	+12.6 C	+11.6 B		5.50	1.17
8.43	−0.09	Growth	GR	+16.4	+2.8	+16.4 B	+12.6 C	+11.6 B	
8.43	−0.09	Midcap Stock	MC	+16.4	+2.8			

● **FUND OBJECTIVE**
(See list on next page.)

● **FUND NAME**

ANNUAL EXPENSES
Shown as a percentage, based on fund annual report. Covers all asset-based charges including distribution (12b-1) fees.

● **RANKING**
Compares performance among funds with same investment objectives and then ranks for time periods listed. Performance is measured from either the closest Thursday or month-end for periods of more than one year. **A** = top 20%; **B** = next 20%; **C** = middle 20%; **D** = next 20%; **E** = bottom 20%.

continued

The Rating Game

The mutual fund rating game works in much the same way as the old dating game on television. Investors use ratings of mutual funds that are listed in newspapers and magazines as a guide to help them pick funds that are the right ones for the portfolio.

Choosing an A-rated fund is a quick and easy way to choose a fund, but are these ratings actually useful? Let's consider mutual fund ratings in *The Wall Street Journal* as compiled by Lipper Analytical Services. Lipper awards

FIGURE 8–8 (continued)   Mutual Fund Objectives

Source: Reprinted by permission of The Wall Street Journal. © *1995 Dow Jones & Company, Inc. All Rights Reserved Worldwide.*

MUTUAL FUND OBJECTIVES

Categories complied by *The Wall Street Journal,* based on classifications by Lipper Analytical Services Inc.

STOCK FUNDS

Capital Appreciation (CP): Seeks rapid capital growth, often through high portfolio turnover.
Growth (GR): Invests in companies expecting higher-than-average revenue and earnings growth.
Growth & Income (GI): Pursues both price and dividend growth. Category includes S & P 500 index funds.
Equity Income (EI): Tends to favor stock with the highest dividends.
Small-Company Growth (SC): Stocks of lesser-known, small companies.
Midcap (MC): Shares of middle-sized companies.
Sector (SE): Health/Biotechnology; Natural Resources; Environmental; Science & Technology; Speciality & Miscellaneous; Utility; Financial Services; Real Estate; Gold Oriented funds.
Global Stock (GL): Includes small-company global; global flexible. Can invest in U.S.
International Stock (IL): (non-U.S.): International; European region; Pacific region; Japanese; Latin American; Canadian; Emerging Markets; International small company.

TAXABLE BOND FUNDS

Short-Term (SB): Ultrashort obligation and short-investment-grade corporate debt.
Short-Term U.S. (SB): Short-term U.S. Treasury; some funds can also hold agency debt.
Intermediate (ib): Investment grade corporate debt of up to 10-year maturity.
Intermediate U.S. (IG): U.S. Treasury and government agency debt.
Long-Term (AB): Corporate A-rated; Corporate BBB-rated.
Long-Term U.S. (LG): Treasury; U.S. government; zero coupon.
General U.S. Taxable (GT): Can invest in different types of bonds.
High-Yield Taxable (HC): High-yield, high-risk bonds.
Mortgage (MG): Ginnie Mae and general mortgage; Adjustable-Rate Mortgage.
World (WB): Short-world, multi-market; short-world, single-market and general-world income foreign bonds.

MUNICIPAL BOND FUNDS

Short-Term Muni (SM): Short municipal debt; Short-term California; single-states short municipal debt.
Intermediate Muni (IM): Intermediate-term municipal debt including single-state funds.
General Muni (GM): A variety of municipal debt.
Single-State Municipal (SS): Funds that invest in debt of individual states.
High-Yield Municipal (HM): High-yield, low-credit quality.
Insured (NM): California insured, New York insured, all other insured.

STOCK & BOND FUNDS

Multi-Purpose (MP): Balanced; convertible securities; income; flexible income; flexible portfolio and other multi-purpose funds that invest in both stocks and bonds.

an A to funds whose returns are in the top 20 percent of their category. The next 20 percent get B's and so on, through C, D, and E. For the period ending December 31, 1997, the Vanguard Index 500 Fund is awarded an A, the highest rating possible, while the Vanguard Index Small Company Fund is only worth a C.

This means that the Vanguard Index 500 Fund is ranked in the top 20 percent of all similar funds, and the Vanguard Index Small Company Fund only ranks in the middle of its peer group. Likewise, for the last 3 years, the Vanguard Index European Fund managed the highest rating of A, while the Vanguard Index Pacific Fund only gets a D for the previous 12 months. So something is odd or wrong with these ratings.

All these funds are pure index funds. They simply track the performance of the predetermined market index. How can one fund deserve an A when the others get D's or C's? The index funds have the lowest cost, and they're widely diversified. They should consistently rank modestly above average compared to other funds in their peer groups. Accordingly, they deserve no better and no worse than a B rating. The only possible explanation for the Lipper rating is that Vanguard funds are not benchmarked properly and are not matched to their correct peer groups.

Index funds should be the easiest of all funds to rank because they simply mirror broad market segments and disclose exactly what's in their portfolios. Active managed funds are much harder to classify than index funds because they have changing styles, moving asset allocation, and other complications. If Lipper can't classify index funds correctly, how accurate can other ratings be? Good ratings bring money into mutual funds, bonuses to managers, and so on. Naturally, managers will do whatever they need to do to improve their ratings.

For example, a recent study[2] by Brown, Harlow, and Starks found that mutual fund managers increase the risk level of their portfolios right in the middle of the year if they are not ranked among peer group performance leaders. If they were successful and their funds' rank improved, the managers would give bonuses and the fund would get increased assets from investors. If the gamble failed, the fund performed worse than it would have if it had not made any changes. But because funds are a winner-take-all industry, fund managers feel it's worth the gamble to take that kind of risk. The mutual fund rating game is a loser's game.

A Barometer of Ups And Downs

When the stock market is said to be up 10 points, what is usually meant is that the venerable Dow Jones Industrial Average (DJIA) went up 10 points. The DJIA is based on the average prices paid for 30 blue-chip stocks. The up-and-down fluctuations of the New York Stock Exchange have been record-

[2] Kelly Brown, Van Harlow, and Laurel Starks, "On Tournaments and Temptations, An Analysis of Managerial Incentives in the Mutual Fund Industry," *Journal of Finance,* March 1996, pp. 85–110.

ed since 1896, and general upward and downward movements of stock prices are symbolized on Wall Street by bulls and bears, respectively.

WHAT IS THE DOW JONES INDUSTRIAL AVERAGE?

Most investors have never heard of 29 of today's companies in the widely watched Dow average. Only one stock, General Electric Co., remains from the original 12 chosen in 1896. The Dow reflects the U.S. economy. When the Dow average ended its first day at 40.94, 12 years before Henry Ford made his first Model T, the average included such stalwarts as U.S. Leather and Tennessee Coal & Iron.

If it hadn't changed, the average wouldn't be an accurate barometer of the economy. It's true that there are only 30 companies, but they are 30 of the best-known and largest companies.

Narrow as it is, the Dow industrial average is easily the most popular gauge of the U.S. stock market. The public follows the Dow more than academics or even the Wall Street crowd do. All three television networks acknowledge the popularity of the Dow as a yardstick by citing it on their nightly news reports.

The Dow industrials are a big brand name, and in that way they have become synonymous with the fortunes of U.S. stocks generally. Investors who want to know if stocks are up or down ask about the Dow just as customers ask for a soft drink or facial tissue. We ask for a Coke, or we ask for a Kleenex.

Rival stock market averages and indexes don't have the Dow's cachet. That was even more true in the 1930s. People watched the stocks, but the Dow in most people's minds was an indicator of what the market was doing.

Dow Jones, publisher of *The Wall Street Journal,* helps ensure that the Dow industrials stay prominent. The biggest newspaper in the country, with a daily circulation of 1.8 million readers, the *Journal* usually features its average first when writing about the stock market. It promoted the Dow average, and once a generation or two was trained on it, it just became the easy thing to follow.

Of late, the Dow industrials have beaten the broader Standard & Poor's 500 Index, the 70-year-old benchmark which gauges 500 stocks. Since the current bull market began in October 1990, the Dow has surged 144 percent, topping the S&P 500's 129 percent gain.

To understand the importance of the Dow Jones Industrial Average, investors must return to the closing years of the 19th century. Charles Dow was ahead of his time. When he decided in 1896 to create the industrial average, he sensed where the country was going. At the time, the NYSE did very little trading of industrial shares. They were too low-brow and were considered speculative—much as we would consider junk bonds today. The only stocks regarded as investment-grade were railroads and utilities. By giving investors a measuring instrument, Dow helped popularize stocks in general.

Big business was relatively unknown before 1880, when most companies were family-owned. The next 25 years saw the creation of national businesses, companies such as General Electric and U.S. Steel. Charles Dow recognized the growing importance of manufacturing and the opportunities available to investors.

The Dow average's popularity grew because investors needed a way to compare their gains with the overall stock market. Professional money managers think of the Dow as a crude average because no allowance is made for the size of a company.

That method doesn't take into account that a 10 percent rise in International Business Machines Corp., whose shares sell for $109, has a far greater impact on the broad market than a 10 percent move in Bethlehem Steel Corp's $12.75 per share stock. By contrast, the S&P 500 Index is weighted by a company's size and is the benchmark by which mutual fund managers usually measure their performance.

The Dow seldom changes its average unless forced to by a merger or acquisition or spin-off. No change has been made in the Dow industrials in the 5 years since Walt Disney Co., Caterpillar Inc., and J.P. Morgan & Co. were added to the average, replacing Navistar International Corp., Primerica Corp., and USX Corp. Others think the Dow industrial average will continue to evolve, perhaps by adopting leading NASDAQ stock market companies, such as Microsoft Corp. or Intel Corp., that are regarded as proxies for the computer industry.

It's also possible that Dow Jones' editors will broaden the average by enlarging it beyond 30 names. After all, they expanded the original list of 12 companies to 20 in 1920 and enlarged the average to the current 30 in late 1928. It's not been a static index. They've added companies and taken companies out. Generally, when they update the index, they add a company that's a little more responsive to what's going on in the economy.

The Standard & Poor's 500 Index, the Value Line Composite Index, and the New York Stock Exchange Composite Index are ostensibly more accurate indices and are also more widely followed. These are broader-based, which should make them somewhat more accurate in a large market. Since the DJIA consists of only 30 large companies, it may not truly reflect market performance.

What If You've Bought a Bad Fund?

What if you're in a mutual fund that isn't performing according to its or your stated goals? I don't want to be going against my own advice on the subject of market timing, but this is an exception—sometimes you just buy a bad fund. Let's look at the tell-tale signs of a bad mutual fund:

- *Above-average expenses.* Those higher costs take a bigger bite out of the return earned by the stocks, meaning lower return to you. If your fund investment loses 3 percent, for example, and has a 2 percent annual expense ratio, you've actually sustained a 5 percent loss for the year. (You can find the expense ratio in your fund's prospectus.) Lipper Analytical says the average stock mutual fund has an annual expense ratio of 1.54 percent. The average fixed income fund is around 0.96 percent.

- *Poor communications.* Troubled funds often fall behind on providing information in a timely fashion. If information isn't arriving on time and you don't get a satisfactory explanation, it's appropriate to get nervous.

- *Lack of discipline.* The best investments all take a consistent approach. The worst type of funds pursues whatever is hot. If your fund has changed its focus, or if the manager has changed his or her style, the fund could be chasing a hot sector, trying to enhance returns.

- *Managers change.* If the managers keep leaving, there's something going on. The fund owes you an adequate explanation. They need to tell you what the new guy can do to help turn it around.

- *And the biggest indicator: shrinking assets.* Funds get bigger when they're making more money, and they shrink when they lose. When investors lose confidence, the shrinking can be dramatic.

MUTUAL FUND NAMES

Titles can mislead investors. There are some strict rules being proposed. When you hear *Fidelity Magellan,* or *Putnam Voyager,* what does it really tell you? Are they going on a voyage? No. You don't have a clue as to what they're investing in. That fact would make them exempt from a proposed federal regulation that would require mutual funds to have at least 80 percent of their assets in securities that match the name of the fund, instead of the 65 percent now required. So, for instance, ABC Japan Fund would have 80 percent of its assets invested in Japan, instead of the 65 percent required now. The point is to prevent investors from being misled by fund names.

Now we will look at the underlying investments that make up these different mutual fund categories. Think of a pyramid. At the top of that pyramid would be stocks. If you combined stocks and bonds for less risk, they would make up the middle. Fixed-interest investments would be at the bottom of the investment pyramid, because of their low risk. See Fig. 8–9. Let's now examine individual stocks and how they work.

FIGURE 8–9   Relationship between Risk and Return

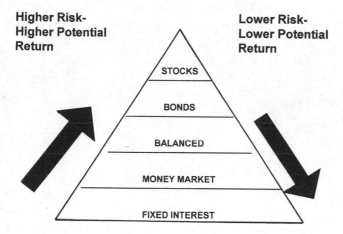

**Higher Risk-
Higher Potential
Return**

**Lower Risk-
Lower Potential
Return**

STOCKS

BONDS

BALANCED

MONEY MARKET

FIXED INTEREST

UNDERSTANDING STOCKS

"Things that have to be together to work,
normally aren't shipped together."

EQUITY MUTUAL FUNDS ARE MADE UP OF MANY INDIVIDUAL STOCKS. A stock is a security issued by a corporation or by a government as a means of raising log-term capital. The ownership is divided into a certain number of shares; the corporation issues stock certificates which show how many shares are owned. The stockholders own the company and elect a board of directors to manage it for them.

The capital that a company raises through the sale of these shares entitles the holder to dividends and to other rights of ownership, such as voting rights. Prices of stocks change according to general business conditions and the earnings and future prospects of the companies that have issued the stock. If the business is doing well, stockholders may be able to sell their stock for a profit. If it is not, they may have to take a loss when they sell.

Large corporations may have many thousands of stockholders. Their stock is bought and sold in marketplaces called *stock exchanges.* A stock exchange occupies an important position in our countries' financial system by providing a mechanism for converting SAVINGS into physical and portfolio INVESTMENT. It also performs two major functions; it provides a primary or new-issues market, in which new capital can be raised by issuing financial securities; plus, a secondary market for trading existing securities which facilitates transferability of securities from sellers to buyers.

The shares of stock represent the value of the corporation. When the corporation has made a profit, the directors may divide the profit among stockholders as dividends, or they may decide to use it to expand the business. Dividends are paid to the stockholders out of the corporation's profits. When profits are used to expand the business, the directors and stockholders may issue more stock to show that there is more money invested in the business. This new stock will be divided among the old stockholders as stock dividends.

Stocks are issued in two forms: *common* and *preferred.*

COMMON STOCK

Common stock represents true ownership shares in a company. Stockholders share directly in growing company profits through increasing dividends and an appreciation in the value of the stock itself. As the holder of common stock, you are a part owner in the company issuing the stock. The purchaser of common stock not only receives a share of any dividends paid by the corporation, but also has the right to vote for corporate directors who, in turn, choose the corporate officers and set the corporation's policies. When a broker uses the term *stock,* he or she is normally referring to *common* stock. Common stock will be the bulk of investments in most mutual funds. See Fig. 9–1.

PREFERRED STOCK

Preferred stock, like common stock, represents ownership or equity, and not debt. Preferred stockholders have a claim on profits which precedes—or is preferred to—the claim of the common stockholder. The preferred stockholder has a right to receive *specified* dividends (for example, 10 percent of the face value of the preferred share) before the common stockholder can be paid any dividend at all.

On the other hand, the preferred stockholder does not have the possibility of large gains open to the common stockholder. While the common stockholder may hope for rising dividends if the corporation prospers, the preferred shareholder will at most receive the specified dividend.

If the preferred stockholders share with the common stockholders in dividends beyond the specified percentage, the stock is called *participating preferred.*

FIGURE 9–1

Preferred stock may also be cumulative. That is, if there are no divi-dends given in a year, the preferred stockholders must be given double their dividend the next year. This is paid before anything is paid to the common stockholders. This principle continues for as many years as dividends are not paid.

Here are some more terms:

Price/Earnings Ratio
This is how you measure the value of a company. The price/earnings (P/E) ratio measures the stock's price divided by the company's earnings per share (EPS) over the past 12 months. If a company is earning $1 per share and the public is buying the stock at $10 per share, the market price is divided by the earnings. In this case, 10 is divided by 1; this tells us that the stock is sell-ing at 10 times earnings (10*P/E,* or 10[ts]). If you invest in this company and pay $10, theoretically you are paying 10 years' worth of earnings to own it. When the market is low, you will see 10[ts] today; in a bull market, the average is 25 to 30 times earnings.

Dividend Payout Ratio

This is the ratio of a company's indicated annual cash dividend per share to its earnings per share (EPS), and it can range from 0 to 100 percent. A utility that pays out $4 in dividends for each $5 of earnings would have a payout of 80 percent. The payout is greater than 50 percent for the average large industrial company and even higher for the typical utility. The higher the dividend payout, however, the less room there is for dividend increases, since less profit is available to reinvest for future growth.

Dividend Yield

This measures the annual dividend divided by the stock price. For example, if a utility's dividend is $4 and its stock sells for $50 per share, the yield will be 8 percent. When the EPS (in general) is high, yields will be low.

BLUE-CHIP STOCKS

These high-quality companies are typically large, old, and well established, such as those represented in the Dow Jones Industrial Average. Blue-chip stocks are often considered income stocks by virtue of their fairly high dividend payouts. Many of the companies included in the S&P 500 would also qualify as blue chips.

Stocks can be lumped into any of several broad categories. These are general classifications, and a stock might simultaneously fit into two or more groups. For example, a blue-chip may also be classified as growth and income and defensive. And a growth company may be categorized as speculative.

WHERE IS THE STOCK TRADED?

The stock exchange is a marketplace in which member brokers (agents) buy and sell stocks and bonds of U.S. and foreign businesses on behalf of the public. A stock exchange provides a marketplace for stocks and bonds in the same way as a commodity exchange does for commodities.

To most investors, "the stock market" means the New York Stock Exchange. The New York Stock Exchange has been in existence for more than 200 years. Needless to say, it has come a long way since 24 merchants and auctioneers met at the site of the present exchange to negotiate an agreement to buy and sell stocks and bonds issued by the new U.S. government, along with those of a few banks and insurance companies. It wasn't until 1817 that the exchange adopted an approved constitution, whereby it named itself the New York Stock and Exchange Board. The exchange did not cross the million-share daily threshold until 1886. Its dullest day ever was March

16, 1830, when only 31 shares changed hands. In 1997, the exchange witnessed the first day in which 1 billion shares were traded.

There are also many other North American exchanges trading stock, from the American Stock Exchange (called AMEX) on down to the Spokane Stock Exchange. In addition, thousands of equities are not traded on any exchange, but rather are sold over the counter (OTC). Prices for OTC stocks are readily available through the NASDAQ, an acronym for the National Association of Securities Dealers Automated Quotations system, the hottest market today. Many unlisted industrial securities are more speculative than listed ones.

There is a distinct difference between OTC stocks and exchange-listed equities, revolving primarily around eligibility requirements. Each stock exchange has listing requirements that must be met before a company may take its place on the exchange floor. For example, before a stock can be listed on the NYSE, the company must have at least 1 million shares outstanding (available to the public). Those shares must be held by at least 2,000 different stockholders, each of whom owns at least 100 shares. The company must also have earned a pretax profit of at least $2.5 million in the year preceding the listing, and the pretax profits in the two prior years must have been at least $2 million each year. The AMEX and the regional exchanges have similar (though less stringent) listing requirements, but no such limitations exist for OTC listings.

HOW DOES A STOCK EXCHANGE OPERATE?
Federal and state laws regulate the issuance, listing, and trading of most securities. The Securities and Exchange Commission (SEC) administers the federal laws.

Stocks handled by one or more stock exchanges are called *listed stocks*. A company that wants to have its stock listed for trading on an exchange must first prove to the exchange that it has enough paid-up capital, is a lawful enterprise, and is in good financial condition.

How Stocks Trade on the Exchange
Probably one of the most confusing aspects of investing is understanding how stocks actually trade. Words such as *bid, ask, volume,* and *spread* can be quite confusing if you do not understand what they mean. Depending on which exchange a stock trades, there are two different systems.

The New York Stock Exchange and the American Stock Exchange (composed of the Boston, Philadelphia, Chicago, and San Francisco exchanges) are both listed exchanges, meaning brokerage firms contribute individuals known as *specialists,* who are responsible for all the trading in a specific stock. This is known as an *open-auction market.* Volume, or the number of shares that trade on a given day, is counted by the specialists.

These individuals control stock prices by matching buy and sell orders delivered by the floor brokers shouting out their orders. The specialists change the prices to match the supply-and-demand fundamentals. The specialist system was created to guarantee that every seller finds a buyer, and vice versa. This process may sound chaotic, but specialists do succeed in their function of maintaining an orderly market and matching sellers to buyers. In return for this service, the specialist charges the buyer an extra fee of 6.25 or 12.5 cents per share, depending on the price of the stock.

Over-the-Counter Market

The NASDAQ stock market, the Nasdaq SmallCap, and the OTC Bulletin Board are the three main over-the-counter markets. In an over-the-counter market, brokerages (also known as *broker-dealers*) act as market makers for various stocks. The brokerages interact over a centralized computer system managed by the NASDAQ, providing liquidity for the market to function. One firm represents the seller and offers an ask price (also called the *offer*), or the price the seller is asking to sell the security. Another firm represents the buyer and gives a bid, or a price at which the buyer will buy the security.

For example, a particular stock might be trading at a bid of $10 and an ask of $10.50. If an investor wanted to sell shares, she would get the bid price of $10 per share; if she wanted to buy shares, she would pay the ask price of $10.50 per share. The difference is called the *spread,* which is paid by the buyer. This difference is split between the two firms involved in the transaction. Volume on over-the-counter markets is often double-counted, as both the buying firm and the selling firm report their activity.

Placing an Order

A person who wishes to buy individual stock or an agent who acts on his own behalf places an order with a licensed representative. The representative gets a quotation (price) by telephone and relays the order to the floor of the exchange. The partner negotiates the sale and notifies the brokerage house. The entire transaction may take only a few minutes.

How do you do it? What types of orders can you place? Let's look at the major types of orders.

- *Buy order.* This is the order you place when, obviously enough, you want to buy shares. Simply tell the broker how many shares you want to purchase.

- *Buy at market.* You instruct the broker to buy a specified number of shares at the prevailing market price.

- *Buy at a limit.* You instruct the broker to buy a specified number of shares, but only at a specified price or lower. For example, you might say, "Buy 100 shares of IBM at a limit of $50." In this case, you are willing to purchase shares of IBM only if you can do so at $50 or less.

- *Sell order.* This is an order you place when you want to sell shares.

- *Sell at market.* This is an order to sell your shares at the prevailing market price.

- *Sell at a limit.* This is an order to sell your shares at only the price that you specify or higher.

- *Sell at a stop limit.* You instruct your broker to sell your stock if it falls to a certain price. For example, you buy IBM at $50 and you instruct your advisor or broker to sell if it falls to $45. This is a *sell stop* at $45.

Shorting Stocks

Shorting a stock is the reverse of buying a stock. In effect, if you sell a stock by borrowing it from a broker, hoping that its share price will go down, you are "short" the stock. The idea is to buy the stock back later at a lower price and then return the shares to the broker and keep the difference. Although shorting is not the place for the first time investor, you should understand how it works.

The basics of the shorting transaction are straightforward. You first contact your brokerage house in order to determine whether it can borrow shares of the stock you want to short. When you receive the borrowed shares, you immediately sell them and keep the cash, promising to return the shares at some future time. The plan is to eventually repurchase the shares at a lower price and return them, keeping the difference yourself. But if the stock's price rises, you might have to buy back the shares at the higher price and thus lose money.

In summary, I think it's worth the time to understand how individual stocks make up equity mutual funds and how they work. Just think of a mutual fund as the house and individual stocks and bonds as the people who live inside.

10

UNDERSTANDING BONDS

W HAT IS A *BOND?* Don't be ashamed if you don't know. A recent survey indicates that more than 90 percent of the general public is in the dark in this area. In fact, the majority of people who have actually invested in stocks and bonds don't really understand what makes a bond different from all other types of investments. A *bond* is the legal evidence of a debt, usually the result of a loan of money.

When you buy a bond, you are in effect lending your money to the issuer of the bond. The issuer agrees to make periodic interest payments to you, the investor holding the bond, and also agrees to repay the original sum (the principal) in full on a certain date, known as the bond's *maturity date.* Interest rates can soar, and you, the customer, will still be repaid the entire principal at maturity. Interest payments are certain, and there will be no volatility with the investment, while even a mutual fund with a stable NAV will be affected to some extent by changes in interest rates.

More important is what "backs" the bond. In the case of many corporate securities, nothing more is behind them than the full faith and credit of the companies that issue them. These bonds, usually called *debentures,* are probably the most common type of debt issued by industrial corporations today.

Public utilities generally issue bonds with specific assets as collateral against the loan. These are called *mortgage* bonds or *collateral trust* bonds.

Some utilities, however, issue debentures, and some industrial corporations issue collateralized bonds.

KINDS OF INDIVIDUAL BONDS

There are three main categories of bonds: the U.S. government or one of its agencies, corporations, and municipalities. While these three types have some different characteristics, they share a basic structure.

U.S. Government Notes and Bonds

The U.S. government issues both Treasury notes (maturities of 2 to 10 years) and bonds (maturities greater than 10 years). U.S. government securities are considered to have no credit risk, and their rate of return is the benchmark to which all other rates of return in the market are compared. The government auctions U.S. government securities on a regular quarterly schedule.

In a normal yield-curve environment, U.S. government notes typically have yields 50 to 250 basis points higher than those on T Bills, and the same spread lower than a U.S. government bond (100 basis points equals 1 percent). Notes are the most likely investment for an individual investor because of the maturity range. Institutional investors and traders actively trade the 30-year bond.

Corporate Bonds

Corporations of every size and credit quality issue corporate bonds, from the very best blue-chip companies to small companies with low ratings. Corporate bonds are not easy to evaluate, especially those with longer maturities when call provisions may apply and the credit outlook is less certain. Many investors simply choose to stay in shorter maturities or with extremely sound companies such as utilities. Corporate bonds may be backed by collateral and are fully taxable at the federal, state, and local levels.

Yields are higher on corporate bonds than on a certificate of deposit (CD) or government-issued or insured debt. The coupon is fixed, and return of principal is guaranteed by the issuer if the investor holds it until maturity. If the investor sells the bond prior to maturity, the bond will be subject to market fluctuation. Investors who want to be able to check the prices of their bonds in the newspaper should buy listed bonds, preferably those listed on the New York Stock Exchange.

The fully taxable nature of corporate bonds (as opposed to municipals or Treasuries) has an effect on yield. When buying a AAA-rated corporate bond, you are buying a security that has more risk than a U.S. government bond. For the risk you are taking, you should receive an additional 25 to 50 basis points in yield.

Municipal Bonds

What are municipal bonds? Very simply, they are investment instruments used to finance municipal government activities. They are not always guaranteed by the municipality.

Investors whose goal is simply to conserve capital and generate returns that keep up with inflation often look to municipal bonds with the idea that these bonds are fairly safe. Investors may believe this because "muni" (municipal) issuances often have language stating they are "backed by the full faith and credit" of the issuing authority. In addition to the safety that conservative investors think they are gaining in municipal bonds, investors may believe that these bonds' tax-free status offers additional rewards. The combination of safety and tax-advantaged reward seems irresistible to many who are not especially sophisticated about the securities markets and who are seeking simply to avoid making an investment mistake.

Munis attract many wealthy investors for the above reasons. They're not looking for growth—they've already made it. The largest part of Ross Perot's holdings is in muni bonds. I'm sure if we asked him, he'd say he's not concerned about growth. But then again, who knows what Perot would say.

I don't like muni investments because if rates fall and prices rise, you're not necessarily going to be able to take advantage of your good fortune because the municipalities may hurry to call the bonds away from you. And tax-free certainly does not mean risk-free: Remember the Orange County debacle of the early 1990s or the New York City municipal difficulties of the 1970s.

Municipal bonds have high trading costs. This is because there are large bid/ask spreads and significant market impact costs in the municipal marketplace. These additional costs eliminate the benefits of using an enhanced trading strategy, such as the matrix pricing strategy we use in our government and corporate bond portfolios. The turnover required would simply be too costly. Because of their high trading costs, municipal bonds are only suitable for buy-and-hold investors who want to hold longer-maturity bonds or high-yield municipals.

Today most investors are better off with taxable securities than municipal bonds. While paying taxes is not pleasant, it's better to pay the tax if one can get higher after-tax returns by doing so.

MUNICIPAL BOND FUNDS

Municipal bond funds are nothing more than a large grouping of various municipal bonds. They may be appropriate when you are in high federal (28 percent and up) and state (5 percent or higher) tax brackets. Most municipal bond funds invest in municipal bonds of similar maturity (the number of years before the borrower, in this case the municipality, must pay back the money to you, the lender).

Most bond funds invest in bonds of similar maturity (the number of years before the borrower must pay back the money to the lender). The key advantage of a bond fund is management. Unlike with individual issues, the fund managers can switch bonds from time to time within a fund. A bond fund is always replacing bonds in its portfolio to maintain its average-maturity objective.

What Are the Risks?
The main form of market risk for a bond is the risk of interest rates changing after a customer buys the bond—called *interest rate risk.* If market interest rates go up, the bond loses principal value; if market rates go down, the bond gains principal value. The longer the term of the bond, the more the price will be affected by changes in interest rates. Regardless of whether the U.S. government, a corporation, or a municipality issues the bond, the risk is similar.

Bonds are also subject to *call risk*—the risk that the bond issuer will choose to redeem (call) the bond before the maturity date. The call provisions must be stated in the prospectus along with other special features—but a prospectus can be hard to understand.

A Look at Interest Rates
A bond's current value is directly affected by changes in the interest rates. The effect of higher interest rates on bonds is to lower their prices. Conversely, lower rates raise bond prices. The fluctuation is due to the fact that the price of the bond must offer a prospective purchaser current market rates.

When Should an Individual Buy a Bond, rather than a Bond Fund?
There is a lot to understand before you buy an individual bond. It is a somewhat different process from buying stocks or mutual funds, because only a certain dollar amount of each bond is issued and that amount is almost certainly much smaller than the amount of equity issued. Large companies have millions of shares of stock outstanding, and all shares of common stock are the same. To buy a bond, on the other hand, the customer can't simply consult *The Wall Street Journal,* pick a particular bond, and place an order. Buying a bond means finding the owner (such as an institutional trading desk) of a bond that meets your needs.

The owner of individual bonds has much greater control of both cash flow and tax consequences. The investor controls when to take profits and losses based on what is in her or his best interest. If it matters to an investor whether a tax gain is taken in December or January, a bond allows that choice.

An individual investor with less than $50,000 to invest in bonds is probably better off in a bond fund (called a *unit investment trust*), receiving the advantages of diversification, professional management, and significant cost benefits. Any institutional investor buys bonds more cheaply than a single individual; and the bonds in a mutual fund have been purchased at the institutional price. The institutional investor also pays a minuscule portion of total price in transaction costs, whereas transaction costs can be significant for an individual—and it gets worse if the individual must pay for safekeeping the securities. A bond fund does, however, pay a management fee that might equal in yield the transaction cost an individual would pay.

The mutual fund pays dividends monthly since it owns bonds with so many different payment dates whereas individual bonds pay out only semiannually.

Following is information an investor should consider before making a bond purchase:

- *Security description:* type of bond, purpose of the bond, and the issuer.
- *Rating:* for example, AA is better than A.
- *Trade date:* the date the bond is purchased in the market.
- *Settlement date:* the date on which the purchaser pays for the bond and interest starts accruing.
- *Maturity date:* the date on which the purchaser will be repaid the principal and last interest payment.
- *Interest payment dates:* dates on which interest payments are made, usually semiannually.
- *Coupon:* fixed annual interest rate (interest income) stated on the bond.
- *Price:* dollar price paid for the bond. (An offer price is the price at which the individual investor buys the bond; the bid price is the price at which the individual can sell the bond.)
- *Current yield:* the coupon divided by price, giving a rough approximation of cash flow.
- *Yield to maturity:* measure of total return on the bond at maturity.

- *Par amount:* face amount of the bond when it was issued, normally $1,000.
- *Accrued interest:* the amount of interest income (coupon income) earned from the date of the last coupon payment to settlement date.
- Whether the bond uses a 360-day or 365-day basis to calculate interest payments.

BOND RATING SERVICES

The two major independent rating services; Moody's and Standard & Poor's. Investment-grade ratings range from AAA to BBB − (Standard & Poor's), or Aaa to Baa3 (Moody's). Lower-rated bonds are considered speculative. Ratings are intended to help you evaluate risk and set your own standards for investment. See Table 10–1.

The price of any bond fluctuates in harmony with the rise and fall of interest rates in general and the stability of the underlying corporation or agency issuing the bond. Grades AAA through BBB are considered investment grade, although many advisors will confine their attention to bonds rated A or above. Ratings attempt to assess the probability that the issuing company will make timely payments of interest and principal. Each rating service has slightly different evaluation methods.

Summary

Almost all muni bonds have had a tough last few years, in part because the stock market continues to steal their thunder. According to the Investment Company Institute, for the first 5 months of 1997, the amount of investor

TABLE 10-1   Bond Ratings

Bond Ratings	Moody's	S&P	Fitch Prime
Credit Risk	Aaa	AAA	AAA
Excellent	Aa	AA	AA
Upper Medium	A-1, A	A+, A	A
Lower Medium	Baa-1, baa, a	BBB+, BBB	BBB
Speculative	Ba	BB	BB
Very Speculative	B, Caa	B, CCC, CC	B, CCC, C
Default	Ca, C	DDD, DD, D	DDD, DD, D

dollars put in muni bond funds shrank from $3.1 billion to $2.5 billion. The outflow followed a similar decline in 1996.

Today, munis offer rare tax breaks for small-to-medium-sized investors, particularly attractive in high-income-tax states such as New York and California. See Fig. 10–1.

Tip

To determine if a muni bond fund makes sense for you, compare your after-tax return to that of another type of bond fund. For example, if a muni fund pays 5 percent versus 6 percent on a corporate bond fund, which fund works better for someone in the 28 percent tax bracket? Divide 5 percent by 0.72 (100 minus the 28 percent tax bracket). The answer, 6.94, is your after-tax return. So the corporate fund needs to yield 6.94 percent to measure up.

Good job. You are now ready to pull it all together, build your core investing strategy and put some advanced strategies to work. In this next chapter, you will learn how to use effective diversification to build your own portfolio—one asset class at a time.

FIGURE 10–1   The Top Three Muni Funds for 1997

Fund	Year to date	3-year	5-year	Morningstar Rating
1. Eaton Vance Muni (800) 225 6265	8.38%	8.91%	7.23%	****
2. Fundamental Calif. (800) 322-6864	8.30	6.08	4.28	*
3. Eaton Vance Mar National (800) 225-6265	8.07	8.77	7.11	****

HOW TO PUT ADVANCED STRATEGIES TO WORK

11

INVESTMENT ARCHITECTURE

*C*OLUMBUS WASN'T LOOKING FOR THE NEW WORLD, *just a faster way to India.*

In Part Two, we took a long look at the major components of investments, stocks, bonds, and mutual funds. Now, with that information, we can consider some additional aspects of those crucial elements as they affect the general architecture of investing. In this chapter, we develop a *passive core investment strategy* to overcome investment noise forever. You can use this same investment strategy, whether your goal is to build your own portfolio for retirement, to protect your assets once you've retired, or to meet other financial goals.

The description of *passive,* meaning no trading or activity, distinguishes this commission-based strategy from the common or historical methods recommended by brokers and advisors. Investors typically only look at each pool of savings on a stand-alone basis [that is, IRA, 401(k), taxable savings]. The investment strategy here involves capturing, through buying and holding a large basket of securities, the risk and return dimensions of an entire asset class. An *asset class* is a group of investment securities that have similar risk factors and expected returns.

This way you don't have to make a leap of faith to invest. There is a body of academically sound knowledge available. By adhering to these principles, shortening bond maturities, and adding small and large U.S. and international companies, it is possible to increase investment returns while lowering investment risks.

YOUR CORE STRATEGY SHOULD START WITH A BASIC INDEX FUND

For simplicity and consistency in your core strategy, choose a simple index fund. (The S&P 500 Index Fund is the most common index fund for both institutional and individual investors.) Index funds run on autopilot.

If the market goes up 30 percent in a year, so does the index fund. Index funds don't try to outguess the market or pick the hottest stocks. You don't play the odds; you play the averages. It's like being in a Las Vegas casino— you're not depending on a manager's expertise. The objective in an index fund remains constant—to match overall market returns.

Actively managed funds, on the other hand, have a manager in charge who selects the specific investment, so we're back to superior stock selection. Anyone other than index fund managers is either a market timer or a stock picker. If the manager has a good year, so does the fund; but the same holds true if the manager has a bad year. Moreover, a fund could change managers, and you wouldn't even know about it. Generally, when a manager changes funds, so do the style and the performance. (Fidelity Magellan has never been the same since Peter Lynch left.)

But if it's true that index funds go up if the stock market goes up, what happens if the market drops? The index fund will *also* drop with the market. The answer is to combine asset classes that *don't move together* within your portfolio. See Fig. 11–1. This will reduce the volatility of the portfolio, enhance your compound returns, and give you a greater ending wealth.

The idea is to follow the principles of asset allocation of modern portfolio theory, minimizing risk by diversifying investments into different asset classes. See Fig. 11–2. While traditional diversification itself cannot ameliorate individual market risk, an investor can spread cash among a number of markets and asset classes so as to not suffer in the collapse of a single market. By combining assets with low correlation, you can lower the overall portfolio risk while enhancing the risk-adjusted rates of return. The most important component of investing is to combine assets with low correlation. These strategies actually simplify the investment decision-making process.

Designing Portfolios that are Efficient

For every level of risk, there is some optimum combination of investments that will yield the highest rate of return. Combinations in a portfolio exhibiting this optimal risk/reward tradeoff form the *efficient frontier* line. See

FIGURE 11–1   Portfolios That Move Dissimilarly

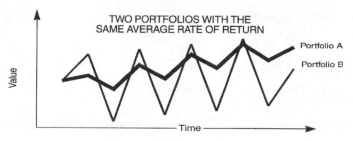

Reprinted with permission from RWB Advisory Services, Inc.

FIGURE 11–2   Correlation for Asset Classes

	Fixed			U.S.		International	
	Money Market	One Year Corp	Five Year Corp	Large Co.	Small Co.	Large Co.	Small Co.
Money Market	1.000						
One-Year Fixed	0.913	1.000					
Five-Year U.S. Government	0.486	0.735	1.000				
U.S. Large-Company Stocks	-0.041	-0.010	0.227	1.000			
U.S. Small-Company Stocks	-0.085	-0.041	0.107	0.763	1.000		
Int'l. Large-Company Stocks	-0.218	-0.181	-0.077	0.487	0.442	1.000	
Int'l. Small-Company Stocks	-0.294	-0.369	-0.286	0.377	0.301	0.821	1.000

Reprinted with permission from RWB Advisory Services, Inc.

Fig. 11–3. The efficient frontier is determined by calculating the expected rate of return, standard deviation, and correlation coefficient for each institutional asset class fund and utilizing this information to optimize the portfolio to get the highest expected return for any given level of risk. That's a mouthful—and could be enough to send you running in the opposite direction! I'll walk you through the process, but this is where a financial advisor can help, if you feel overwhelmed.

By plotting each portfolio representing a given level of risk and expected return, you are able to create a line connecting all efficient portfolios. In Fig. 11–3 I have illustrated how the efficient frontier would actually have performed. I've identified three model portfolios along the efficient frontier. For lack of better terms, I've called them conservative, moderate, and aggressive. (See Fig. 11–4.) The equity allocation in each is 50, 70, and 85 percent, respectively. While the terms *conservative, moderate,* and *aggressive* mean different things to each of us, they are convenient working titles for various combinations of asset classes.

FIGURE 11–3   Efficient Frontier

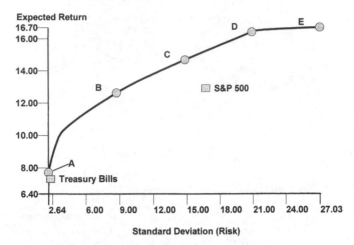

Standard Deviation (Risk)

Reprinted with permission from RWB Advisory Services, Inc.

As an example, the aggressive portfolio is no more risky than the S&P 500 Index. Many investors might consider a portfolio with the same risk as blue-chip stocks not that aggressive. Once you determine your risk tolerance, then you can look at the efficient frontier line and select the model portfolio. Don't be swayed by what we call the *model portfolio*. Each investor has her or his own risk tolerance. It is the tradeoff between the risk the investor is willing to take to receive a specific expected rate of return and the investor's financial conditions, objectives, and needs.

Generally, younger people have the greatest tolerance for risk and retirees the least. Often, younger people feel that they have both time and earning capability to recover from any loss, while retirees may feel they do not. Retired individuals are dependent on income from their investment principal, and any loss would represent a reduction in income. However, as investors become more sophisticated and understand asset class investing, they often are more comfortable with risk because they understand investing for the long-term will mitigate the volatility of their portfolios as a whole.

Most investor portfolios fall significantly below the efficient frontier. Remember the earlier chart where we showed that more than 90 percent of the return on invested capital comes from the allocation of various combinations of investments, rather than from the purchase of individual equities.

As I mentioned earlier, Harry Markowitz is credited with forging a new way of looking at how to divide assets which has the effect of minimizing risk and maximizing returns. Markowitz knew investors faced an especial-

FIGURE 11–4   Three Model Portfolios

	Conservative	Moderate	Aggressive
Money Market	5%	5%	5%
One-Year Fixed	20	20	10
Five-Year U.S. Government	25	5	0
U.S. Large-Company Stocks	20	25	25
U.S. Small-Company Stocks	5	10	15
Int'l. Large-Company Stocks	20	25	25
Int'l. Small-Company Stocks	5	10	20

Reprinted with permission from RWB Advisory Services, Inc.

ly tough question: *How can one earn attractive returns without accepting undue amounts of risk?* Using mathematics to solve this puzzle, Markowitz was guided by the fairly radical assumption that there was a scientific way to improve returns without increasing risk. Based upon his study of historical investment performance, Markowitz eventually made his breakthrough, creating the best combination of securities in a portfolio.

Let's start moving toward putting together your own advanced asset class portfolio. We'll begin very conservatively, copying what the endowments and foundations, such as colleges, universities, churches, and nonprofits, do. Endowment and foundation funds are managed to sustain the research, capital spending, and operations of their underlying institutions. They need their portfolios to exist in perpetuity as well as to pay out sufficient income each year. In the end, they must not spend more than the real return on their investments. This is the only way they can be assured that their assets will last forever.

You have similar goals. Like endowment funds, most investors want to get as much income as they can, without reducing principal in real terms.

1.   Assets should be invested in both fixed-income and equity securities. The typical endowment fund is invested 60 percent in equities and 40 percent in fixed-income securities.

2.   Assets need to be effectively diversified. Endowments diversify their equity investments into asset classes that are relatively uncorrelated to reduce risk. They have multiasset, total-return investment policies.

So, let's use their tried-and-true formula. *But how do you know which ones you should utilize for your portfolio?*

Let's review each of the key concepts that must be incorporated in your portfolio. Then we will compare how the introduction of each new asset class fund will increase the average rate of return with less risk.

Concept 1: Don't pick all your investments in the same asset class
If your investments all move together, then you've got ineffective diversification. It's as if you didn't diversify. When your investments *do not* move in tandem, you've accomplished effective diversification.

Concept 2: Don't pick similar funds
Invest in different asset class mutual funds. To build your portfolio, you need cost-effective building blocks that make use of these concepts. Institutional asset class funds are designed to meet these goals. Similar to index fund managers, asset class mutual fund managers do not actively buy and sell securities to try to take advantage of the latest guesses of what's going to happen in the future. They recognize that the best way to add value to their mutual funds is to provide you with a cost-effective representation of the particular asset class you want. These asset class funds have been designed from the ground up, to provide you with dissimilar price movement that will allow you to effectively diversify.

Concept 3: Add global index or asset class funds
When the U.S. market periodically moves down, it tends to take most investors with it. With the introduction of international asset classes, you can provide for greater protection against risk with an all-U.S. portfolio.

Concept 4: Be comfortable
Take small, incremental steps. Gradually rebalance your allocation or increase your long-term investment according to your experience.

In Fig. 11–5, I have simulated how each of these asset classes would have performed in the accompanying model portfolios.

FIGURE 11–5

Conservative

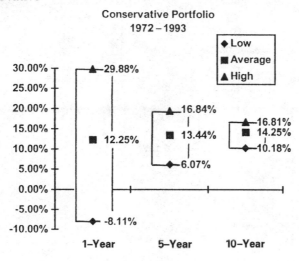

Conservative Portfolio
1972 – 1993

◆ Low
■ Average
▲ High

Moderate

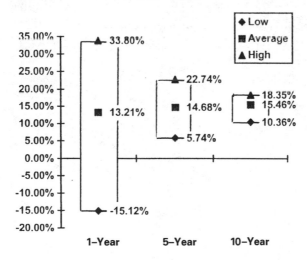

Moderate Portfolio
1972 – 1993

◆ Low
■ Average
▲ High

Aggressive

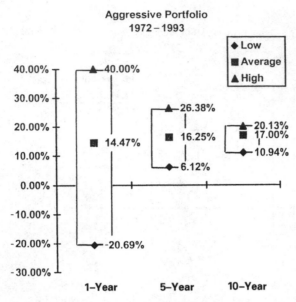

Aggressive Portfolio
1972 – 1993

To obtain current numbers read *The Prudent Investor's Guide to Beating Wall Street at Its Own Game, Second Edition,* by John J. Bowen and Dan Goldie, pages 127–129, (McGraw-Hill) or email John Bowen at jbowen@rwb.com.

Reprinted with permission from RWB Advisory Services, Inc.

12

BUILDING YOUR PORTFOLIO ONE ASSET CLASS AT A TIME

N OW THAT YOU HAVE ACCESS TO ASSET CLASS MUTUAL FUNDS, which ones should you utilize for your own portfolio? A good starting point is an examination of the historical performance of each investment category. This will allow you to better understand how each asset class has performed over long periods. I'm not saying that the past indicates future performance; what I want you to look for are the relationships between various asset classes.

Time series information on domestic asset classes is readily available for you to review, starting with 1926 through 1996. This time period includes the Great Depression, World War II, the Korean war, the Vietnam war, and numerous other major world crises. How did the investment markets perform? In the following graph, you will see that, historically, equities asset classes have far outperformed fixed-income asset classes.

For example, if you had invested $1 in Standard & Poor's 500 Index at the beginning of 1926, it would be worth $1,366 (assuming reinvestment of dividends) by the end of 1996, while an investment in small-company stocks would be worth almost $3,863. See Fig. 12–1. Fixed-income investment asset classes had trouble keeping pace with inflation. Investments over

FIGURE 12–1   Equities Asset Classes Have Far Outperformed Fixed-Income Asset Classes

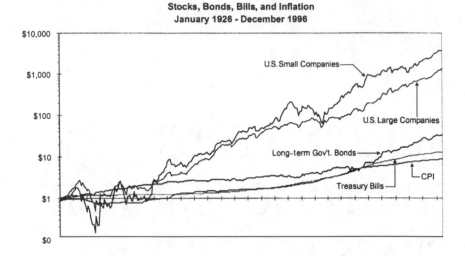

Stocks, Bonds, Bills, and Inflation
January 1926 - December 1996

this period required an increase in value of $9 simply to maintain purchasing power. The inflation rate is the absolute minimum goal for any investor.

Figure 12–2 illustrates that not only has the S&P 500 Index outperformed fixed-income asset classes, but also it easily outpaced inflation. Shown in Fig. 12–2 is a series of time periods. Over each of the periods, the S&P 500 Index increased more than both long-term U.S. government bonds and inflation. In most periods, the long-term U.S. government bond market barely exceeded inflation. Even in the years during which government bonds substantially beat the inflation rate, the S&P 500 Index beat both.

Figure 12–3 takes a look at the inflation-adjusted returns of 15-year periods. Stocks dominated bonds in all periods. This time, however, both U.S. government and corporate issues are examined. In each period, equities beat fixed income by varying degrees. Interestingly, even in the period ending in 1980, when all three assets had negative returns after adjusting for inflation, the equities lost the least. In fact, the stock market, which has often been stereotyped as too risky, ironically had only one negative 15-year period, while U.S. Treasury bonds and corporates both had two.

Modern portfolio theory states that investments in equities will produce higher expected returns than investments in fixed income, given the higher risks inherent in equity markets. These risks are primarily due to the cyclical swings of the stock market.

FIGURE 12–2   Nominal Annualized Total Returns

Number of Years	Time Period	S&P 500	Long-term Gov't Bonds	Inflation (CPI)
71	1926-96	10.7%	5.1%	3.1%
50	1947-96	12.6%	5.4%	4.1%
40	1957-96	11.2%	6.5%	4.5%
30	1967-96	11.8%	7.8%	5.4%
20	1977-96	14.6%	9.6%	5.2%
10	1987-96	15.3%	9.5%	3.7%
5	1992-96	15.2%	9.3%	2.9%

Reprinted with permission from RWB Advisory Services, Inc.

The minimum time horizon for you to invest in equities should be 5 years. For any portfolio with less than a 5-year horizon, the portfolio should be comprised predominantly of fixed-income investments. This 5-year minimum investment period is critical. The investment process must be viewed as a long-term plan for achieving the desired results. This is because 1-year volatility can be significant for certain asset classes. However, the range of probable returns over a 5-year period is greatly reduced. Since fixed investments tend to be less volatile than equities, fixed investments should be used to reduce the overall level of risk to your comfort level.

Long-term vehicles, such as U.S. Treasury bonds, are thought to be attractive because of their safety and higher yields. They are considered "safe" because of the high credit quality of these bonds, which are backed by the full faith and credit of the U.S. government. But long-term bonds have many different types of risk that must be considered, such as reinvestment risk, call risk, purchasing power risk, liquidity risk, and interest rate risk. The major risk in bonds is interest rate risk. Prices of bonds move in the opposite direction from interest rates; thus, when interest rates rise, prices of bonds fall—and vice versa.

Figure 12–4 illustrates the historical rates of total return for 20-year Treasury bonds over six decades. During the 1980s, long-term bond investors enjoyed their best decade in history, with gains averaging 12.7 percent per year. What even the smartest investors don't understand is that the volatility of long-term bonds, particularly over long periods, approaches the volatility of common stocks. Clearly, long-term U.S. Treasury bonds don't have the price stability which many bond investors are seeking.

When the marketplace values a bond, the length of time to maturity is critical. The longer the term to maturity, the longer the expected stream of

FIGURE 12–3   (Inflation Adjusted) Annualized Returns
15-Year Periods Ending In...

	1996	1995	1994	1993	1990	1980	1970	1960
S&P 500 Index	13.2%	10.7%	9.8%	10.3%	7.7%	-0.5%	5.6%	10.1%
Long-term corp. bonds	9.9%	9.2%	6.5%	5.9%	3.6%	-3.9%	0.6%	-1.9%
30 Day Treasuries	2.9%	3.2%	2.9%	2.6%	2.2%	-0.6%	1.0%	-2.0%

Reprinted with permission from RWB Advisory Services, Inc.

interest payments to the bondholder. The market price of any bond represents the present value of this stream of interest payments, discounted at the currently offered interest rates. As interest rates fluctuate, the present value of this stream of interest payments constantly changes. The longer stream of interest payments, which long-term bonds have versus short-term bonds, creates higher price volatility for the long-term bonds.

The higher risk of long-term bonds is acceptable, provided we are sufficiently compensated with higher rates of return for the additional risk. Eugene Fama has studied the rates of return of long-term bonds from 1964 to 1996. Fama has shown that long-term bonds historically have had wide variances in the rate of total return without sufficiently compensating investors with higher expected returns. He found that bonds with maturities beyond 5 years actually have had lower total returns than those with maturities of less than 5 years and higher standard deviations.

The main buyers in long-term bond markets are institutions, including corporate pension plans and life insurance companies. These investors are interested in funding long-term debt obligations such as fixed annuity payments or other fixed corporate responsibilities. They are not concerned with volatility of principal or with the effects of inflation since their obligations are a fixed amount. But you are.

In terms of variability of total return, long-term bonds look more like stocks than like shorter-term fixed-income vehicles such as Treasury bills. And yet, over long periods, their respective total returns have consistently lagged those of equities.

A look at Fig. 12–5 will help illustrate the higher standard deviations and lower total returns of bonds with maturities beyond 5 years.

Replacing the traditional long-term bond holdings with a combination of common stocks and short-term fixed-income vehicles will maintain your portfolio's expected rates of return, while decreasing volatility.

Studies show that the efficient market hypothesis holds true not only for stocks, but for bonds as well. There appears to be no ability to predict future changes in interest rates. Interest rate changes, as well as equity price changes, are immediately priced into the market. The best estimate of the future price of any fixed instrument is the price of a similar instrument today.

FIGURE 12–4   Long-Term Treasury Bond Returns

Long-Term Treasury Bond Returns through Six Decades

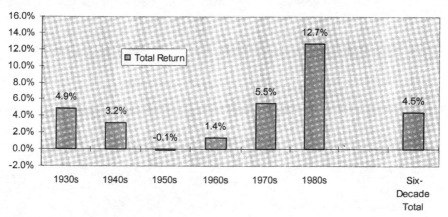

Reprinted with permission from RWB Advisory Services, Inc.

Fixed investments should be in your asset class portfolio simply to mitigate risk. But it makes no sense to have longer-maturity instruments. Because of the risk of inherent greater volatility with long-term bonds without the reward for that risk, you should avoid all debt instruments with maturities beyond 5 years.

GLOBAL INVESTING

Global investing is a hot topic on Wall Street and among money managers, many of whom for various reasons would rather have U.S. investors park their funds at home and therefore discourage international investing for their clients. These clever managers and advisors have even come up with ways that investors can seemingly play markets abroad by using domestic assets. This theory holds that the way to make a global play—without taking on true global securities exposure—is to buy the stocks of U.S. multinational firms doing a great deal of business abroad.

This idea seems clever on first glance, but there are difficulties. What most undermines this concept is that stocks of multinational firms tend to follow the movements of their local markets rather than the international market. This is true regardless of the degree to which their operations are globally diversified. For example, Colgate gets about 80 percent of its revenues from foreign operations, yet its stock price still closely follows the U.S. market. Because stocks of U.S. multinational firms are so highly correlated with the U.S. market, the stocks lose their diversification power.

To capture the diversification benefits of foreign equities, you must purchase shares of companies headquartered in foreign countries.

FIGURE 12–5   Risk versus Reward

Risk & Reward Examined for Bonds, 1964–1996

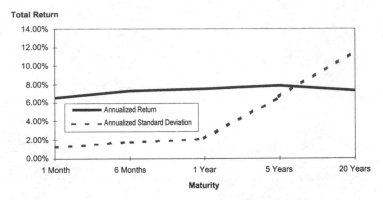

Reprinted with permission from RWB Advisory Services, Inc.

Let's look at the three main arguments against global diversification to see if they make sense. The first is efficiency. Many U.S. managers argue that the international markets are not efficient. This logic assumes that local investors in foreign countries can't figure out the correct prices for their securities. For some reason, U.S. managers think they can sit at a desk in New York City and value German companies more accurately than a German banker in Munich can. They believe that they can take advantage of market inefficiencies to generate superior returns. Empirical evidence shows that this is not true.

There appears to be no credible study that documents the consistently superior performance of active managers in any major international market.

The higher costs associated with international investing make it harder for the pros to beat foreign benchmarks than domestic benchmarks. Foreign markets are as well developed and liquid as our own. Information there moves quickly and prices rapidly adjust to new information, just as they do here. Market efficiency is not just limited to U.S. markets.

The second argument against global diversification is overseas costs. Despite the evidence, international equity managers still argue that the markets are not efficient. Even if they are correct, the cost of capturing these inefficiencies would most likely negate their efforts. Estimated costs of a buy-side trade of $50,000 range from a high of 139 basis points in Singapore and Malaysia to a low of 38 basis points in the Netherlands. Given the already high fixed costs of international investing, high turnover rates for international portfolios can have a severe negative effect on returns.

The significantly higher cost of investing overseas makes it even more important for you to be aware of the turnover ratio of the international mutual funds you use. An active manager trying to be competitive in Singapore with a 200 percent turnover rate would experience a 2.78 percent cost of doing business, without considering market impact costs. Combining these costs with the average expense ratio of international equity mutual funds of 1.80 percent results in a total cost to the investor of 4.58 percent. Active management probably cannot overcome this expense.

The discipline of asset allocation itself, which may only call for reallocation once per year for smaller international exposures, makes asset allocation investing the cheapest and most effective way to organize overseas investing. Unlike the active manager, the asset allocator has logical, long-term reasons for his or her exposure; and thus, the costly and often hyperactive trading that often takes place among global managers is avoided.

Currency risk is the third argument against global diversification. "The dollar is flying, making sushi in Osaka cheaper, Hermes scarves in Paris more affordable, and a room in the Gritti Palace in Venice less of a strain on your wallet. That same dollar is also blowing big holes in many mutual funds that invest in European and Japanese securities." These were the opening lines of an April 17, 1997, article in *The Wall Street Journal.* The author, Michael Sesit, goes on to note that, at a certain point, Fidelity's United Kingdom Fund was down 1.4 percent when measured in U.S. dollars, and the London stock market was up 3 percent when measured in British pounds. And while shares in Tokyo were down 8 percent when measured in yen, some Japanese mutual funds were down as much as 26 percent when measured in U.S. dollars.

Many sophisticated investors hedge the so-called currency risk of foreign stocks. (*Hedging* is the process of reducing uncertainty about future market prices by effectively covering a bet through an offsetting bet.) For example, to reduce exposure to losses from exchange rate movements, a U.S. company investing overseas may match the investment in a country with an equivalent amount of loans raised locally in that country. Then if an adverse exchange rate movement reduces the dollar value of the company's overseas assets, it will simultaneously reduce the dollar value of its liabilities.

Options can also be used to hedge against uncertainty about future prices. An option offers the right to sell or buy a commodity at an agreed price within some specified future time. Once the option has been purchased, it can be exercised at the discretion of the option holder.

Sometimes investors win by hedging foreign currencies, and sometimes they lose. Do investors win more often than they lose? Consider returns on hedged and unhedged portfolios over the period from 1980 through 1996 with a simulated "moderate" portfolio and an "aggressive" portfolio. The moderate portfolio is composed of 30 percent fixed-income securities (2-year Treasury notes) and 70 percent stocks (35 percent in the S&P 500, 17.5 percent in the Japanese Nikkei, 8.75 percent in the British FTSE, and 8.75

percent in the German DAX). The aggressive portfolio is composed of 15 percent fixed-income securities and 85 percent in stocks, divided in proportions identical to those in the moderate portfolio.

In such a situation, the hedged portfolios would do better than the unhedged ones in 1995 and 1996. However, the unhedged portfolios would do better than the hedged ones in 1993 and 1994. Over the entire period from 1980 to 1996, the unhedged portfolios would provide somewhat higher returns than the hedged ones. However, the unhedged portfolios also would have somewhat higher standard deviations. Thus, the analysis of returns and standard deviations shows no clear advantage to the hedged or unhedged portfolios, but other considerations give an advantage to the unhedged portfolios.

Modern portfolio theory has taught us to look at assets not in isolation, but rather as part of an overall portfolio. An unhedged portfolio is a better choice for diversification reasons because it has a lower correlation than a hedged portfolio when combined with U.S. equities. This being the case, an investor or money manager who is pursuing a disciplined asset allocation strategy will probably choose not to hedge overseas investments.

International markets are efficient, asset allocation strategies allow investors to allocate globally without excessive costs, and hedging is probably unnecessary—and even counterproductive for those involved in truly disciplined asset class investing.

Modern portfolio theory shows us that overseas investing is part of building a portfolio with appropriate risk and reward at any level of investment. There are no valid arguments against it.

If you have read this far, you understand a good deal about asset class investing from a conceptual standpoint. In this section of the book, we will actually put an asset allocation program together. We will examine the necessary stages that one goes through and will take a look at some of the investment products—in particular, asset class mutual funds that can be used to facilitate your asset class investment strategy.

The next question should be, How do you determine the most desirable combination of asset classes? Here's how:

1. Determine the expected rate of return of the asset class. You want to know that the expected rate of return would justify the inclusion of that investment, so you will have a targeted rate of return against which you can measure your realized performance.

The rate of return is going to be a direct result of your willingness to take risk and your search for the long-term nature of your objectives. I have identified the specific return risk profiles of each asset class. Use these ranges of returns for each risk level as the framework to determine your return expectation for your overall portfolio. See Fig. 12–6.

FIGURE 12–6   Rate Of Return & Risk Objectives

Asset Class	Expected Return	Standard Deviation
Money Market	4.90%	3.30%
Fixed Income	6.70%	3.90%
U.S. Large	13.60%	20.30%
U.S. Small	19.40%	38.50%
International Large	13.60%	20.30%
International Small	19.40%	38.50%
Emerging Markets	16.00%	29.00%

Reprinted with permission from RWB Advisory Services, Inc.

2. Know the (standard deviation) risk of each asset class. Risk is the uncertainty of future rates of return. Historical variance or risk of an investment can be statistically measured by using the standard deviation. The current price of the security reflects the expected total return of an investment and its perceived risk. The lower the risk, the lower the return.

3. Determine the price movements of each specific asset class. Are they dissimilar? Many asset class mutual funds, representing total market segments, have historically shown a pattern of moving dissimilarly in time, degree, or direction. When these asset class mutual funds are combined with low correlation to each, they average out the volatility of the portfolio.

4. Identify your risk tolerance. Many questionnaires have been developed by advisors to quantify the risk level that investors are willing to take. Typically the questionnaires utilize different *qualitative* measures. I've found that these are subjective at best and are influenced significantly by how you feel the day you are completing the questionnaire.

I like the *quantitative* approach. It's much more effective and reliable. If you are working with an advisor, get her or him to determine what your proposed combination of assets would have done during 1973 and 1974. For example, assume that your portfolio would have lost 30 percent during the 1973–1974 period and you have $200,000 invested. That means your portfolio is now worth $140,000. Would you have closed your account because of the downturn and fired your financial advisor? Probably, if you didn't understand the risks ahead of time. You are in control if you predetermine the risk level that you are willing to accept. Over the long term, the more risk you take, the higher the rate of return, but only if you stay with the strategy.

Most first time investors can get sidetracked by formulas. If you are already working with an advisor, you do not need to know how to calculate each of the four steps—you just need to understand the end result.

INVESTMENT IMPLEMENTATION

You are ready to implement your investment program. You have three key decisions to make:

1. You must decide whether to work with an investment advisor (see Chap. 18 on selecting an investment advisor for more information), work directly with the mutual fund provider, or work with a broker or dealer who has many mutual fund families.

2. Decide which specific asset class mutual funds you will select. To assist you in this process, see the end of this chapter for a list of currently available mutual funds.

3. Pick out your asset classes, call the mutual fund company that offers the ones you want, and ask the company to send you a review of their performance in each of the asset classes. Compare these reports with the expectation of your investment goals to make sure you are on track. If one of your asset class mutual funds is outside your expectation, it is likely that it is using an active management strategy and should be avoided.

We are now ready to build and implement your portfolio. The next step is to decide what the allocation (formula) should be between equity and bond mutual funds. I have chosen the traditional institutional portfolio allocations in these examples.

FORMULA 1: THE 60–40 PERCENT INVESTOR

The most often recommended portfolio allocation from investment professionals has been 60 percent in the equity market and 40 percent in the bond market. See Fig. 12–7. An investor who began with $10,000 in January 1976, in a combined portfolio of 60 percent in the average return of all equity and 40 percent of all bond mutual funds, would have earned the following average rate of return through the end of 1996:

FIGURE 12–7   The 60%–40% Investor

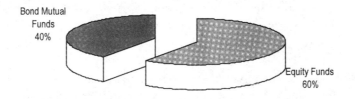

Bond Mutual
Funds
40%

Equity Funds
60%

The 60–40% Percent Investor

Portfolios	Geometric Mean, %	Risk: Standard Deviation, %	Growth of $1
60 percent equity, 40 percent bond mutual funds	12.56	9.29	$11.99

FORMULA 2: THE INDEXED PORTFOLIO

If the investor did nothing more than use the most basic of asset class mutual funds [the S&P 500 and the Shearson Lehman (S/L) Intermediate Government and Corporate Index], she or he would have accomplished approximately the same return at the same level of risk. See Fig. 12–8.

FIGURE 12–8   The Indexed Portfolio

60% S&P 500 - 40% Intermediate Bonds

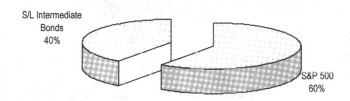

S/L Intermediate
Bonds
40%

S&P 500
60%

However, we now have many tools that will increase the expected return substantially without increasing risk. In the next few steps, we will add asset classes, using simple percentage allocations.

The Indexed Portfolio

Portfolios	Geometric Mean, %	Risk: Standard Deviation, %	Growth of $1
60 percent equity, 40 percent bond mutual funds	12.56	9.29	11.99
60 percent S&P 500, 40 percent S/L intermediate bonds	12.88	9.52	12.74

FORMULA 3: SUBSTITUTE SHORT-TERM FIXED INCOME

Substituting short-term fixed income for long-term fixed income significantly reduces risk while increasing expected returns. In this example, we
have replaced the Shearson Lehman Intermediate Government and Corporate
Bond Index, which has a weighted-average maturity of 3½ to 4½ years, with
a 2-year fixed-income strategy that further reduces the average maturities
for the portfolio. This lowers the risk. In addition, this new asset class has
taken advantage of the matrix pricing strategy we discussed in order to
increase expected returns. See Fig. 12–9.

FIGURE 12–9   Substitute Short-Term Fixed Income

2 yr Fixed Income
40%

S&P 500
60%

Substitute Short-Term Fixed Income

Portfolios	Geometric Mean, %	Risk: Standard Deviation, %	Growth of $1
60 percent equity, 40 percent bond mutual funds	12.56	9.29	11.99
60 percent S&P 500, 40 percent S/L intermediate bonds	12.88	9.52	12.74
Shorten fixed maturities	12.88	8.71	12.73

This reduction in risk (standard deviation) will allow you to introduce
other riskier asset classes, such as international.

FORMULA 4: ADD GLOBAL ASSET CLASS FUNDS

Foreign markets and domestic markets do not move in tandem. You can add
international investments that will increase the effective diversification. In
this example, we divided the 60 percent allocation in equity between the
S&P 500 Index and the EAFE (EAFE; Europe, Australia, Far East markets,
Japan, Pacific Rim, Singapore, United Kingdom, France, Germany, Italy,
Switzerland, Belgium, Spain) Index. See Fig. 12–10.

Utilize Global Diversification

Portfolios	Geometric Mean, %	Risk: Standard Deviation, %	Growth of $1
60 percent equity, 40 percent bond mutual funds	12.56	9.29	11.99
60 percent S&P 500, 40 percent S/L intermediate bonds	12.88	9.52	12.74
Shorten fixed maturities	12.88	8.71	12.73
Add global diversification	13.10	8.82	13.27

FIGURE 12–10   Utilize Global Diversification

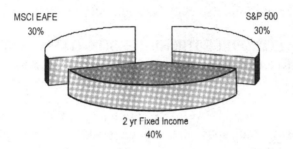

MSCI EAFE
30%

S&P 500
30%

2 yr Fixed Income
40%

FORMULA 5: INTRODUCE THE SIZE EFFECT

The second risk factor that academics Gene Fama and Ken French used to explain market returns was the size factor. In this next example, we have reduced each of the large equity asset classes by one-half and reallocated that in small asset classes around the world. See Fig. 12–11.

Introduce the Size Effect

Portfolios	Geometric Mean, %	Risk: Standard Deviation, %	Growth of $1
60 percent equity, 40 percent bond mutual funds	12.56	9.29	11.99
60 percent S&P 500, 40 percent S/L intermediate bonds	12.88	9.52	12.74
Shorten fixed maturities	12.88	8.71	12.73
Add global diversification	13.10	8.82	13.27
Introduce size effect	14.74	8.79	17.93

FIGURE 12–11   Introduce the Size Effect

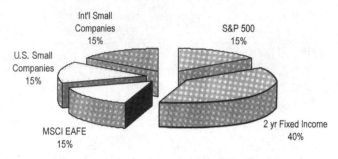

It is interesting to note that the introduction of this risky asset class actually reduces the portfolio risk while substantially increasing returns.

FORMULA 6: INTRODUCE THE HIGH BOOK-TO-MARKET EFFECT
The third risk factor that Fama and French used to explain market returns was the relative book-to-market (BTM) ratio. They found that this risk factor was rewarded most significantly outside the United States. The replacement of the S&P 500 Index and EAFE Index with a high BTM asset class again increased returns significantly while reducing risk. This is an advanced strategy and may require the help of an advisor.

Introduce the High Book-to-Market Effect

Portfolios	Geometric Mean, %	Risk: Standard Deviation, %	Growth of $1
60 percent equity, 40 percent bond mutual funds	12.56	9.29	11.99
60 percent S&P 500, 40 percent S/L intermediate bonds	12.88	9.52	12.74
Shorten fixed maturities	12.88	8.71	12.73
Add global diversification	13.10	8.82	13.27
Introduce size effect	14.74	8.79	17.93
Utilize the high BTM risk factor	15.93	8.76	22.30

This comprehensive strategy represents more than a 75 percent increase in the ending value of the portfolio compared to simply using a pure index fund. Most investors will not typically experience returns anywhere near this.

In summary:

1. *The indexed portfolio.* If you had simply used two of the most basic passively managed funds, one that tracks the S&P 500 Index and one that tracks the Shearson Lehman Intermediate Government and Corporate Index, you would have received approximately the same results with the same level of risk.

2. *The 60–40 percent principle.* We begin with a traditional, balanced portfolio allocation: 60 percent stocks and 40 percent bonds.

3. *Use short-term fixed income.* The reduction in risk allows you to introduce other, more risky, higher-expected-return asset classes without exceeding your risk tolerance level. This is one way to increase your overall returns while keeping risk in check.

4. *Introduce the size effect.* Small stocks have delivered higher long-term returns in every country around the world. First, reduce your allocation to large-company asset classes by one-third, and reallocate it to small stocks both in the United States and overseas. The introduction of this risky asset class increases returns with only a slight increase in overall portfolio volatility.

5. Replace the S&P 500 Index with U.S. large value stocks as defined by Fama and French. The result is higher returns with only a small increase in standard deviation.

6. *Diversify globally.* Foreign markets and domestic markets do not move in tandem with one another. Therefore, international investments can increase returns while reducing risk.

In this exercise, we increased our returns more than 3 percent per year, from 12.56 to 15.93 percent, by using asset class investing techniques. (A 15 percent return means your investments will double in 4.8 years.) With these additional strategies, we significantly increase the growth of a dollar invested from $11.99 to $22.30, more than an 85 percent increase in the ending value of the portfolio. See Fig. 12–11.

Asset class investing adds value by allowing you to effectively diversify both across and within asset categories and to fully capture the returns delivered by the capital markets. You can do all this without the cost and uncertainty of conventional investment strategies.

As promised, Fig. 12–13 is a list of asset class mutual funds and their phone numbers. You will find this list on page 138.

Last, a critical component to asset class investing in order to maintain your chosen level of risk is rebalancing.

REBALANCING

Rebalancing is an important part of a successful diversification strategy. It is necessary because the asset classes in your portfolio will not move in tan-

FIGURE 12–12

Portfolios %	Years	Average Compound Return %	Standard Deviation (Risk) %	Growth of $1
60% Equity Funds, 40% Bond Mutual Funds	21	12.56	9.29	11.99
60% S&P 500 Index, 40% S/L Intermediate Bond Index	21	12.88	9.52	12.74
Shorten Fixed Maturities	21	12.881	8.71	12.73
INTRODUCE SIZE EFFECT	21	13.77	8.90	15.01
60% Equity Funds, 40% Bond Mutual Funds	21	12.56	9.29	11.99
60% S&P 500 Index, 40% S/L Intermediate Bond Index	21	12.88	9.52	12.74
Shorten Fixed Maturities	21	12.881	8.71	12.73
Introduce Size Effect	21	13.77	8.90	15.01
ADD VALUE STOCKS	21	14.82	9.49	18.23
60% Equity Funds, 40% Bond Mutual Funds	21	12.56	9.29	11.99
60% S&P 500 Index, 40% S/L Intermediate Bond Index	21	12.88	9.52	12.74
Shorten Fixed Maturities	21	12.881	8.71	12.73
Introduce Size Effect	21	13.77	8.90	15.01
Add Value Stocks	21	14.82	9.49	18.23
Diversify Globally	21	15.80	8.56	21.78

In the above statistical examples, you see how adding additional asset classes to a portfolio increases return while decreasing volatility.

dem. Therefore, the amount of money you have in each asset category will change as markets fluctuate. In other words, your allocation will drift much as a sailboat without a rudder. The process is just as important as the initial allocation. Efficient asset class investors use systematic rebalancing strategies and stick with them.

Rebalancing is a challenge for most investors since it is the inverse of the natural and historical inclination to buy and sell. Sometimes this step requires selling assets that have recently done well and buying assets that have recently done poorly. It is emotionally difficult to sell winners and buy losers. It is easy to fall back into our old way of believing that there are trends in the market, to think that what has gone up will continue to go up, and that what has gone down will continue to go down. Unfortunately, investing with discipline is not that easy. The market is too efficient for such simple observations to work.

Over long periods, that asset class performance tends to be *mean reversionary.* Periods of above-average returns are often followed by periods of below-average returns—the opposite of a trending market. Rebalancing helps take advantage of these cycles, and most important, it maintains the chosen level of risk. If left unchecked, because stocks outperform bonds in the long run, the portfolio's relative allocation to stocks would increase, making the portfolio inherently more risky.

DOES ASSET CLASS INVESTING MEET YOUR INCOME NEEDS?

The biggest mistake most people make when they reach retirement age and require income is to assume what is needed is some kind of high-yielding fixed investment vehicle. But here's the rub: The moment an investor buys that high-yielding investment, his or her investment portfolio stops growing.

That also happens to be the biggest challenge financial advisors face everyday—to show clients how to create income to meet their retirement objectives while still maintaining a sufficient capital base to achieve growth.

They forget to plan for a significantly increasing life expectancy or the systematic erosion of capital by inflation. It is a big challenge. As you approach retirement, you need to properly deploy your assets to provide a consistent, spendable income stream to meet your retirement objectives without being overweighted in fixed-income securities.

While most investors realize the importance of building a sufficient capital base to achieve their retirement goals, they do not fully realize the importance of a properly constructed portfolio and its ability to deliver income through total return. They understand that interest and dividend income provides a regular check in the mail but don't feel comfortable with the concept of total return and systematic withdrawals because that requires "invading

FIGURE 12–13

Asset Class Mutual Funds Available To The Public

Fund Name	Investment Objective	Fund Inception Date	Fund Family	Phone
Ambassador Indexed Stock Ret A	Growth-Inc.	12/92	Ambassador Funds	800-892-4366
American Gas Index	Sp.Nat. Res.	5/89	Rushman Group	800-343-3355
Asm	Growth-Inc.	3/91	Asm Fund	800-445-2763
Benham Global Natural Res Index	Sp. Nat. Res.	9/94	Benham Broup	800-331-8331
Benham Gold Equities Index	Sp. Metals	8/88	Benham Group	800-331-8331
Biltmore Equity Index	Growth-Inc	5/93	Biltmore Funds	800-462-7538
Bt Investment Equity 500 Index	Growth	12/92	Bt Funds	800-943-2222
California Investment S&P Midcap	Growth-Inc	4/92	California Investment Trust Group	800-225-8778
Capital Market Index	Growth-Inc	11/92	Capital Market Fund	800-328-74088
Composite Northwest 50a	Growth	11/86	Composite Group Of Funds	800-543-8072
Composite Northwest 50b	Growth	3/94	Composite Group Of Funds	800-543-8072
Dean Witter Value-Add Market Equity	Growth Inc	12/87	Dean Witter Funds	800-869-3863
Domini Social Equity	Growth-Inc	6/91	Domini Social Equity Trust	800-762-6814
Dreyfus Edison Electric	Sp. Util	12/91	Dreyfus Group	800-645-6561
Dreyfus-Wilshire Lrg Co Grth	Growth	10/92	Dreyfus Group	800-645-6561
Dreyfus-Wilshire Lrg Co Val	Growth	10/92	Dreyfus Group	800-645-6561
Dreyfus-Wilshire Sm Co Grth	Small Company	10/92	Dreyfus Group	800-645-6561
Dreyfus-Wilshire Sm Co Val	Small Company	10/92	Dreyfus Group	800-645-6561
Fidelity Market Index	Growth-Inc	3/90	Fidelity Group	800-544-8888
First American Equity Index A	Growth-Inc	8/94	First American Investment Funds	800-637-2548
First American Equity Index B	Growth-Inc	12/92	First American Investment Funds	800-637-2548
Galaxy II Large Co. Index Ret	Growth-Inc	10/90	Galaxy Funds	800-628-0414
Galaxy II Small Co Index Ret	Small Company	10/90	Galaxy Funds	800-628-0414
Galaxy II U.S. Treasury Index Ret	Gvt Treasury	6/91	Galaxy Funds	800-628-0414
Galaxy II Utility Index Ret	Sp Util	1/93	Galaxy funds	800-628-0414
Gateway Index Plus	Growth-Inc	12/77	Gateway Group	800-345-6339
Gateway Mid Cap Index	Growth	9/92	Gateway Group	800-345-6339
Gateway Small Cap Index	Small Company	6/93	Gateway Group	800-354-6339
Goldman Sachs Core F/I Instl	Corp General	1/94	Goldman Sachs Asset Management Group	800-621-2550
Jackson National Growth	Growth	11/92	Jackson National Capital Management Funds	800-888-3863
Kent Index Equity Investment	Growth-Inc	12/92	Kent Funds	800-633-5368
MainStay Equity Index	Grown-Inc	12/90	MainStay Funds	800-522-4202
Monitrend Summation	Growth-Inc	2/88	Monitrend Mutual Funds	800-251-1970

FIGURE 12–13

Fund Name	Investment Objective	Fund Inception Date	Fund Family	Phone
Nations Equity-Index Tr A	Growth	12/93	Nations Funds	800-321-7854
Peoples Index	Growth-Inc	1/90	Dreyfus Group	800-645-6561
Peoples S&P Midcap Index	Growth	6/91	Dreyfus Group	800-645-6561
Pnc Index Equity Inv	Growth-Inc	6/92	Pnc Family Of Funds	800-422-6538
Portico Bond Immdex	Corp Hi Qlty	12/89	Portico Funds	800-228-1024
Principal Pres S&P 100 Plus	Growth-Inc	12/85	Principal Preservation Portfolios	800-826-4600
Schwab 1000	Growth-Inc	4/91	Schwab Funds	800-526-8600
Schwab International Index	Foreign	9/93	Schwab Funds	800-526-8600
Schwab Small Cap Index	Small Company	12/93	Schwab Funds	800-526-8600
Seven Seas Matrix Equity	Growth	5/92	Seven Seas Series Fund	800-647-7327
Seven Seas S&P 500 Index	Growth-Inc	12/92	Seven Seas Series Fund	800-647-7327
Seven Seas Small Cap	Small Company	7/92	Seven Seas Series Fund	800-647-7327
Smith Breeden Mkt Tracking	Growth-Inc	6/92	Smith Breeden Family Of Funds	800-221-3138
Stagecoach Corporate Stock	Growth-Inc	1/84	Stagecoach Funds	800-222-8222
STI Classic Intl Equity Index Inv	Foreign	6/94	STI Classic Funds	800-428-6970
T. Rowe Price Equity Index	Growth-Inc	3/90	Price T. Rowe Funds	800-638-5660
United Svcs All American Equity	Growth-Inc	3/81	United Services Funds	800-873-8637
Vanguard Balanced Index	Balanced	9/92	Vanguard Group	800-662-7447
Vanguard Bond Index Int-Term	Corp General	3/94	Vanguard Group	800-662-7447
Vanguard Bond Index Long-Term	Corp General	3/94	Vanguard Group	800-662-7447
Vanguard Bond Index Short-Term	Corp General	3/94	Vanguard Group	800-662-7447
Vanguard Bond Index Total Bd	Corp Hi Qlty	12/86	Vanguard Group	800-662-7447
Vanguard Index 500	Growth-Inc	8/76	Vanguard Group	800-662-7447
Vanguard Index Extended Market	Small Company	12/87	Vanguard Group	800-662-7447
Vanguard Index Growth	Growth	11/92	Vanguard Group	800-662-7447
Vanguard Index Small Cap Stock	Small Company	10/60	Vanguard Group	800-662-7447
Vanguard Index Total Stk Mkt	Growth-Inc	4/92	Vanguard Group	800-662-7447
Vanguard Index Value	Growth-Inc	11/92	Vanguard Group	800-662-7447
Vanguard International Equity Emerg Mkt	Foreign	3/94	Vanguard Group	800-662-7447
Vanguard International Equity European	Europe	6/90	Vanguard Group	800-662-7447
Vanguard International Equity Pacific	Pacific	6/90	Vanguard Group	800-662-7447
Vanguard Quantitative	Growth-Inc	12/86	Vanguard Group	800-662-7447
Victory Stock Index	Growth-Inc	12/93	Victory Group	800-539-3863
Woodward Equity Index Ret	Growth-Inc	7/92	Woodward funds	800-688-3350

Reprinted with permission from RWB Advisory Services, Inc.

their principal." Often these investors chase yield and overlook the combined risk of living longer and inflation. That's when trouble starts; it's also
where an investment advisor who understands these concepts can add substantial value.

In building portfolios for retirement, almost all financial advisors create
diversified portfolios that focus primarily on total return and providing growth.
Many advisors do a great job of both explaining the need for asset allocation
to their clients and helping them understand the important role of equity. There
is often, however, a missing piece that many advisors don't adequately explain
to their clients: the role of volatility in achieving their success.

First, let's take a look at a simple example of the effect of differences
in variances between two portfolios with the same average return (variances
meaning the difference between average return and the actual results). If
both portfolios had an average rate of return of 10 percent for 3 years, we
would expect the ending value to be the same. But it is not.

Let's assume that you invest $100,000 at the beginning of the 3-year
period and earn 10 percent each year with no volatility. The simple average
return is the total of the annual returns divided by the number of periods, or
0.30 / 3=10 percent. The ending value is $133,100. Let's say that my portfolio earns the same average return of 10 percent over the 3-year period but
with a lot more volatility—up 20 percent the first year, down 20 percent the
second year, and up 30 percent the third. The average is $(0.20 - 0.20 + 0.30)$
$/ 3 = 10$ percent, which is the same percentage rate as that for the first portfolio. The terminal wealth created in my portfolio, however, is significantly less at $124,800. Ouch!

The impact of volatility was actually substantially understated in the
above example because of the relatively short time period used and because
the impact of withdrawals was not considered.

One of the benefits of asset class investing is that you can invest in exact
asset classes you find in your historical research. This allows you to reliably estimate the degree of risk inherent in your portfolio. See Table 12–1.
Most Wall Street model portfolios I've seen are nothing more an asset mix
composed of securities of several different asset class categories. This makes
it virtually impossible to recreate a portfolio that has the characteristics of
their historical model portfolio.

Let's test it and look at how one asset class model portfolio stacks up
against 90-day Treasury bills and Standard & Poor's 500 Index. I'm using
Reinhardt Werba Bowen's global conservative portfolio of indexes (before
any fees). I have chosen the period beginning with 1972 so that we include
the recession of 1973–1974. See Fig. 12–14.

TABLE 12–1   Asset Class Composition

	Global Conservative, %	Global Moderate, %	Global Aggressive, %
Money market	5	5	5
Two-year fixed	45	25	10
U.S. large-company stocks	18	25	30
U.S. small-company stocks	7	10	13
International large-company stocks	16	22	27
International small-company stocks	6	9	11
Emerging market stocks	3	4	4

FIGURE 12–14   Growth of a Dollar

January 1972–December 1997

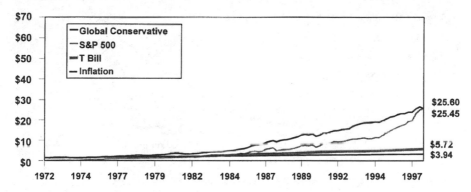

Reprinted with permission from RWB Advisory Services, Inc.

Many first time investors will find it surprising that the global conservative portfolio has a greater ending value than the S&P 500 Index for this period. Global conservative for every dollar invested grew to $25.60 versus S&P 500 at $25.45. The compound returns were very close, but the average simple returns were significantly different. During the 26-year period from January 1, 1972, through December 31, 1997, U.S. Treasury bills earned an average annual compound rate of return of 6.9 percent. During this same period, Standard & Poor's 500 Index and the global conservative portfolio earned 13.3 percent. The global conservative portfolio ended with a greater terminal value due to the lower volatility.

But what if you took systematic withdrawals, as you would during retirement? Let's examine each of the portfolios after a quarterly systematic withdrawal of $2,000. Figure 12–15 shows that Treasury bills presented the greatest problem for a retired investor because they failed to earn at a high enough rate to pay out income and maintain principal. The initial investment of $100,000 fell to $31,566, and this was before adjusting for inflation and taxes! The investment in the S&P 500 did better, netting an ending balance of $232,859, but this is not much reward for the significant risk taken owing to greater volatility. Even though the global conservative portfolio is relatively low-risk, it finishes with an ending balance of $891,827, significantly higher!

FIGURE 12–15   Global Conservative vs. S&P 500 & T-Bills

Global Conservative vs S&P 500 and T-Bills
Less Quarterly Income of $2,000
January 1972–December 1997

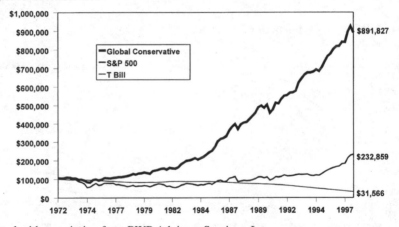

Reprinted with permission from RWB Advisory Services, Inc.

Why is there such a dramatic difference between the global conservative portfolio and the S&P 500 when their rates of return were virtually identical? The answer is that the lower volatility of the global conservative portfolio prevents it from being depleted too far in down markets. The severe market declines in 1973–1974 caused the S&P 500 to fall much farther than the other two investments. The continued income withdrawals during such severe down periods made it very difficult for the account to rebound when the markets recovered.

The most important message contained in this comparison is that investors who are retiring should not assume that a fixed-investment vehicle is necessary to provide a dependable income. And income investors must use diversified portfolios with lower variances than pure equity accounts when they seek total rates of return.

Asset class investing, by design, provides an answer to the retirement dilemma of living longer combined with inflation.

INVESTING
TAX-DEFERRED

13

INVESTING FOR A LONGER RETIREMENT

I CAN STILL REMEMBER THE WAY I FELT THE DAY MY DAD RETIRED from the service. After 30 years of hard work, two wars, and many personal sacrifices, he handed my mother a pension check for $800.

"This is it?!" She actually pulled on the check in an attempt to make it stretch longer. "This is what they expect us to live on!" Tears filled her eyes as if she suddenly realized an irreversible mistake. My dad hung his head, dropped his shoulders, and walked out of the kitchen. I felt her pain and his bitter disappointment, but at the time I didn't understand there was something they could have done differently.

My dad had trusted the system, depended on someone else's plan for his retirement, and ended up working as a security guard at Kmart until the day he died. I supplemented their income as well. They never understood how to invest.

When it comes to retirement planning, most people have overly ambitious goals, inadequate funding, and either no investment strategy or the wrong kind of strategy, as we have seen. In the unlikely event that you stay with the same employer all your working years (although statistics say that you won't), the best you can hope for is to retire on one-half your average annual earnings. You can't expect Social Security to fill in the gaps, since most employers' retirement formulas count one-half of the monthly Social Security benefit as part of your pension income.

To reach your financial goal, you will have to develop a dependable income stream, control costs, and beat the inflation robber. Asset class investing, with its automatic reallocation procedures, precludes the need to predict rates of inflation. Investors need only make the decision to invest and then decide how much risk they can tolerate in a given time span.

Figure 13–1 shows how much you would need to save every month, starting now, to have $1 million at age 65. It also shows that the earlier you start, the richer, by far, you'll be.

With tax deferral, your money will grow faster than the same return rate without the tax deferral. See Fig. 13–2. Even after withdrawing all your money and paying current taxes, you will most likely still have more dollars than you would by paying taxes as you go. The reason is that you are able to earn interest on dollars that would have normally gone to pay taxes.

Figure 13–3 shows the tax equivalent yield and helps you calculate what you will need to earn on a taxable investment to achieve the same annual growth. For instance, let's say you are in the 28 percent bracket and have a tax-deferred or tax-free investment earning 5 percent. Find the 28 percent tax rate and the 5 percent interest rate, and you will see they meet at 6.94 percent. This means you would need to find a taxable investment paying 6.94 percent to achieve the same growth rate, after paying taxes, as that for the tax-deferred or tax-free investment.

RETIREMENT PLANS

There are a number of special plans designed to create retirement savings, and many of these plans allow you to deposit money directly from your paycheck before taxes are taken out. Employers occasionally will match the amount (or a percentage of that amount) you have withheld from your paycheck up to a certain percentage. Some of these plans permit you to with-

FIGURE 13–1   How To Have A Million

Starting Age	AMOUNT YOU HAVE TO SAVE PER MONTH 8% return	10% return	15% return
25	$310	$180	$45
30	$470	$300	$90
35	$710	$490	$180
40	$1,100	$810	$370
45	$1,760	$1,390	$760
50	$2,960	$2,500	$1,640
55	$5,550	$5,000	$3,850
60	$13,700	$13,050	$11,600

FIGURE 13–2   Tax-Deferred Accumulation: A Powerful Financial Tool

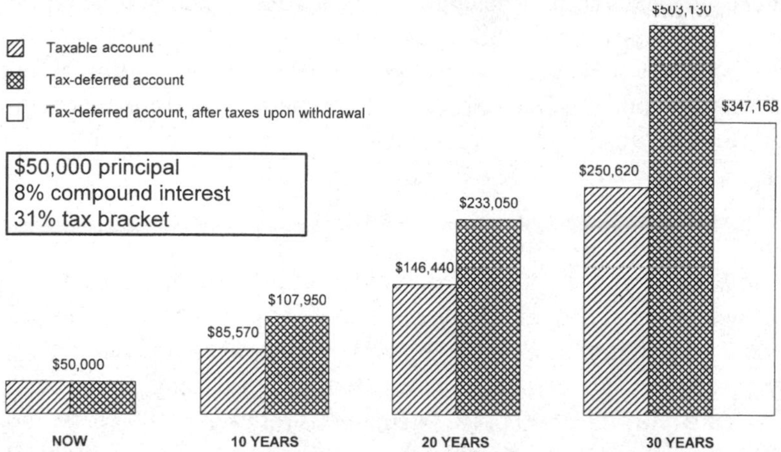

Reprinted with permission from McGraw-Hill, *Guaranteed Income for Life,* Michael F. Lane

draw money early without a penalty in order to buy a home or pay for education. For those that do not allow early withdrawals without penalty, sometimes you can borrow money from the account or take out low-interest secured loans with your retirement savings as collateral. Rates of return vary on these vehicles depending on what you invest in, since you can invest in stocks, bonds, mutual funds, CDs, or any combination.

Why start now? The age at which you begin does make a dramatic difference. If at age 25 you start putting $150 per month into a retirement account that's tax-deferred, by the time you're 65 years old, you'll have $840,000. If you wait until you're 35 years old to begin, you'll have $300,000.

FIGURE 13–3   Tax-Deferral Calculator

A tax rate of:	15%	28%	31%	36%	39.6%
Interest rate					
		What a taxable investment must earn during accumulation:			
2.5%	2.94	3.47	3.62	3.91	4.14
3.0%	3.53	4.17	4.35	4.69	4.97
3.5%	4.12	4.86	5.07	5.47	5.79
4.0%	4.70	5.56	5.80	6.25	6.62
4.5%	5.29	6.25	6.52	7.03	7.45
5.0%	5.88	6.94	7.25	7.81	8.28
5.5%	6.47	7.64	7.97	8.59	9.11
6.0%	7.06	8.33	8.70	9.38	9.93
6.5%	7.65	9.03	9.42	10.16	10.76
7.0%	8.24	9.72	10.14	10.94	11.59
7.5%	8.82	10.42	10.87	11.72	12.42
8.0%	9.41	11.11	11.59	12.50	13.25
8.5%	10.00	11.81	12.32	13.28	14.07

Equivalent yield formula: Tax-deferred rate divided by (1 - tax rate)

Example: 6.0 (tax-deferred) divided by (1 - 28%) = 6.0 divided by .72 =8.33%

Reprinted with permission from National Association of Home Builders

You can do it yourself or use brokers or investment advisors. They screen investment managers across the country and across investment disciplines to ensure compatibility with the investor's financial goals. They not only monitor the money managers on an ongoing basis, but also help you monitor and evaluate your personal portfolio with a quarterly performance report. Next let's look at the different types of retirement plans and which one best fits your needs. See Fig. 13–4.

Individual Retirement Account

IRA contributions are no longer deductible if either you or your spouse is covered by another retirement plan, such as corporate pension plan, SEP IRA accounts, Keogh plans, or 401(k) company-sponsored plans.

If your adjusted gross income is less than $35,000 (single) or $50,000 (joint), you are allowed $1.00 in IRA deductions for each $5.00 below those limits. In other words, you can still get a tax credit for the full $2,000 IRA contribution if your adjusted gross income is no higher than $25,000 (single) or $40,000 (joint) and you or your spouse are covered by a pension plan or a Keogh.

IRA CHECKLIST

Consider putting money in an IRA if:

- Your contributions are fully deductible—couples filing jointly with gross income of less than $40,000, singles who make less than $25,000, or anyone who is not covered by a pension, profit-sharing, or other tax-advantaged retirement plan.
- You qualify for a partial deduction and are sure that you will not need the money in your IRA before age 59½.

Contributing to an IRA is probably not worthwhile if:

- You are ineligible for a deduction, especially if you think that your tax rate when you retire will be higher than it is now.
- You can use other tax-favored retirement savings plans such as a 401(k).
- You don't want to worry about the lifelong burden of paperwork required to document a nondeductible or partially deductible IRA for the Internal Revenue Service (IRS).

FIGURE 13–4 Retirement Plans

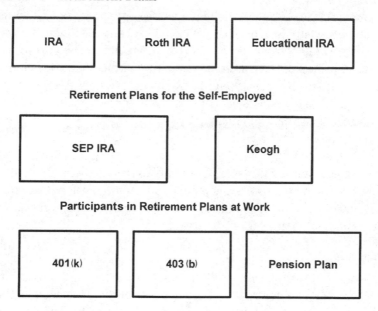

The basic rules of contributing to any type of IRA (with the exception of educational IRAs which are really not retirement accounts) are based on taxable compensation. This includes wages, salaries, tips, professional fees, commissions, and self employment income. Your annual contribution to all IRA accounts cannot exceed $2,000 plus up to an additional $2,000 for a non-working or low-earning spouse. The IRA is simply a tax shelter, because all the earnings in every type of IRA compound are completely tax-deferred. For example, say you accumulate $50,000 in a deductible IRA by the time you reach age 40. If your account averages a 10 percent annual return for the next 25 years, you'll generate $492,000 of earnings. And if you withdraw that as a lump sum and pay a 30 percent average tax rate, you'll net around $344,000. On the other hand, if you have that $50,000 in a taxable account, then your earnings are subject to an average tax rate of 30 percent, and you net only 7 percent per annum instead of 10 percent. At that rate, $50,000 earns about $221,000 over the next 25 years. So that's the benefit of compounding. You get an extra 3 percent provided by the IRA tax shelter.

IRAs are also a great place for an aggressive growth mutual fund because you want to strive for high returns to maximize the advantage of the tax-deferred compounding. Even though your stocks are riskier in the short run and there may be volatility over the long run, they may participate in the growth of the economy.

Educational IRAs

Educational IRAs limit contributions to $500 per year; and while the earnings compound tax-free, they have to be used for tuition or other allowable college costs. The IRS would penalize you if your child decided to buy a car with it instead. If the funds are used for any purpose other than education, income taxes and a 10 percent penalty are slapped on the earnings. Also, when you cash in an educational IRA, you become ineligible for new tuition tax credits during that calendar year. And finally, if you're ready or not, you must withdraw any remaining funds by your youngest child's thirteenth birthday.

Another idea for your children's education might be to set aside your spare change, unused dimes, and quarters everyday. Once a month, write a check equivalent to the total to a mutual fund company. It will accept a small contribution of $50 per month. If you earn 8 percent per year, in 10 years your child could net $9,064.

The Roth IRA

The Roth IRA, available in 1998, is a valuable new kind of IRA. It differs from others in that contributions are not deductible. However, distributions of funds held in the IRA for more than 5 years from the date you set up the Roth IRA will be totally *tax-free* if used for up to $10,000 of first-time home-buying expenses or after the occurrence of death, disability, or attainment of age 59½.

The Roth IRA will be most valuable when it holds investments that compound at a high rate, such as growth stocks, for a long time. That's because the ultimate value of the compound investment returns will be distributed *tax-free,* instead of being taxed at normal rates, as are distributions from regular IRAs and other retirement accounts.

Children's IRA Opportunity

A Roth IRA is an excellent investment account to open for children as soon as they have earned income. The extra years of compounding available to a child can produce a tax-free payoff that will give the child a big headstart on lifetime financial security.

While a child must have earned income to open a Roth IRA, the IRA need not be funded with the child's earned income. It can be funded with money received as a gift—from parents, grandparents, etc. This gives the child the chance to "double up" by also saving the earned income in another account.

Roth IRA for Yourself

You can make a full $2,000 contribution to a Roth IRA if your adjusted gross income (AGI) is less than $150,000 for a joint return or $95,000 for a sin gle return. The contribution gets phased out from $150,000 to $160,000 (joint) and $95,000 to $110,000 (single). If your AGI doesn't exceed $100,000, you'll be able to convert existing IRAs to Roth IRAs. To do this, you'll have to first withdraw your IRA assets and pay the taxes on the gains. If you convert after 1998, you must pick up all the income in the year of conversion.

Whether it will pay to convert a regular IRA to a Roth IRA will depend on several factors, such as

- Your current and expected future tax rates
- The length of time you expect to keep your funds in the IRA
- The rate of return that you expect to earn
- Whether you can pay the tax due on the conversion from non-IRA funds

A Roth IRA offers advantages in addition to the tax-free distributions— you can withdraw the amount of your regular contributions to a Roth IRA at any time.

A good comprehensive booklet on IRAs is available from Schwab: *Schwab IRA Answers, New Laws, More Choices.* Just call 1-800-806-8481.

Retirement Plans for the Self-Employed
Keogh
This is a special type of IRA that doubles as a pension plan for a self-employed person. The self-employed person can put aside up to $30,000 per year, significantly more than the normal $2,000 cap on an individual IRA. You can do this asset class investment program inside a self-directed Keogh.

If you are self-employed, sock away 20 percent of your income—up to a maximum of $30,000—in a Keogh plan. You can establish a Keogh plan with any bank, brokerage firm, or mutual fund. You may also want to explore the advantages of a simplified employee pension (SEP) plan.

Simplified Employee Pension Plan
A SEP plan is like a giant IRA. SEP plans were created so that small businesses could set up retirement plans that were a little easier to administer than normal pension plans. Both employees and the employer can contribute to a SEP plan.

The reason you don't hear more about these plans is that the brokers don't make money selling them.

You can actually save more in a SEP account than you can in a 401(k). A SEP plan allows you to put away as much as 13.034 percent of pretax self-employed earnings or $24,000 per year, whichever is less. The nice thing about a SEP account is that you can wait until the last minute to invest. The cutoff date is April 15.

Participate in Retirement Plans at Work
The 401(k)
Things have changed dramatically in the last few years. If you participate in a 401(k) retirement plan at work, you need to know that any investment mistakes you make come out of your retirement nest egg. In other words, investment results are your responsibility, and not that of the sponsor of the plan. This makes it even more important for you to understand your investment choices and make smart decisions.

Some employers will match your contribution. That's like found money. So your contribution and your employer's contribution could be compounding tax-deferred until you retire.

The 403(b)
The nonprofit version of a 401(k) plan is the 403(b). Local and state governments offer the 403(b) plan.

Whatever you're doing, add to it. If your company sponsors a 401(k) or 403(b), make an appointment with the human resources office, and sign up or increase the amount of your contribution as soon as you can. You can put up to a maximum of $10,000 per year directly from your paycheck into your retirement account. The benefits of saving pretax dollars are huge. Now with the 28 percent tax bracket, that $10,000 contribution represents $2,800 in tax savings. So the full annual contribution really costs you only $7,200. The same investing and selection of mutual funds as outlined in the book would apply inside the plan.

The problem is that time does not permit you to absorb and evaluate the vast amounts of information required to make astute investment decisions. Meeting your personal production schedules, sales, and service commitments must take priority. Often, these problems ultimately push you, the plan participants, to choose expedient, short-term solutions that seem reasonable but may not produce the results you desire.

The following investment-oriented steps are set forth to help you to accomplish your investment goals.

Participants normally have the right to move their funds in a 401(k) plan from one alternative to another periodically. One caution: By moving from equities to cash or fixed income and back, you unknowingly become your own personal market timer. (Aside from everything in the book about market timing, this type of activity also causes you to get "whipsawed" by market moves you may not understand, to the detriment of your long-term investment success).

The best approach is to decide upon one strategy and stick with it. Work with your 401(k) plan's financial consultant and develop a personal strategy, in the form of a statement of investment objectives for each alternative and commit to it in writing. Such a statement should articulate clearly what the fund may and may not invest in, the expected long-term goals (in terms of performance and volatility) and the general approach to be taken by the manager (whether a private investment manager or a mutual fund manager) in achieving those results.

Most 401(k) plans have a long-term, systematic manner of monitoring any plan's investment progress. You should inquire into how your assets are to be monitored. If mutual funds are used as an investment vehicle, then you should be provided performance results periodically. Otherwise, periodic meetings or telephone conferences with your financial consultant should be requested.

These kinds of questions should form the basis of such meetings:

- Is your manager continuing to apply the style and strategy that you understood would be used in the management of your assets?
- Do you find the reporting clear, logical, and understandable? Does it show clearly what your plan owns?
- Do you feel comfortable that your overall communications with the financial consultant are good, and that your queries and needs are attended to promptly?
- Is your 401(k) plan's performance roughly in line with the performance you expected? Or is the fund apparently doing much better or much worse than expected? Why? Is the explanation satisfactory?
- If there are investment restrictions in your guidelines, are these being adhered to?

Your financial consultant can be called upon to meet with participants to explain the advantages of various investment alternatives as well as how the plan has progressed. This, of course, would be at the option or request of the sponsoring company. As a participant, you should understand that, over long periods, common stocks—although more volatile—tend to produce overall returns almost twice as high as those of high-quality bonds.

You may be able to run your own asset class strategy. An alternative is a balanced portfolio which may combine elements of cyclical stocks, large and small growth stocks, and others with good-quality bonds (fixed-income securities). It will seldom involve an element of market timing. Balanced portfolios are often used by major funds and charitable endowments as well as individuals. They provide great flexibility.

The 401(k) plans are much more attractive to many companies since the company's investment committee is not directly liable for any losses sustained by the plan.

Many employees like the sense of control they get from a 401(k) plan. But serving as one's own money manager can also be overwhelming to people who have trouble managing their own checkbooks, let alone their financial future. Unfortunately, with so much at stake, many participants feel intimidated about making investment decisions. That is why the most popular choice in 401(k) plans is low-risk, fixed-rate guaranteed investment contracts (GICs) offered by insurance companies.

Luckily for plan investors, back in the 1980s fixed-rate contracts were paying unusually high rates, around 9 percent. But in the 1990s, interest rates came down. Participants coming out of a 5-year, 9 percent contract had to reinvest at lower rates, which means they will be coming up short at retirement. Still, many investors who are given a choice with their retirement money prefer to play it safe with a fixed income. That's fine, if it's the only way you can sleep at night; but don't forget, there is a tradeoff in results.

WHAT SHOULD A PARTICIPANT INVESTOR BE AWARE OF?

Faced with a number of investment decisions, an employee should get prepared:

1. Identify investment goals.
2. Select and set appropriate risk parameters, and choose an option to meet your financial needs.
3. Look at all the options—not just the guaranteed ones. Remember that, in fixed-investment vehicles, low risk often means low return.
4. If provided, get investment counseling.
5. Monitor your investment manager's progress.

In most 401(k) plans, participants are offered short-term investment vehicles that neglect their long-term investment needs. This can spell trouble 20 years from now when many plan participants may learn, too late, the ruthless rules of investing.

The reality is that guaranteed fixed-income investment contracts and market timing or daily switching produce, over the long run, only negligible investment returns. Unfortunately, this is what's being sold to the 401(k) investing public.

Warning: The Pension Benefits Guaranty Corporation (PBGC) does not cover 401(k) plans. About 40 percent of all money in 401(k) plans is invested in a product called a *guaranteed insurance contract* (GIC), which is like a certificate of deposit issued by an insurance company. GICs offer a guaranteed yield. Most investors mistakenly think that their principal is guaranteed; what is actually guaranteed is the rate of interest for a set period. The principal is secured by the insurance company's general fund, which is used to secure all policies.

Many insurance companies have huge investments in noninvestment-grade junk bonds—8 to 11 percent of their portfolio is typical. If forced to liquidate today, one in five insurance companies would not have enough money to meet its obligations.

Not Being Properly Advised

It's a sad fact that most 401(k) participants are not being properly advised and cannot be expected to make appropriate investment allocations or choices. The feature of daily switching [a feature offered by 401(k) service providers which gives the participant the freedom to transfer between investment options on a daily basis] offers plan participants the greatest control over their assets.

Regulations Give no Guidance

Beyond the minimum requirement of tossing a prospectus that offers the standard three investment choices on the lunchroom table, there is absolutely no incentive for employers to inform employees of investment options. This forces the employee-participants to fend for themselves in the rough investment seas of the 1990s. In most cases, participants act as their own asset allocators or market timers, deciding each quarter—or sometimes each day—how much money should be invested in each class.

What to Do

How can an employer with a 401(k) plan get the best ongoing investment advice?

- Have your plan reviewed for investment performance. Begin the year by having a qualified financial firm review your 401(k) plan.
- Request investment counseling regarding asset allocation appropriate to the participant's individual objectives, his or her retirement horizons, and his or her risk tolerance.

- Set up an educational program to acquaint participants with the capital markets, and provide specific investment counseling regarding an appropriate mix of investments.
- Encourage participants with long-term investment horizons, or younger participants, to invest to some extent in equities.

Pension Plan

In a defined benefit pension plan, the sponsoring company takes full responsibility for providing a guaranteed benefit for you as a participant. The sponsoring company shoulders all the investment risks and promises to make specific payouts. To many companies that have abandoned pension plans, retirement benefits generated from these plans didn't seem worth the extensive amount of government paperwork and the fiduciary risk that the sponsoring company had to shoulder.

Retirement Checkup

Pension miscalculations are a growing problem that affects people of all ages, not just retirement age. Anytime someone changes jobs or takes a lump-sum pension cash-out, she or he is at risk. Women are especially vulnerable to pension mistakes because they tend to move in and out of the workforce more often than men. For the most part, pension mix-ups aren't intentional. Federal pension laws are incredibly difficult even for expert number crunchers.

How would you know if there was an error which had been compounding for many years? How can you ensure that you'll get what's rightfully yours when retirement arrives? It's up to you to keep track of your own pension. Know your rights and monitor your retirement plan before the "golden years" creep up on you. Learn the details. Ask for a summary plan description. This will show how your pension is calculated. If you're in a workplace 401(k), get a description of your program from the administrator of your benefits plan. Also, an individual benefits statement will tell you what your benefits are currently worth and how many years you've been in the plan. It may even include a projection of your monthly check.

Check for obvious errors such as wrong years of service. If you're stashing money away in a 401(k), you'll get periodic statements just as you do with your checking accounts. Save all your statements. You should keep any pension documents your company gives you over the years. Also keep records of dates when you worked and your salary, since this type of data is used by your employer to calculate the value of your pension. Ask for professional help, if you still think something might be wrong. Ask for the name of a qualified specialist in your area. Call the American Society of Pension Actuaries at (703) 516-9300 or the National Center for Retirement Benefits at (800) 666-1000.

Most of the time companies won't intentionally fudge; sometimes the blame can be on simple errors. Here are nine common pension mistakes to watch for:

1. Company forgot to include commission, overtime pay, or bonuses in determining your benefit level.
2. Your employer relied on incorrect Social Security information to calculate your benefits.
3. Somebody used the wrong benefit formula (i.e., an incorrect interest rate was plugged into the equation).
4. Calculations are wrong because you've worked past age 65.
5. You didn't update your workplace personnel officer about important changes that would affect your benefits such as marriage, divorce, or death of a spouse.
6. The firm's computer software is flawed.
7. The year 2000 computer problem is also something you should be aware of. Consult with your pension administrator to make sure that the computer software doesn't lose your precious data.
8. The company neglected to include your total years of service.
9. Your pension provider just made a basic mathematical mistake.

If you do not have a qualified retirement plan available, you should look to invest in a private IRA. With the new limits and options, you may find one that you qualify for. Be very careful to avoid the insurance salespersons who sell the "private pension plans" as an alternative to qualified retirement plans. These are a scam; and if you read the papers, you will note that most of the major insurance companies are being sued for misleading sales practices relating to these plans.

Another Option within Your Control—Retire for a Lot Less

Often experts are quoted as saying a minimum of a $1 million in assets will be needed—a conclusion that is regularly accompanied by selling a product, funding a 401(k) plan, or buying an annuity. But not everyone needs $1 million for a secure retirement. There are many people who can retire on a lot less, as little as $300,000, and live the life they please, enjoy retire ment to the fullest, and die with $100,000 or more still safely tucked away. Maybe it will mean not taking that trip to Europe or buying a new car or jewelry or joining the country club. I put away my golf clubs and took up swimming. It's fun and inexpensive and keeps me in shape.

Put away the traditional concept of retirement. Several years ago, I read somewhere that you should live in a smaller town and simplify your life. On that strategy, as I went through my midlife changes, I moved to the town of Ojai, California, slowed my pace—sold my Porsche—and started writing books on investing.

In 1997, a study conducted by Alliance Management and Louis Harris Associates, both of New York, revealed that 84 percent of respondents either didn't know or grossly underestimated how much they would need to retire. A study by William F. Mercer, Inc., an employee benefits consulting firm in New York, showed that one-half of the executives polled predicted that the average 65-year-old salaried employee would not have enough assets to retire comfortably in the year 2000. You might be in stable shape financially, but when you read these stories, it makes you feel badly and prompts you to make a decision to invest in possibly inappropriate or aggressive-type investments.

In general, people spend on impulse while juggling bills; and they postpone investing until next year, then walk around feeling guilty about it. Once you control your financial condition, you can start to measure or gauge your progress toward whatever you call your dreams.

An article entitled "Living High on the Hog for a Lot Less" by Gary Gentry (*Financial Planning Magazine,* April 1998) talks about several investors who rolled out of their companies' profit-sharing plans with $300,000, which was more than enough to meet their needs. In one case, a woman receives $700 per month plus $750 Social Security per month and is living very well. Her asset base is not depleting—in fact, she goes out to dinner, shops, and enjoys life and still is able to let her assets grow. The author also mentions an advisor with 600 clients who share a common trait: They're savers. What a great goal to have as your mission statement for an investment advisor's client base. This particular advisor counseled his clients to accumulate $100,000 in savings as their first goal—not to invest with him, not to buy an annuity, but to save money first. Other investors had nest eggs of only $60,000 to $70,000 and were living comfortably in towns just a few minutes away from major cities. Their savings were mostly due to the lower cost of living in certain parts of the country, the article points out. In areas where the median family income is $46,000, they could afford to buy

94.6 percent of the homes sold in the fourth quarter of 1997. In contrast, in San Francisco, where the median household income was $64,000, they could only afford 20 percent of the area's homes. So one strategy of first time investors is to think about where you want to live, and plan for that—not when you turn 65, but in your forties and early fifties.

Another consideration is state income tax. The highest per capita state tax is on residents of the District of Columbia, Alaska, Hawaii, and Mexico. Figure 13–5 lists 15 of the most affordable as well as 15 of the least afford-able metropolitan areas in 1997 according to the National Association of Home Builders.

The whole scenario is to live within your means. A lot of people are going to retire on $1,500 per month; and if they plan correctly, they can be satisfied. A lot of people are going to retire on $3,500 to $5,000 a month. Rather than feeling badly about this, just look at it realistically. Use your investments to make up the difference between Social Security and your retirement benefits.

Start by completing the form to request the Social Security Administration to send an accounting of your benefit payments, so you can know ahead of time how much you're going to be making when you retire. Also request from your company that same information regarding your pension plan, if you have one. Subtract the total of those two amounts from what you anticipate needing in retirement, and the difference is your investment goal.

FIGURE 13–5   Where Living Is Cheap—And No So Cheap

Most Affordable	Least Affordable
Kokomo, Ind.	San Francisco, California
Davenport-Moline-Rock Island, Iowa	Portland-Vancouver, Ore. - Wash.
Anchorage, Alaska	Santa Cruz-Watsonville, California
Wilmington-Newark, Del. - Md.	San Luis Obispo-Atascadero-Paso Robles, California
Lima, Ohio	Santa Rosa, California
Baton Rouge, La.	San Jose, California
Beaumont-Port Arthur, Texas	Salem, Ore.
Rockford, Ill.	Salinas, California
Utica-Rome, N.Y.	Santa Barbara-Santa Maria-Lompoc, Ca.
Jamestown, N.Y.	Provo-Orem, Utah
Kansas City, Mo.	San Diego, Calif.
Elkhart-Goshen, Ind.	Oakland, Calif.
Newburgh, N.Y.	Laredo, Texas
Duluth-Superior, Minn.	Honolulu, Hawaii
Lakeland-Winter Haven, Fla.	Salt Lake City, Utah

LAST NOTES ON RETIREMENT PLANNING

Since qualified plans all have contribution limits, what do you do if you have already contributed, or are contributing, the maximum amount into your retirement plans and will still have a shortfall?

I personally would avoid any get-rich-quick plan or the sure bets—they probably are not what they appear to be. Believe it or not, millions of dollars are contributed every year to scams. What may appear as a great conversation piece at a cocktail party may very well put you in a position of not being able to afford to attend the next one.

After your qualified retirement plan is fully funded, you have two general options: investing in a taxable account versus a tax-deferred account. Examples of taxable accounts are CDs, mutual funds, stocks (if traded), and bonds. Examples of tax-deferred vehicles are fixed and variable annuities.

Some may include variable life as a tax-deferred vehicle for analysis purposes, but I will not. My conclusion to date is that there is not a life insurance policy on the market that has expenses low enough to make it an attractive investment solution. If you *need* life insurance and are planning to invest the difference anyway, a *versatile universal life* (VUL) policy may make sense. If you do not need the life insurance, why pay for it, and in most cases, give a life insurance agent a 50 percent commission or more on your contribution?

If you have at least 10 years before you need to receive retirement income, invest in variable annuities. If you need the funds prior to this, use mutual funds. Variable annuities have expenses that mutual funds do not have and are also taxed differently. If you have less than 10 years before you begin distributions (notice that I do not say 10 years until retirement), the cost and less favorable taxation of the annuity may negate the benefits of the tax deferral and the death benefit. You may have other sources of capital to use for retirement income, such as a 401(k), that would enable you to continue to defer the use of the annuity for income and maximize the benefit of the variable annuity.

14

WHAT ARE ANNUITIES?

ANNUITIES ARE A POPULAR RETIREMENT SAVINGS VEHICLE. But first time investors should consider their options and costs carefully before purchasing one. You won't get into too much trouble as long as you think of yourself as a sheep drinking from the wolves' stream.

In general, there are two types of annuities: fixed and variable. A fixed annuity provides a specific income for life. With a variable annuity, payouts are dependent on investment return, which is not guaranteed. Variable annuities offer the choice of several investment divisions such as stocks, bonds, and money market funds, which can cause the rate of return to fluctuate according to market conditions.

In both fixed and variable annuities, you do not have to pay income tax on the accumulated earnings until payouts start. But keep in mind that withdrawals are taxable and, if you are under age 59½, may be subject to a 10 percent tax penalty.

Fixed Annuities

The word *fixed* is used to describe the type of annuity referred to by the interest rate paid by the issuing insurance company. The fixed annuity offers security in that the rate of return is certain. Typically, with a fixed annuity the insurance company declares a current interest rate and sets the interest rate. It promises to pay at a lower rate than the rate it expects to earn on its investment. The difference in rates is sometimes referred to as the *spread*. It allows the insurance company to recover its administrative costs and to profit.

The fixed aspect of the annuity also offers security in that the annuity holder does not take responsibility for making decisions about how the money should be invested. Also, the amount of the benefit that will be paid out of the annuity when the contract is annuitized is fixed. The settlement options that the annuitant receives from the insurance company are the same each year during the annuitization phase. If the annuitant chooses a settlement option based on life expectancy, the same amount will come to that annuitant each month for the rest of his or her life without any investment decisions or risk on the participant's part.

Example: A customer has accumulated $50,000 in an annuity. She owns a 6 percent fixed annuity and wants to make consistent monthly payments over the next 15 years. She can plan on payments of $421 each month to the annuity. At her retirement her original $50,000 lump sum will grow to approximately $76,000.

Variable Annuities

Variable annuities are often called *mutual funds with an insurance wrapper.* A variable annuity combines the best aspects of a traditional *fixed* annuity (tax deferral, insurance protection for beneficiaries, tax timing of controlled income options) with the benefits of traditional mutual fund type of portfolios (flexibility in selecting how to invest funds and the potential for higher investment returns).

Let's say you are a 35-year-old investing $10,000 in a low-cost tax-deferred variable annuity, and you're fortunate enough to get a return of 12 percent. By your sixty-fifth birthday, you could accumulate more than $240,000. If you are able to add $5,000 per year all along the way, your $160,000 of total invested capital, compounding tax-free, could balloon to more than $1,282,558. If you continue working and don't retire until age 70, your variable annuity could hold more than $2,224,249. That's what is made possible by investing in a variable annuity.

Variable annuity investors control their contract options. They dictate the amount, frequency, and regularity of their contributions; how their contributions are invested; and when the money is disbursed. The investor pays a premium to the insurance company which then buys *accumulation units,* similar to mutual fund shares, in an investment fund. The IRS imposes no limits on the annual nonsheltered amount that an individual may contribute to a variable annuity funded with after-tax dollars. In other words, you can put in as much money as you can afford. This is particularly important when it comes to supplementing retirement assets beyond the annual tax-free contribution limitation.

The variable annuity investor directs those funds in subaccount portfolios consisting of stocks, bonds, or cash money market funds. Diverse investment options make it possible to structure an investment portfolio to meet a variety of needs, goals, and risk tolerances. These investments may be managed by a mutual fund company or by the insurance company. With the important advantage of tax-free rebalancing, investors can adjust their portfolios at any time. This allows an investor's advisor to carefully plan and manage the asset allocation strategy based on changing needs or market conditions, without having to worry about generating current tax. See Fig. 14–1.

Unlike a mutual fund, an annuity does not pay out earnings or distribute any capital gains, so these are compounded on a tax-deferred basis. The ability to reallocate assets without current tax ramifications, combined with the tax-deferred compounding of potential earnings, makes variable annuities a highly competitive investment vehicle.

A variable annuity's rate of return is not guaranteed, but rather is determined by the performance of the investments selected. As the value of the

FIGURE 14–1   Investing Tax-Deferred vs. Taxable

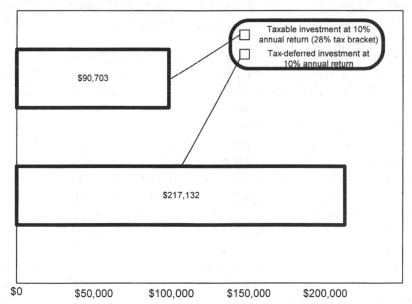

Taxable investment at 10% annual return (28% tax bracket)

Tax-deferred investment at 10% annual return

$90,703

$217,132

$0 $50,000 $100,000 $150,000 $200,000

$1,200 annual investment over 30 years

Reprinted with permission from McGraw-Hill, *Guaranteed Income for Life,* Michael F. Lane.

stocks in the portfolio varies, each unit will be worth more or less. Today's variable annuity managers, along with their affiliate mutual fund managers, seek diversification, consistent performance, and competitive returns by maximizing a portfolio's return and also minimizing the level of risk. Variable annuity investments are often balanced by investing a percentage of assets in the annuity fixed-income option to provide a less volatile investment return. These fixed annuity investments tend to smooth out extreme fluctuations; investors won't profit as much from a good year in the market with such an annuity, but neither will they suffer as great a loss of income during a bad year.

Payouts from variable annuities reflect the investment experience of the underlying portfolios. The amount of variable payments is not guaranteed or fixed and may decline in periods of market decline. However, if the annuitant dies during the accumulation phase (i.e., prior to receiving payments from the annuity), the investor's designated beneficiary is guaranteed to receive the greater of the account's accumulated value or the full amount invested less any withdrawals and applicable premium taxes. Some annuities also offer *enhanced death benefits,* such as options that would enable a client to receive a step up every 6 years until age 75, to lock in gains. Also, in most states, this built-in benefit generally bypasses the delays and costs of probate.

When withdrawals do begin, taxes are generally paid only on the amounts withdrawn that represent a gain at ordinary tax rates, while the remainder of the account value can continue to grow tax-deferred. However, if the investor takes funds from the variable annuity before age 59½, there is the additional 10 percent IRS penalty on the withdrawal of any gain.

Most variable annuities offer a free annual withdrawal provision that gives the investor access to up to 10 percent of the annuity value yearly without paying any surrender charges. Any distributions in excess of that 10 percent are subject to the surrender charges. No-load variable annuities that do not impose a surrender charge are 100 percent liquid but, like all annuities, may be subject to a 10 percent federal penalty for withdrawal prior to age 59½.

Despite their inherent advantages, not all variable annuities are created equal. They can vary widely in terms of costs and available investment options. Because of their insurance benefits, variable annuities generally cost more than traditional taxable investments, such as mutual funds. There may be front-end charges (loads), management fees, and sometimes back-end surrender charges for early withdrawals from the policy. These charges and the length of time that they apply to the policy vary widely across the industry. The average policy probably has a 6 to 7 percent first-year surrender charge that declines one percentage point per year. Some have *rolling surrender charges,* which means that each investment made has a new surrender charge schedule. For example, if you invested $1,000 every year, each $1,000 contribution would have a new surrender charge schedule. I would avoid these if possible.

In addition to portfolio management fees, variable annuities charge a fee to cover the issuing insurance company's administrative costs and mortality and expense (M&E) charges. According to the 1997 Morningstar Benchmarks, annual M&E charges for the current industry average are around 1.3 percent and are increasing.

The higher the overall costs, the longer it takes for the benefit of tax deferral to compensate for those costs. A no-sales-load, low-cost variable annuity can help shorten that breakeven holding period. In general, variable annuities are designed to be held as long-term investment vehicles so a breakeven of 10 to 15 years may be affordable for those investors with that type of time frame. Remember, the time horizon is measured not by when you will retire, but according to the time at which you need to start withdrawals. Income distributions from a variable annuity are best used to supplement conventional retirement benefits or as a reserve until other payouts are exhausted.

A variable annuity receives varying interest on the funds placed inside the annuity depending upon the choice of investment options. In addition, the holder of the variable annuity assumes the risk associated with the underlying investments made at the investment decision. Understanding how returns are credited on money invested in the framework of variable annuities can be a little more complicated than the case of a fixed annuity.

One of the main differences between a fixed annuity and a variable annuity is that the variable annuity is considered to be a security under federal law and, therefore, is subject to a greater degree of regulation. Anyone selling a variable annuity must have acquired securities licenses. Any potential buyer of a variable annuity must be provided with a prospectus—a detailed document that provides information on the variable annuity and the investment options.

In a variable annuity, the annuity holder may choose how to allocate premium dollars among a number of investment choices including stocks, bonds, a guaranteed account, income, growth fund, and various funds called subaccounts. Any funds placed in the guaranteed account of a variable annuity are credited with a fixed rate of interest in much the same manner as funds in a fixed annuity contract. There's a guaranteed interest rate and a current interest rate, and the current rate changes periodically. If it drops below the floor set by the guaranteed rate, then the annuity holder receives at a minimum the guaranteed rate.

The variable annuity typically offers the annuity holder several different subaccounts in which to invest all or a portion of the premiums paid into the annuity. The terms *subaccount, flexible account,* and *flexible subaccount* are certainly interchangeable. When an annuity holder purchases a variable annuity, he or she determines what proportion of the premium payments, usually on a percentage basis, will be allocated or paid to the different variable subaccounts. Once a percentage is determined, it remains in effect until the annuity holder notifies the insurance company of a desire to alter the allocation arrangement. Many variable annuities offer an option called *dollar cost averaging* which provides a method of systematic transfer of dollars from one fund to another inside the variable annuity.

In contrast to the fixed annuity option, an annuity holder who elects to receive all or part of the benefit payments under the variable option receives a check for the same amount each month.

The accumulation phase is a period of time from the purchase of the annuity until the annuity holder chooses to begin receiving payments from the annuity. It is during this period that the annuity builds up and accumulates the funds that will provide the annuity holder with future benefits. This works for both the fixed annuity and the variable annuity.

Deferred Annuities

Deferred annuities are the most popular. They allow people to accumulate money without paying current income tax on their earnings. This means that the amount can grow faster, due to the tremendous power of compound interest. Most deferred annuity contracts provide greater flexibility in the timing of premium payments and benefit payouts.

A tax-deferred annuity is an interest-bearing contract between an investor and an insurance company. When an investor purchases an annuity, the insurance company pays interest which is tax-deferred until withdrawal. The investor may withdraw the money at regular intervals or at a specific time in a lump sum or through random withdrawals.

One feature of an annuity that is unique and is not found in any other investment vehicle is that the annuity provides a stream of income that an annuitant cannot outlive. Annuities offer protection against living too long. (This statement about living too long refers to the person's financial situation only.) Dollars inside the annuity remain tax-deferred until withdrawal, which is at the complete discretion of the owner of the annuity.

For example, if you have $10,000 to invest in a deferred annuity that is earning 5 percent per year, at the end of the first year your annuity will be worth $10,500. That full amount will be available to earn interest the following year. If, instead, you invest in a currently taxable investment that is also earning 5 percent and your marginal tax rate is 28 percent, then at the end of the year, only $10,360 will be available for reinvestment. The remaining $140 will be paid to the government for income tax on the $500 you earn. This may seem like a small sum of money, but if this process continues for 10 years, the difference between the values of the tax-deferred annuity and those of the currently taxable investment will be $2,046! (Of course, taxes must still be paid when the earnings inside the annuity contract are distributed. If the annuity were cashed in after 10 years, the income tax would be $1,761, assuming a 28 percent rate and no penalty taxes.)

Immediate Annuities

An *immediate* annuity is one which begins paying benefits very quickly, usually within 1 year of the purchase date. By nature, it is almost always a *single-premium* purchase. The immediate annuity can be useful for an individual who has received a large sum of money and must count on these funds to pay expenses over a period of time.

METHODS OF PURCHASE

Single-Premium Annuity

A single-premium annuity is purchased with one premium. Usually the loan premium is fairly large. The single-premium option may be used to purchase either a fixed annuity or a variable annuity. A single-premium annuity requires an initial lump-sum deposit (generally a minimum of $1,000 to $5,000) and does not accept any future contributions.

As an example, Jovita Fontanez recently received a settlement from an insurance claim—a lump sum of $150,000. She does not need the money currently, so she uses the funds to purchase a single-premium annuity for $150,000 and chooses to receive benefits at her retirement age by electing one of the income settlement options.

Other types of individuals might be athletes, actors, or artists who receive a large payment at one time; they purchase a single-premium annuity that begins paying benefits when the person's career ends. Or it might be a business owner who recently sold her or his company. Once a single-premium annuity has been purchased, the annuity holder can choose to begin receiving the benefit payments from the annuity at any time. If it is an immediate annuity, benefit payments will usually begin within 1 year of the annuity's purchase. However, if the annuity is a deferred annuity, the annuity holder may delay the receipt of benefits for several years. See Fig. 14–2.

Flexible Premium Annuity

A flexible premium annuity allows payments to be made at varying intervals and in varying amounts. Flexible premium annuities can accept future contributions and often require a smaller initial deposit. This type of annuity is usually used for accumulating a sum of money that will provide benefits at some point in the future. As with a single-premium annuity, the flexible premium annuity can purchase either a fixed or variable annuity. See Fig. 14–3.

Annuity Stages

There are two phases of an annuity: the asset-building, or accumulation, phase and the payout, distribution, or benefit phase.

A variable annuity is generally more appropriate for a customer with longer time horizons to allow a substantial accumulation of wealth through equity investments on a tax-deferred basis.

In the accumulation phase, you buy units similar to those of mutual fund shares. But unlike a mutual fund, the annuity does not pay out income or distribute any capital gains, so the customer accumulates unit values over a period of years. These also grow tax-deferred, making the compound effect even more dramatic.

During the payout phase, the insurance company starts making a series of payments consisting of principal and earnings for a defined period to the annuitant or to the main beneficiary. Taxes are assessed on only the portion of each payment that comes from earned interest (except with qualified contracts).

FIGURE 14–2   Single-Premium Annuity Accumulation Phase

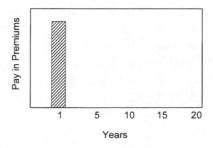

FIGURE 14–3   Flexible Premium Annuity Accumulation Phase

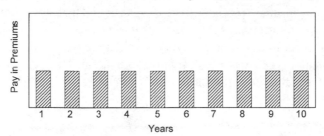

The following are payout options:

- *Lifetime income*—the entire account value is converted to a monthly income stream guaranteed for as long as the annuitant lives.

- *Lifetime income with period certain*—income stream is guaranteed for a specified number of years or for as long as the annuitant lives, whichever is longer.

- *Refund life annuity*—the entire account value is converted to a monthly income stream guaranteed for as long as the annuitant lives. If the annuitant dies prior to the principal amount's being annuitized, the balance is paid to the beneficiary.

- *Joint and survivor*—income stream is guaranteed for as long as either annuitant lives (e.g., you or your spouse).

- *Fixed period certain*—the entire account value is fully paid out during a specified period.

- *Fixed-amount annuity*—equal periodic installments are withdrawn until the account balance is exhausted.

Unlike regular life insurance, which pays out a lump sum upon premature death, the lifetime payout option protects you against the danger of outliving your money. Once a guaranteed income option is elected, the investor cannot withdraw money or surrender his or her contract.

The single exception to this is the immediate annuity which does not actually pass through an accumulation phase, but moves immediately after it is purchased into the annuitization phase.

Parties to an Annuity

Generally, there are four potential parties to an annuity contract: the owner, the annuitant, the beneficiary, and the issuing insurance company. The rights and duties of each of these entities will be discussed in a general overview. The *owner* purchases the annuity, and the *annuitant* is the individual whose life will be used to determine how payments under the contract will be made.

The *beneficiary* is the individual or entity that will receive any death benefits, and the issuing insurance company is the organization that accepts the owner's premium and promises to pay the benefits spelled out in the contract.

The most common situation involves only three parties, since the owner and the annuitant are most often the same individual. Thus, the three parties are the owner-annuitant, the individual or beneficiary, and the insurance company.

The Owner

Every annuity contract must have an owner. Usually the owner is a real person, but there's no requirement that the owner be a real person as there is with the annuitant. In most instances where the owner and the annuitant are the same person, the owner pays money in the form of premiums into the annuity during the accumulation phase. See Fig. 14–4.

Also, the owner has the right to determine when the annuity contract will move from the accumulation phase into the payout or annuitization phase and begin making payments. Most annuity contracts do not specify a maximum age past which annuity payments cannot be deferred. But in most annuities, the age will usually be well past retirement age.

FIGURE 14–4   Owner and Annuitant

Accumulation Phase

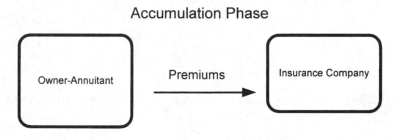

Payout or Annuitization Phase

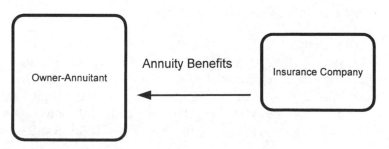

The Annuitant

According to the Internal Revenue Code, the annuitant is the individual whose life is of primary importance in affecting the timing and the amount of payout under the contract. In other words, the annuitant's life is the measuring life.[1] The annuitant, unlike the owner and the beneficiary of the annuity contract, must be a real person. See Fig. 14–5.

The Beneficiary

Similar to the conditions of a life insurance policy, in the annuity contract, beneficiaries receive a death benefit when the annuitant dies prior to the date upon which the annuity begins paying out benefits. In effect, the payment of the death benefit allows the owner to recover her or his investment and pass it along to the beneficiaries if the annuitant does not live long enough to begin receiving annuity contract benefits. The death benefit is equal generally to the value of the annuity contract at the time of death.

The beneficiary has no rights under the annuity contract other than the right to receive payments of the death benefit. He or she cannot change the payment settlement options or alter the starting date of the benefit payments, or make any withdrawals or partial surrenders against the contract. The owner, under most annuity contracts, has the right to change the beneficia-

FIGURE 14–5   The Relationship of Various Parties to the Annuity Contract

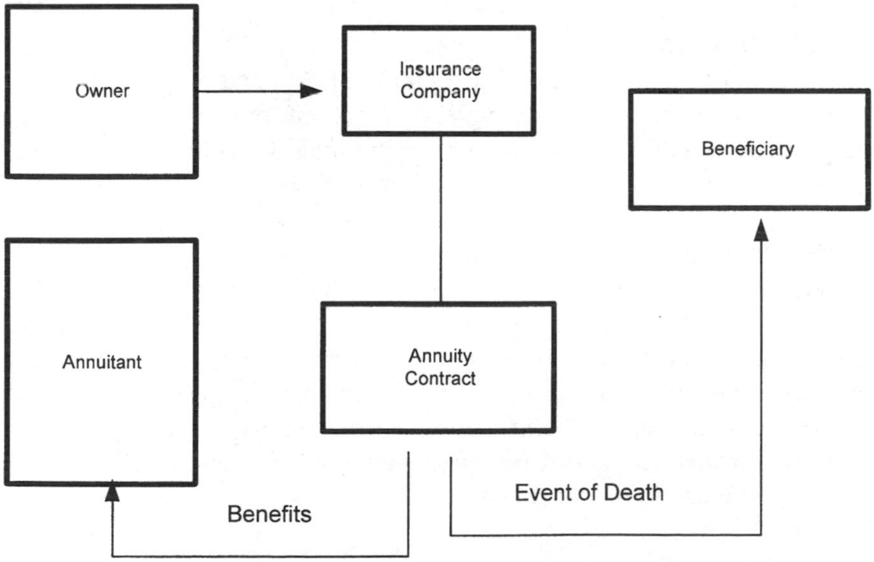

[1] See IRC, Section 72-S6.

ry designation at any time. In a very general sense, the insurance company that issues the annuity contract promises to invest the owner's premium payments responsibly, credit interest to the funds placed in the annuity, pay the contract death benefit in the event of the death of the owner prior to annuitization of the contract, and make benefit payments according to the contract settlement options selected by the contract owner.

The Internal Revenue Code requires that all annuities contain certain provisions in order to be eligible for the tax benefits associated with the annuity contract, but there is considerable variation among companies. For example, all companies have a maximum age beyond which they will not issue an annuity contract. If an individual is 80 years old, he or she will not be able to purchase an annuity contract from a company whose maximum age is, say, 75. Financial planners should request a sample contract for each annuity product they work with to maximize their understanding.

The financial strength and the investment philosophy of the issuing company should be examined. To evaluate the financial strength, you could look at the AM Best companies, Moody's, Standard & Poor's, or Duff and Phelps. The rating services examine the items connected with the insurance company that are important in gauging the effectiveness and probability of the company's performing in the future. It includes a list of information evaluating the company's profitability and capitalization and its liquidity. In addition, rating services examine the company's investment strategy and marketing philosophy as well as its business practices and history.

Premium Payments
Most annuity contracts require each premium payment to be at least a certain minimum amount. For example, under a deferred annuity the contract might require a minimum monthly premium of $50, while another annuity might require a minimum single premium of $5,000.

Settlement Options
A settlement option in the annuity contract is the method by which the annuity owner selects to receive payments of benefits under the annuity contract. Most annuity contracts allow the settlement option to be changed with proper notice to the insurance company. Although not a complete list, following are the most common settlement options: life annuity, life with period certain guaranteed, refund life annuity, joint survivor annuity, fixed-period annuity, and fixed-amount annuity.

Maintenance Fees
The annual contract maintenance fee generally ranges from $25 to $40.

Insurance-Related Charges

Many fixed annuity contracts levy a charge against partial or full surrender of the contract for a period of years after the annuity is purchased. This charge is usually referred to as a *surrender charge* or a *deferred sales charge.* It can range from 0.5 to 1.5 percent per year of the average account value. There are also no-load annuities that do not have surrender charges. The surrender charge is usually applicable to surrender made for an annuity for a certain number of years. Typically, a surrender charge is a percentage decreasing with each passing year, similar to vesting.

For example, a fixed annuity contract might provide the following surrender charges: year 1, surrender/withdrawal charges, 8 percent; year 2, 7 percent; year 3, 6 percent; year 4, 5 percent; year 5, 4 percent; year 6, 3 percent; year 7, 1 percent.

Loans

Most annuity contracts do *not* offer the option of taking a loan against the annuity value.

Death Benefits

There are certain standard provisions common to most annuity contracts. They require distribution after the death of the owner to be made in a particular manner as requested by the Internal Revenue Code.

If the annuitant dies, the value of the death benefit is the greater of the amount originally invested in the contract or the annuity's account value. The death benefit is guaranteed never to be lower than the total amount invested in the annuity. In this sense, annuities look a bit like life insurance.

Interest Rates

Typically, a fixed annuity contract will offer two interest rates: a guaranteed rate and a current rate.

The guaranteed rate is the minimum rate that will be credited to the funds in the annuity contract regardless of how low the current rate sinks or how poorly the insurance company fares. Typically, the guaranteed rate is 3 to 4 percent.

The current interest rate varies with insurance companies. The current rate might be 7 percent, and its guaranteed rate could be 4 percent. On the anniversary of the purchase of the annuity, the company notifies the owner of the new current rate. If, for some reason, the interest rate drops below the guaranteed rate, a bailout provision provides the contract holder to fully surrender the annuity contract and not incur any surrender charges under the annuity contract. The name for this is a *bailout provision* or *escape clause.*

For example, an annuity offering a bailout clause allows the contract to be surrendered if the current interest rate drops 1 percent below the interest rate of the previous period. Assuming that the prior interest rates were 6.5 percent, if the current rate for the next period falls below 5.5 percent, the annuity holder could surrender the annuity contract completely and not be subject to any contract charges. The 10 percent penalty tax on premature withdrawals may still apply to a surrender under the bailout provision.

Competitive Return

Fixed annuities offer a competitive interest rate because their rate is more closely tied to the medium- or long-term maturities than typically lower rates of short-term maturities associated with products such as CDs. The current rate, which is actually the annualized rate, is usually guaranteed for 1 year, although other options may be available. At the end of the guaranteed period of the current or initial rate, the annuity will renew with a new rate that is the best rate the company can offer under the current economic conditions. The minimum guaranteed rate also applies, usually around 3 to 4 percent, which is the lowest rate possible regardless of where the current rates are. And that rate is also tax-deferred.

As we have discovered, because annuities have many different features, there are a number of factors to examine. For example, you should ask if there are penalties for early withdrawals. Are there graduated withdrawal charges over a period of years? How much can you withdraw at any one time without a penalty?

In addition, if you are considering the purchase of an annuity, you should ask these questions:

- What is the current interest rate, and how often does it change?
- What is the minimum interest rate guaranteed in the contract?
- Is there a bailout option that permits you to cash in the annuity, without withdrawal penalties (there may be tax penalties), if the interest rate drops below a specific figure?
- Are there front-end load charges or annual administrative fees? How much are they, and how will they affect your return?

WHAT IS A SUBACCOUNT?

Subaccount is a term that describes the mutual fund portfolio held inside a variable annuity.

Variable annuities offer anywhere from 5 to 35 subaccount investment options. Mutual fund account managers select individual securities inside the subaccounts; the investor then selects the most appropriate subaccount based on the security selection for her or his portfolio. If this sounds exactly like a mutual fund, that's because it is. The same, or *clone,* as they're commonly called, mutual funds tend to have the same managers inside variable annuity subaccounts, so the same criteria exist for choosing a mutual fund as for choosing a subaccount—and the same benefits also exist, such as professional money management, convenience, economies of scale, and diversification. Subaccount exchanges do not create taxable events and do not entail sales or transfer charges, Most companies do set limits, usually 12, on the number of annual exchanges before a transfer fee is charged.

The variable annuity, however, gives the added benefit of tax-deferred wealth accumulation. Subaccounts usually include a list of the primary investment objectives, and it's relatively easy to determine what the fees are applied for. It is required for a subaccount to specify the primary group of securities held as well as the issuing insurance or mutual fund company.

Investment Flow of a Subaccount

All investment funds flow through the insurance company into the various subaccounts, depending on those chosen by the investor or investment advisor. See Fig. 14 6.

Each subaccount has a specific investment objective. Combined with other subaccounts, this gives the investor a chance for diversification and the ability to select different portfolios to meet asset allocation and diversification needs. Subaccount managers purchase stocks, bonds, or cash which is valued daily as an accumulation unit, another name for fund shares of the mutual fund.

Accumulation units—shares—are purchased by the contract owner at the *accumulation unit value* (AUV), which is very similar to the mutual fund equivalent known as net asset value (NAV), without commissions, in full and fractional units.

TYPES OF SUBACCOUNTS

Subaccounts may be divided into several broad categories: asset classes seeking aggressive growth; asset classes seeking more stable growth; asset classes seeking low volatility utilizing fixed-income bonds; a combination; and asset classes featuring money market rates. Inside each of these classes, categories are broken down further.

Fixed-income accounts are established to decrease risk for those in need of meeting current income requirements. Fixed-income subaccounts include

FIGURE 14–6   Typical Variable Annuity Investment Option

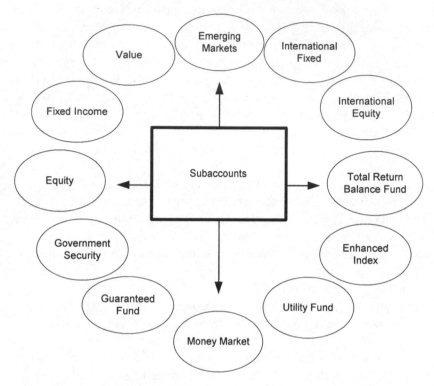

Reprinted with permission from McGraw-Hill, *Guaranteed Income for Life*, Michael F. Lane.

government agencies, corporate rate bonds, high-yield, foreign government corporate bonds, and certain fixed-income choices.

Equity or stock investing would be in funds for growth of principal. Since variable annuities are long-term investments, the equity subaccounts will be most important to review.

Other asset classes could include cash and cash equivalents, which would be more short-term. Figure 14–7 illustrates the investment options available in a variable annuity offered to consumers through investment advisors.

You still may have questions about subaccounts and mutual funds, how they work, and what makes up a mutual fund. As you read the next chapter, think of a subaccount inside the variable annuity and a mutual fund as being the same thing. Although they are kept separate, and the fund within each cannot be commingled, for ease of understanding how these work, we will look at the predecessor to the subaccount, the mutual fund.

FIGURE 14–7   No-Load Variable Annuities Offered through Advisors

Product Name	Subaccounts	Insurance Expense	Portfolio Fees	Insurance Company	Phone Number
No load					
Dimensional Variable Annuity	7	0.65%	.40 - 1.00%	Providian Life & Health*	800-797-9177
Galaxy	4	0.55%	.70% - 1.40%	American Skandia	800-541-3087
The Adviser's Edge	17	0.65%	.40% - 1.50%	Providian Life & Health	800-797-9177
Scudder Horizon	6	0.70%	.50% - 1.08%	Charter National	800-242-4402
T. Rowe Price	5	0.55%	.70% - 1.05%	Security Benefit	800-469-6587
Touchstone	7	0.80%	.50% - 1.25%	Western-Southern	800-669-2796
JW Value Advantage Plus	21	0.45%	.80% - 1.47%	Fortis	800-827-5877
Vanguard Variable Annuity Plan	7	0.55%	.23% - .34%	Providian Life & Health	800-462-2391
The Schwab Variable Annuity	21	0.85%	.35% - 1.75%	Great West Life	800-838-0650
Vanguard VAP	9	0.38%	.22%-.49%	Providian Life & Health	800-523-9954

* Providian Life & Health is now AEGON Financial Services Group, Inc.

How Mutual Funds and Subaccounts Work

The manager of the mutual fund uses the pool of capital to buy a variety of stocks, bonds, or money market instruments based on the advertised financial objectives of the fund. The mutual fund manager uses the investment objectives as a guide when choosing investments. These objectives cover a wide range. Some follow aggressive policies, involving greater risk in search of higher returns. Others seek current income and little risk.

When you purchase mutual fund shares, you pay the *net asset value,* which is the value of the fund's total investment minus any debt, divided by the number of outstanding shares. For example, if the fund's investment value is $26,000, it has no debt, and there are 1,000 shares outstanding, then the net asset value is $26 per share. In a regular mutual fund, which includes thousands and often millions of shares, the NAV is calculated on a daily basis, with values moving up or down along with the stock or bond markets. The NAV is not a fixed figure because it must reflect the daily change in the price of the securities in the fund's portfolio. In contrast, a variable annuity issues shares at the accumulation unit value (AUV). The only difference between the two is that inside a mutual fund you will sometimes pay higher than the NAV for shares that have front-end commissions, and in annuities this is not an option.

Costs

It's simply common sense that lower expenses generally translate to higher overall returns. The goal of the smart investor is to keep his or her acquisition costs as low as possible. There are four basic kinds of costs: sales charges, operating expenses, M&E charges (Mortality and Expense), transaction charges.

Sales Charges

Sales charges (or loads) are commissions paid on the sale of mutual funds. All commissions used to be simply charged up front, but that's all changed. There are now several ways in which mutual fund companies charge fees. Annuities and mutual funds are similar if you compare the B share mutual fund option. This option has no front-end sales charges, but has higher internal costs. If you decide to redeem your shares early, usually within the first 5 years, you pay a surrender charge. This is very similar to annuity investing.

Some sales charges, as in B shares, are levied on the back end as a contingent deferred sales charge. The load is charged when the investor redeems shares in the fund. A customer who redeems shares in the first year of ownership typically pays a 5 percent sales charge. The amount drops by an equal amount each year. After 6 years, the shares can be redeemed without further charge. For large purchases, you should never purchase B-share mutual funds. There are less-than-ethical brokers out there who will tell you it is a better deal to invest in B shares since you will not pay an up-front charge.

Class C shares typically have even higher internal expenses, but pay the selling broker up to 1 percent per year based on assets. This fee comes directly from your investment performance and is paid to the selling broker. C shares may have no up-front fee, possibly a 1 percent deferred sales charge in year 1 (sometimes longer), and higher annual expenses (up to 1 percent extra per year).

No-load mutual funds do *not* mean *no cost.* Some no-load funds charge a redemption fee of 1 to 2 percent of the net asset value of the shares to cover expenses mainly incurred by advertising. Fee comparisons are particularly important. Every dollar charged comes directly from the performance of the subaccount. Remember to compare the proverbial apples to apples in this case: similar equities to equities subaccounts and similar bonds to bonds subaccounts.

Operating Expenses
These are fees paid for the operational costs of running a fund. These costs
can include employees' salaries, marketing and publicity, servicing the toll-
free phone line, printing and mailing of published materials, computers for
tracking investments and account balances, accounting fees, and so on. A
fund's operating expenses are quoted as a percentage of your investment;
the percentage represents an annual fee or charge. You can find this number
in a fund's prospectus in the fund expenses section, entitled "Total Fund
Operating Expenses" or "Other Expenses."

A mutual fund's operating expenses are normally invisible to investors
because they're deducted before any return is paid, and they are automatically charged on a daily basis. Beware, though, a subaccount can have a
very low management fee, but have exorbitant operating expenses. A fund
that frequently trades will have more wire charges, for instance, than a fund
that does not.

M&E (Mortality and Expense)
An annual charge, 1 to 1.5% of the daily asset value of each subaccount, is
charged for the mortality risk that arises from the obligation to pay guaranteed death benefits or guaranteed lifetime income payments to annuitants.

Transaction Charges
Transaction charge is another term for execution costs. Total transaction
costs (or the cost of buying and selling stocks) have three components: (1)
the actual dollars paid in commissions; (2) the market impact, i.e., the impact
a manager's trade has on the market price for the stock (this varies with the
size of the trade and the skill of the trader); and (3) the opportunity cost of
the return (positive or negative) given up by not executing the trade instantaneously.

For example, when an individual investor places an order to buy 300
shares of a $30 stock ($9,000 investment), she or he is likely to get a commission bill for about $204, or 2.3 percent of the value of the investment. Even
at a discount broker, commissions are likely to cost between $82 (0.9 per-
cent) and $107 (1.2 percent). A mutual fund, on the other hand, is more like-
ly to be buying 30,000 to 300,000 shares at a time! Its commission costs
often run in the vicinity of one-tenth of the commission you would pay at a
discount broker! Where the commission might have been $0.35 per share,
the mutual fund could pay only $0.05 per share or even less! The commis-
sion savings can (and should) mean higher returns for you as a mutual fund
shareholder. See Fig. 14–8.

FIGURE 14–8   Subaccounts

Portfolio	Objective	Type of Investment	Asset Class Represented
Small Cap Value	Capital appreciation	Equity securities of small U.S. and foreign companies	U.S. Small Cap
Enhanced Index	Total return modestly in excess of the performance of the S&P 500 Index	Primarily equity investments of large and medium-sized U.S. companies	U.S. Large Cap
Domestic Blue Chip	Primarily long-term growth of capital; secondarily providing income	Common stocks of "blue chip" companies	U.S. Large Cap
Utility Fund	High current income & moderate capital appreciation	Equity & debt securities of utility companies	Energy
Money Fund	Current income with stability of principal and liquidity	High-quality money market instruments	Cash
High-Yield Income Bond Fund	High current income and overall total return	Lower-rated fixed income securities	High-Yield Fixed Income
U.S. Government Securities	Current income	U.S. government securities	Short-Term Fixed Income
Emerging Markets	Capital appreciation	Equity securities of companies in countries having emerging markets	Emerging Markets
Growth Equity	Capital appreciation	Primary equity securities of domestic companies	U.S. Large Cap
Domestic Small Cap	Capital appreciation	Primarily common stocks, convertibles and other equity-type securities with emphasis on small company stocks	U.S. Small Cap
International Fund	Capital growth	Primarily equity securities of companies located outside the U.S.	International Large Cap
Value Fund	Primarily long-term capital appreciation; secondarily current income	Equity securities of medium to large-sized companies, primarily in the U.S.	U.S. Large Cap Value
International Small Cap	Long-term capital appreciation	Primarily equity securities of small and medium-sized foreign companies	International Small Cap
International Equity	Capital appreciation	Equity securities of non-U.S. companies	International Large Cap
Small Company Growth	Capital growth	Equity securities of small-sized U.S. companies	U.S. Small Cap

Reprinted with permission from McGraw-Hill, *Guaranteed Income for Life,* Michael F. Lane.

THE 20 BEST VARIABLE ANNUITIES ON THE MARKET TODAY

The following variable annuities have no front-end load, below-average costs, and a wide selection of mutual fund subaccounts with good performance, and are issued by insurance companies rated A (excellent), B (good), or C (fair) by Weiss Ratings. When you select individual funds within these annuities, be sure to make comparisons based on the funds' total cost (insurance cost plus annual expense). See Fig. 14–9.

FIGURE 14–9   The 20 Best Variable Annuities

The 20 Best Variable Annuities					
Name of Variable Annuity Name of Insurer *(Phone Number)*	Front- end Load	Surrender Charge	Number of Funds	Number of Strong Funds	Weiss Safety Rating
(1) **Jack White Value Advantage Plus** Fortis Benefits Insurance Co. *(800-622-3699)*	none	none	24	10	B+
(2) **Vanguard Variable Annuity Plus** Providian Life & Health Insurance Co. *(800-523-9954)*	none	none	9	5	B-
(3) **Schwab Variable Annuity** Great West Life & Annuity Insurance Co. *(800-838-0650)*	none	none	20	14	B+
(4) **Janus Retirement Advantage VA** Western Reserve Life Assurance of Ohio *(800-504-4440)*	none	none	9	5	B
(5) **USAA Life Variable Annuity** USAA Life Insurance Co. *(800-531-6390)*	none	none	7	5	A
(6) **Providian Advisor's Edge VA** Providian Life & Health Insurance Co.* *(800-866-6007)*	none	none	17	10	B-
(7) **Ameritas No-Load VA** Ameritas Life Insurance Co. *(800-255-9678)*	none	none	10	4	A
(8) **Touchstone Variable Annuity II** Western-Southern Life Assurance Co. *(800-669-2796)*	none	none	7	5	B+
(9) **Pacific Mutual One VA** Pacific Life Insurance Co. *(800-722-2333)*	none	none	13	6	A
(10) **Guardian Value Guard II VA** Guardian Insurance & Annuity Co. *(800-221-3253)*	none	none	9	6	A

* Providian Life & Health is now AEGON Financial Services Group, Inc.

(continued)

Note: In arriving at the list of "best" variable annuities in Fig. 14–9, mutual fund subaccount performance played an important role in the selection process. After all, a variable annuity can have low costs and a strong Weiss safety rating, while at the same time offering only mediocre fund performance. Likewise, when researching other variable annuities, you will want to include in your evaluation the performance of the funds in which you are interested.

FIGURE 14–9 *concluded*

The 20 Best Variable Annuities					
Name of Variable Annuity Name of Insurer *(Phone Number)*	Front- end Load	Surrender Charge	Number of Funds	Number of Strong Funds	Weiss Safety Rating
(11) T. Rowe Price No-Load VA Security Benefit Life Insurance Co. *(800-469-6587)*	none	none	7	5	C+
(12) Scudder Horizon Plan VA Charter National Life Insurance Co. *(800-225-2470)*	none	none	7	5	C
(13) Fidelity Retirement Reserves VA Fidelity Investments Life Insurance Co. *(800-544-2442)*	none	5% declining over 5 yrs	13	8	B
(14) AARP Variable Annuity American Maturity Life Insurance Co. *(800-396-5552)*	none	rolling 5% declining over 5 yrs	9	7	B
(15) Ohio National Top Plus B (NQ) Ohio National Life Insurance Co. *(800-366-6654)*	none	6% declining over 6 yrs	13	6	B
(16) Best of America IV - Nationwide Nationwide Life Insurance Co. *(800-848-6331)*	none	rolling 7% declining over 7 yrs	34	14	B+
(17) Hartford - The Director Hartford Life Insurance Co. *(800-862-6668)*	none	rolling 6% declining over 7 yrs	10	6	B+
(18) Mass Mutual Panorama Plus Mass Mutual Life Insurance Co. *(800-234-5606)*	none	5% declining over 10 yrs	6	3	A-
(19) Security Benefit Variflex LS Security Benefit Life Insurance Co. *(800-888-2461 x.3112)*	none	none	11	6	C+
(20) WRL Freedom Bellwether VA Western Reserve Life Assurance of Ohio *(800-851-9777)*	none	none	16	8	B

Reprinted with permission from Weiss Ratings Inc.

THE 10 WORST VARIABLE ANNUITIES ON THE MARKET TODAY

On the whole, the variable annuities offered today are much better than those available only a couple of years ago. Nevertheless, the variable annuities in Fig. 14–10 possessed one or more drawbacks which made them unattractive investment options at the time of this publication.

Note: The list in Fig. 14–10 is intended to provide a sample of those variable annuities that contain one or more unattractive features. Exclusion from this list does not mean that a particular variable annuity is a good investment choice. Likewise, some of the insurance companies listed above offer several other variable annuity policies which may be worthy of consideration.

FIGURE 14–10 The 10 Worst Variable Annuities

Name of Variable Annuity / Name of Insurer	Front-end Load	Surrender Charge	Number of Funds	Number of Strong Funds	Weiss Safety Rating	Primary Draw-backs
(1) PaineWebber Milestones B/D / PaineWebber Life Insurance Co.	none	rolling 5% declining over 5 yrs	9	3	D	high cost and weak rating
(2) American Skandia Advisor's Plan / American Skandia Life Assurance	none	rolling 7.5% declining over 7 yrs	28	18	D+	high cost and weak rating
(3) First Investors VA / First Investors Life Insurance Co.	7.0%	none	10	4	C+	high load
(4) Principal Banker's Flex VA / Principal Mutual Life Insurance Co.	7.0%	none	1	1	B+	high load and only one fund
(5) John Hancock Accommodator VA / John Hancock Mutual Life Ins. Co.	8.0%	none	18	9	A-	high load
(6) United Investors Advantage II VA / United Life & Annuity Ins. Co.	8.5%	rolling deferred	11	6	C	high load
(7) Providian Life Prism VA - A units / Providian Life & Health Insurance Co.	5.75%	none	6	4	B-	high load
(8) Golden America Fund for Life VA / Golden American Life Insurance Co.	1.5%	none	1	1	C+	load and only one fund
(9) Allmerica Variable Annuity / Allmerica Financial Life Ins. & Annuity	none	7% declining over 9 yrs	3	1	C	only three funds
(10) Farm Bureau Variable Annuity / Farm Bureau Life Insurance Co.	none	6% declining over 6 yrs	6	1	A-	poor performing funds

Reprinted with permission by Weiss Ratings Inc.

Weiss Safety Ratings Defined

The Weiss safety ratings assigned to the above insurance companies are defined as follows:

A   **Excellent.** The company offers excellent financial security. It has maintained a conservative stance in its investment strategies, business operations, and underwriting commitments. While the financial condition of any company is subject to change, Weiss Ratings believes that the company has the resources necessary to deal with severe economic conditions.

B   **Good.** The company offers good financial security and has the resources to deal with a variety of adverse economic conditions. It comfortably exceeds the minimum levels for all our rating criteria and is likely to remain healthy for the near future. However, in the event of a *severe* recession or major financial crisis, Weiss Ratings feels that this assessment should be reviewed to make sure that the firm is still maintaining adequate financial strength.

C   **Fair.** The company offers fair financial security and is currently stable. But during an economic downturn or other financial pressures, Weiss Ratings feels the company may encounter difficulties in maintaining financial stability.

D   **Weak.** The company currently demonstrates what Weiss Ratings considers to be significant weaknesses which could negatively impact policyholders. In an unfavorable economic environment, these weaknesses could be magnified.

E   **Very Weak.** The company currently demonstrates what Weiss Ratings considers to be significant weaknesses and has also failed some of the basic tests that Weiss Ratings uses to identify fiscal stability. Therefore, even in a favorable economic environment, it is Weiss Ratings' opinion that policyholders could incur significant risks.

F   **Failed.** The company is under the supervision of state insurance commissioners.

+   **The plus sign** is an indication that with new data, there is a modest possibility that the company could be upgraded.

−   **The minus sign** is an indication that with new data, there is a modest possibility that the company could be downgraded.

CONCLUSION

The variable annuity appears to be the answer to the shortfall retirement problems of longer life expectancies and longer retirement periods. Why? Because of reductions in expected pension benefits, as both corporations and government are getting out of the retirement benefits business.

YOU SHOULD KNOW

A variable annuity's rate of return is not guaranteed, but rather is determined by the performance of the investments selected. As the value of the stocks in the portfolio varies, each unit will be worth more or less.

More and more variable annuity companies are offering asset class investing to provide a less volatile investment return. As we have already pointed out, these asset classes tend to smooth out extreme fluctuations; investors won't profit as much from a good year in the market with such an annuity, but neither will they suffer as great a loss of income during a bad year.

Any distributions in excess of that 10 percent are subject to the surrender charges. No-load variable annuities that do not impose a surrender charge are 100 percent liquid; but, like all annuities, they may be subject to a 10 percent federal penalty for withdrawal prior to age 59½.

WARNING

Despite any inherent advantages, not all variable annuities are created equal. They can vary widely in terms of costs and available investment options. Because of their insurance benefits, variable annuities generally cost more than traditional taxable investments, such as mutual funds. There may be front-end charges (loads), management fees, and sometimes back-end surrender charges for early withdrawals from the policy. These charges and the length of time they apply to the policy vary widely across the industry. The average policy probably has a 6 to 7 percent first-year surrender charge that declines one percentage point per year. Some have *rolling surrender charges* which means that each investment you make has a new surrender charge schedule. For example, if you invested $1,000 every year, each $1,000 contribution would have a new surrender charge schedule. I would avoid these if possible.

The higher the overall costs, the longer it takes for the benefit of tax deferral to compensate for those costs. A no-sales-load, low-cost variable annuity can help shorten that break-even holding period. In general, variable annuities are designed to be held as long-term investment vehicles so a breakeven of 10 to 15 years may be affordable for those investors with that type of time frame. What does this mean?

HISTORY

Prior to the 1997 Taxpayer Relief Act, the breakeven for investors in the 28 percent tax bracket (during both the accumulation and withdrawal phases of a variable annuity) was about 12 years. Today, the break-even period is extended to about 18 years. (The break-even point is where you are better off with a variable annuity than investing in a mutual fund.) The mainstream media predicted the demise of the variable annuity because it was so long. But I would have to argue that the capital gains tax cuts won't have the effect that the media predict. Maximum advantage is centered on your ability to reduce your long-term capital gains tax to 20 percent while extending the maximum holding period to 18 months.

TAX CHANGES

The tax changes have created a three-tier schedule for taxing capital gains. If you hold an investment for less than 12 months and realize a gain when you sell, you will pay tax on the gain at your ordinary income tax rate (which now can be as high as 39.9 percent). If you sell a holding between 12 and 18 months after buying it, gains will be taxed at the 28 percent long-term capital gains rate. If you sell the holding after 18 months, your gains will be taxed at 20 percent.

The reduction of the long-term capital gains tax rate to 20 percent on an 18-month holding gives you the opportunity to halve the tax penalty for your high-tax-bracket clients. Take, e.g., a client in the 39.9 percent tax bracket whose $100,000 investment of taxable dollars returns 10 percent, producing a $10,000 gain.

Gain taxed as ordinary income at 39.9 percent	$3,990 tax
Gain taxed at 28 percent capital gains tax rate	$2,800 tax
Gain taxed at 20 percent capital gains tax rate	$2,000 tax

Investors who realize their gains within the 12- to 18-month window and pay the 28 percent capital gains tax have a 30 percent savings over the regular income tax rate at which short-term capital gains are taxed. If the investors hold investments for 18 months or longer, the 20 percent tax rate reduces the amount of federal taxes by almost 50 percent compared to ordinary income tax rates.

This savings is predicated solely on not realizing the gain for a minimum of 18 months. What's not talked about is that most stock market investing is influenced by institutional investors, not taxable investors. Most mutual fund managers employ very active day-to-day short-term trading to maximize total return. This approach will take away any advantage of the new lower capital gains tax rate and still leave their taxable investors exposed to nearly 40 percent.

It's human nature. Mutual fund managers are going to try to get the highest returns because their jobs depend on it. They are judged quarter by quarter; not every 18 months. If they can take a short-term profit, they will—which creates happy institutional investors and ordinary income to taxable investors. The last thing mutual fund managers are concerned about is whether they should hold a security for 12 months or 18 months. So all cases being equal, we are right back where we started.

SO WHAT DO YOU DO TODAY?

Say you just received a lump sum of $500,000, you invested it in a variable annuity, and it grows to $1 million. You do not have to cash it all in and pay tax on the $500,000 of growth at one time. If you annuitize, that $1 million will be paid to you in monthly installments from a portion of the original $500,000 and a portion of the $500,000 gain. This means that taxes are paid at a lower rate. What's even better is that you do not have to keep track of when you bought which shares and how long you held them. That's a huge advantage.

WHAT THE EXPERTS SAY

I asked Jeff Saccacio, partner-in-charge of West Coast Personal Financial Services Practice for PricewaterhouseCoopers L.L.P., to comment:

> Assuming tax rates remain the same and that you are invested in an equity income type mutual fund, a large amount of your dividend income will be taxed at ordinary income rates. The alternative is to invest in a variable annuity product, which invests in the same type of mutual fund, but you are taxed later on the distribution.

- This makes a big difference. If you get taxed now and you are in a high-income-tax state, you're going to pay anywhere between 46 and 48 cents out of every dollar, which gets taken right off the top before reinvestment. If you invest in a variable annuity product, that 46 to 48 cents doesn't get taken out until the annuity product pays out in the future. So you get the benefit of compounding on what you otherwise would have paid in tax.

- You will accumulate more, even though you are going to pay tax on the gains in the future. This is a simple present-value calculation, i.e., the present value of that future accumulation versus the present value of your earnings stream if you don't elect to use this deferral-type variable annuity product. The variable annuity works if you do not need access to your money right away, you have an emergency cash reserve, and your goal is to accumulate funds for retirement. A variable annuity provides you with a tax shelter on an accumulation basis.

- The investor who has maxed out her or his 401(k) and is cut off from contributing to a Roth IRA is left with the choice of after-tax contributions to the retirement plan, or after-tax contributions to an IRA, both of which are extremely limited. The logical choice is to consider a variable annuity product which gives the sheltered-growth benefits of a qualified plan.

Survey after survey reveals that building a retirement nest egg is the number one financial concern of most U.S. households. Since most people are concerned about outliving their retirement funds, accumulating money is only one side of the retirement coin. Positioning assets to provide sufficient income during retirement is equally critical.

THE MOST OVERLOOKED BENEFIT IS THE DEATH BENEFIT

No, this is not a sick joke. Obviously, no one can predict if you will die when the market is up or down. But the *standard* death benefit provided by variable annuities guarantees that if the policyholder dies while still saving for retirement, his or her heirs will receive the greater of either the amount of money invested or the policy's value at the time of death. Many variable annuities go even further and offer *stepped-up* benefits that actually lock in investment gains every year.

This means that if an investor buys a variable annuity today with $100,000 but dies when it's worth only $80,000, then the insurance company is on the hook for the difference of $20,000. A variable annuity is, in effect, insuring the heirs against a market downturn, and the investor is paying for that benefit. Mortality expense charges finance the whole support function, including commissions on commission products, the processing of paperwork, customer service, and the guarantee of insurance benefits.

SHOULD YOU BUY THE UNDERLYING FUNDS AND PAY TAXES?
Whether the breakeven between a mutual fund and a mutual fund inside a variable annuity is 5, 10, or 18 years is virtually irrelevant. What I'm interested in is what will save me time and still provide a high probability of my retiring comfortably. Using the variable annuity, I don't need to know which of the three tax rate bands I'm in, and I don't need to keep track of every single purchase to report to my accountant. After all, I bought the variable annuity in order to accumulate assets *over and above* what I could place in my retirement account.

The primary goal of a retirement plan, of course, is to provide employees with a lifetime stream of retirement income. Variable annuities were specifically created to satisfy that goal and are recognized by the IRS as a tax-advantaged income vehicle.

WHAT CAN YOU DO TO BECOME BETTER INFORMED?
Revisit your recent Monday issues of *The Wall Street Journal* and look at the variable annuities listed. Notice the subheadings which indicate names of insurance products and investment subaccounts. Instead of focusing only on past performance or unit price, look at the total expense column (the last column listed). Total expense includes management, operations, and insurance-related expenses. You will see that these costs wander all over the board, as high as 2.79 and as low as 0.79. Now check the prospectus of the annuity you are considering, in order to uncover any up-front costs or surrender charges. Armed with this simple guide, you will be able to increase your returns by lowering your costs. Not all variable annuities are shown in the *Journal*; only ones that have 3 years of performance numbers are listed.

BEST ADVICE: CUT COSTS

There's a commonsense way to shorten that break-even period. Buy no-load or low-cost variable annuities. Obviously, higher fees counter the benefits of tax deferral. But despite their lower costs, no-load variable annuities aren't that popular, commanding only 1 percent of all variable annuity assets. Why? Because many investors are willing to pay a load for the extra education and service that come with the added cost.

Tax deferral offered by a variable annuity works over the long run. Maximize your variable annuity's rate of return by lowering expenses. Find variable annuities that offer high dividend-producing mutual funds and high short-term capital gain realization portfolios. Avoid all other types of low-turnover funds or index funds. These should be held outside the variable annuity. Narrow your search by finding the annuity with the lowest marketing and administrative expenses which allows you to invest in asset classes.

Let's move on to Social Security.

15

SOCIAL IN-SECURITY

SOCIAL **S**ECURITY **CAN'T CONTINUE TO EXIST** in its present form. So what's new—neither can Medicare, Medicaid, or welfare. These and other "entitlements," heretofore politically sacrosanct, will be drastically altered and benefits reduced. The handwriting is on the wall.

Social Security can be likened to a giant pension fund that we all pay into. Theoretically, the assets taken in will grow to fund the liabilities that the fund will have down the road when you retire. However, Social Security was never set up to be a retirement plan. It was meant to be a safety net, a last resort.

Social Security originated in 1936 during the depression years. Working people would pay a small portion of their wages into the Social Security system with the idea that the current working population would support the retirees of that time. So money went in and right back out again. It worked because in 1937, the first full year of operation, there were 33 workers for every one retiree. The annual contribution of a working person was only $30.00, so the system was workable. The problem is that, given the demographics of the following years including the slowing down of the birthrate and the fact that wages grew more slowly, strains on the system started to build. Our political and economic system forced the Social Security system to become a pension plan for every U.S. citizen.

In 1960, there were 15 workers for every one person retired. It's estimated that in the year 2029, there will be 2½ workers for every one person retired. You can see that something has to give.

BUT FOR NOW LET'S ASSUME CONGRESS WILL DO SOMETHING ABOUT SAVING THE SYSTEM

Before you buy an expensive insurance policy, remember to check into your Social Security benefits. Obtain estimates of your future benefits based on what you have been credited for and what you will be credited for by the time you reach retirement age.

We don't want to debate whether Social Security will be here. We could have the same debate about your insurance company. What we discovered was that if one of us were to die today, each of his or her children and the surviving spouse would get almost $900 per month; and if one of us were to become disabled, he or she would get more than $800 per month. When we figured the cost of how much insurance it would take to duplicate those benefits, Social Security looks very good. A policy that would give you a $2,100 monthly death benefit for your family would cost you a small fortune.

The point is that you may not even need expensive life insurance—and you don't even know it. You can take the money you would save and invest it in a mutual fund instead of contributing it to an insurance company's coffers. Figures 15–1 to 15–3 show how Social Security calculated my benefits.

It will take you about five minutes to complete the Request for Earnings and Benefits Estimate Statement. This includes the time it will take to read the instructions, gather the necessary facts, and fill out the form. You can send this form to your nearest Social Security office or to

Social Security Administration
Wilkes-Barre Data Operations Center
P.O. Box 20
Wilkes-Barre, PA 18711-2030

Or Social Security HCDP://www.ssa.gov

FIGURE 15–1   Social Security Estimated Benefits

Facts, Credits, and Earnings
November 7, 1990

THE FACTS YOU GAVE US

Your Name	Raymond L. Chambers
Your Social Security Number	XXX-XX-XXXX
Your Date of Birth	July 20, 1947
1989 Earnings	$45,000
1990 Earnings	Over $51,300
Your Estimated Future Avg. Yearly Earnings	Over $51,300
The Age You Plan to Retire	70
Other Social Security Numbers You've Used	None

YOUR SOCIAL SECURITY CREDITS
To qualify for Social Security benefits and Medicare, you need credit for a certain amount of work covered by Social Security. The number of credits you need will vary with the type of benefit. Under current law, you do not need more than 40 credits to qualify for any benefit or for Medicare.

Our review of your earnings, including any 1989 and 1990 earnings you told us about, shows that you now have at least 40 Social Security credits.

YOUR SOCIAL SECURITY EARNINGS
The chart on the next page shows the earnings on your Social Security record. It also estimates the amount of Social Security taxes you paid in each year to finance benefits under Social Security and Medicare. If you have government earnings that help you qualify for Medicare, those earnings also are shown on the chart.

We show earnings only up to the maximum yearly amount covered by Social Security. These maximum amounts are shown on the chart. The chart may not include some or all of your earnings from last year because they may not have been added to your record yet.

YOUR EARNINGS RECORD

Years	Maximum Yearly Earnings Subject to Social Security Tax	Your Social Security Taxed Earnings	Est. Taxes You Paid: Retirement, Survivors & Disability Insurance	Est. Taxes You Paid: Medicare Hospital Insurance	Your Medicare Qualified Government Earnings
1963	4,800	1,276	46	0	0
1964	4,880	1,469	53	0	0
1965	4,800	1,040	37	0	0
1966	6,600	1,475	56	5	0
1967	6,600	1,255	48	6	0
1968	7,800	1,247	47	7	0
1969	7,880	2,110	88	12	0
1970	7,800	612	25	3	0
1971	7,800	1,574	72	9	0
1972	9,000	2,177	100	13	0
1973	10,800	1,442	69	14	0
1974	13,200	7,187	355	64	0
1975	14,100	14,100	697	126	0
1976	15,300	15,300	757	137	0
1977	16,500	16,500	816	148	0
1978	17,700	17,700	893	177	0
1979	22,900	22,900	1,163	240	0
1980	25,900	25,900	1,315	271	0
1981	29,700	30	1	0	0
1982	32,400	0	0	0	0
1983	35,700	4,020	217	52	0
1984	37,800	0	0	0	0
1985	39,600	39,600	3,603	1,069	0
1986	42,000	42,000	3,948	1,218	0
1987	43,800	0	0	0	0
1988	45,000	45,000	4,554	1,305	0
1989	48,000	45,498	2,757	659	0
1990	51,500				

*Earnings were taxed for Hospital Insurance beginning 1966

(continued)

FIGURE 15–1 *Concluded*

Estimated Benefits
RETIREMENT
You must have 40 Social Security credits to qualify for retirement benefits. This is the same number of credits you need to qualify for Medicare at age 65. Assuming that you meet all the requirements, here are estimates of your retirement benefits based on your past and any projected earnings. The estimates are in today's dollars, but adjusted to account for average wage growth in the national economy.

If you retire at 62, your monthly benefit in today's dollars will be about:	$965

The earliest age at which you can receive an unreduced retirement benefit is 66 years of age. We call this your full retirement age. If you wait until that age to receive benefits, your monthly benefit in today's dollars will be about: — $1,355
If you wait until you are 70 to receive benefits, your monthly benefit in today's dollars will be about: — $1,855

SURVIVORS
If you have a family, you must have 21 Social Security credits for certain family members to receive benefits if you were to die this year. They may also qualify if you earn 6 credits in the 3 years before your death. The number of credits a person needs to be insured for survivors benefits increases each year until age 62, up to a maximum of 40 credits.

Here is an estimate of the benefits your family could receive if you had enough credits to be insured, they qualified for benefits, and you died this year:

Your child could receive a monthly benefit of about:	$705
If your child and your surviving spouse who is caring for your child both qualify, they could each receive a monthly benefit of about:	$705
When your surviving spouse reaches full retirement age, he or she could receive a monthly benefit of about:	$945
If more family members qualify for benefits (other children, for example), the total amount that we could pay your family each month is about:	$1,655
We may also be able to pay your surviving spouse or children a one-time death benefit of:	$255

DISABILITY
Right now, you must have 21 Social Security credits to qualify for disability benefits. And 20 of these credits had to be earned in the 10-year period immediately before you became disabled. If you are blind or received disability benefits in the past, you may need fewer credits. The number of credits a person needs to qualify for disability benefits increases each year until 62, up to a maximum of 40 credits.

If you were disabled, had enough credits, and met the other requirements for disability benefits, here is an estimate of the benefits you could receive right now:

Your monthly benefit would be about:	$895
You and your eligible family members could receive up to a monthly total of about:	$1,340

These estimates may be reduced if you receive workers' compensation of public disability benefits.

IF YOUR RECORDS DO NOT AGREE WITH OURS
If your earnings records do not agree with ours, please report this to us right away by calling the 800 number shown below. We can usually help you by phone. When you call, have this statement available along with any W-2 forms, payslips, tax returns or any other proof of your earnings.

IF YOU HAVE ANY QUESTIONS
If you have any other questions about this statement, please read the information on the reverse side. If you still have questions, please call 1-800-937-7005.

Social Security considers all calls confidential. We also want to ensure that you receive accurate and courteous service. That is why we may have a second Social Security representative listen to some calls.

FIGURE 15–2   How Social Security Income Builds

These figures represent the approximate yearly income from Social Security benefits for a single person and, on the following line, for a worker and a nonworking spouse of the same age, when they become eligible for full Social Security benefits at age 65 to 67. All of the amounts in the table are Social Security Administration projections in 1988 dollars, based on continuous employment throughout an adult lifetime.

		Annual Social Security Benefit				
Your earnings in 1987		$20,000	$25,000	$30,000	$35,000	$45,000+
Your age in 1988						
25	Individual	11,796	13,548	14,568	15,600	17,652
	Couple	17,688	20,316	21,852	23,400	26,472
35	Individual	10,896	12,540	13,476	14,436	16,296
	Couple	16,344	18,804	20,208	21,648	24,444
45	Individual	9,972	11,496	12,360	13,104	14,412
	Couple	14,952	17,244	18,540	19,656	21,612
55	Individual	9,048	10,344	10,920	11,352	12,036
	Couple	13,572	15,516	16,380	17,028	18,048
65	Individual	8,100	9,216	9,564	9,792	10,056
	Couple	12,144	13,824	14,340	14,688	15,084

FIGURE 15–3   Request for Earnings and Benefit Estimate Statement

---

Request for earnings and benefit estimate statement

1.   Name shown on your Social Security card:

First   Middle Initial   Last

2. Your Social Security number as shown on your card:

☐☐☐ - ☐☐ - ☐☐☐☐

3. Your date of birth:

Month   Day   Year

4. Other Social Security numbers you have used:

☐☐☐ - ☐☐ - ☐☐☐☐

☐☐☐ - ☐☐ - ☐☐☐☐

5. Your Sex: ☐ Male ☐ Female

6. Other names you have used (including a maiden name):

First   Middle Initial   Last

7.   Show your actual earnings for last year and your estimated earnings for this year. Include only wages and/or net self-employment income covered by Social Security.

A. Last year's actual earnings:
$ ☐☐☐☐ ☐☐☐ ☐☐
Dollars only

B. This year's estimated earnings:
$ ☐☐☐☐ ☐☐☐ ☐☐
Dollars only

8. Show the age at which you plan to retire: ☐☐☐

(Show only one age)

9.   Below, show the average yearly amount that you think you will earn between now and when you plan to retire. Your estimate of future earnings will be added to those earnings already on our records to give you the best possible estimate.

Enter a yearly average, not your total future lifetime earnings. Only show earnings covered by Social Security. Do not add cost-of-living, performance or scheduled pay increases or bonuses. The reason for this is that we estimate retirement benefits in today's dollars, but adjust them to account for average wage growth in the national economy.

However, if you expect to earn significantly more or less in the future due to promotions, job changes, part-time work, or an absence from the work force, enter the amount in today's dollars that most closely reflects your future average yearly earnings.

Most people should enter the same amount that they are earning now (the amount shown in 7B).

Your future average yearly earnings:

$ ☐☐☐ , ☐☐☐☐ . ☐☐
Dollars only

(continued)

FIGURE 15–3 *Concluded*

10. Address where you want us to send the statement:

Name

Street Address (Include apt. no., P.O. Box, or Rural Route)

City   State   Zip Code

I am asking for information about my own Social Security record or the record of a person I am authorized to represent. I understand that if I deliberately request information under false pretenses I may be guilty of a federal crime and could be fined and/or imprisoned. I authorize you to send the statement of earnings and benefit estimates to the person named in item 10 through a contractor.

Please sign your name (Do not print)

Date   (Area Code) Daytime Telephone No.

ABOUT THE PRIVACY ACT
Social Security is allowed to collect the facts on this form under Section 205 of the Social Security Act. We need them to quickly identify our record and prepare the earnings statement you asked us for. Giving us these facts is voluntary. However, without them we may not be able to give you an earnings and benefit estimate statement. Neither the Social Security Administration nor its contractor will use the information for any other purpose.

5

HOUSE CLEANING

This last part I call *house cleaning.* It covers all the other little things you need to do to put your investment plan in place, including *Do It Yourself—On-line* and where you can go for help. We'll discuss other types of nonliquid assets, plus the crucial qualifications you should look for in a financial advisor or broker.

There's also a chapter in this part on how to analyze an investment—for those of you who still want to buy an individual stock from time to time, instructions on how to read that boring prospectus and, of course, a discussion on how to pay for college. Finally, we pull it all together with a quick-start plan to get you going safely and smartly, plus an investment calendar with important dates and a schedule to keep you on track. This last part will help make investing much less mysterious—even user-friendly.

16

DO IT YOURSELF—
ON-LINE

WARNING! While the Internet offers tremendous opportunities, it also is a spawning ground for investment fraud. Just
apply what you have learned about investing and ask yourself, "Why am I getting such a great deal?"

If you do find you've been duped, the Internet makes it
easier to go for help. Investors can e-mail complaints to the Office of Investor
Education and Assistance at Help@sec.Gov. Complaint-inquiries numbered
600 during the second half of 1996, then ballooned to 5,000 inquiries in
1997 and double that in 1998. The office evaluates the complaints and if
there is fraud, the office refers the case to the Division of Enforcement,
which can be reached at enforcement@sec.gov. There is also the National
Fraud Information Center at www.fraud.org.

I just pulled this unsolicited e-mail (Fig. 16–1) off my computer as I
was writing this chapter. Many, many sites are little more than ads—move
on quickly when you see these. But no matter what the site, check the legitimacy of any organization you find yourself thinking of doing business with.
Beware, e.g., of a Web site belonging to some brokerage selling penny stocks
from New York, Vancouver, or Denver that you've never heard of. You can
bet that the Web site won't tell you if the firm is under investigation by the
Securities and Exchange Commission.

Now to the good guys.

FIGURE 16–1   RE:E-ALERT

RE:E-ALERT: URGENT BUY RECOMMENDATION

Wall Street analysis from Harvard Equity Research has issued a STRONG
BUY recommendation on XXX stock.   XXX was quoted as predicting a $2.50-$3.00 price near-
term with "sustained momentum into the $5.00 plus range by the 4th quarter of 1998".

Harvard Equity Research's recommendation of this stock went from $3 to $9.00 in ten trading days!
(*The big promise*)

Harvard Equity Research is so confident of their projections that they
are offering their subscribers a money-back guarantee on their
subscription if XXX doesn't at least double within the next year.
(*Please, where's the SEC when you need them?*)

For further information go to: or send a SASE, for a free issue of Harvard Equity Research's latest
top-rated newsletter, to XXX, a P.O. Box in Toronto, Canada.
(*Right!*)

*When you see names tossed around like "Harvard" you can bet your last whatever, it has
nothing to do with Harvard University but the promoter wants you to believe his research came
from Harvard but why a Toronto P.O.Box?... Give me a break.*

FINANCIAL PLANNING ON THE INTERNET

Think of the Web as a gigantic computerized Yellow Pages with colorful graph-
ics and links that, at the click of a mouse, let you connect with Web sites containing related information. You'd have to go to the library and search through
dozens of books and periodicals to get the same information.

Back to the Last Phases of Our Simple Plan

I asked Louis Schiff, the founder, and Doug Gerlach, senior editor, of the
Armchair Millionaire Web site to help after you've set the book down. Louis
Schiff is an advocate of a methodology called "Common Sense Saving and
Investing" and he has a great Web site (www.armchairmillionaire.com). He
also understands asset class investing.

They have a five-step plan to financial freedom. Their Web site will
teach you great savings methods in the first four steps. In the fifth step you
begin to implement the plan. They recommend a basket of index funds and
tell you how to approach a broker, fill out applications, and answer confusing and intimidating questions that are more designed for the broker than
the investor—they've got a whole community of regular people who have
already gone through it.

They will help define commonsense saving and investing. Investing
experience is not unlike other consumer experiences. When you buy a television, you compare remote controls, prices, and features, and you choose

the one that fits your needs. In investing, however, people seem to choose investments with their eyes closed and then cross their fingers. That doesn't have to be the case. You can actually make consumer-style investment decisions based on a fair comparison of features.

Each of the five steps is very understandable. But if you don't understand it, don't do it. Every component of the plan is useful in and of itself. It's not as though the whole plan hangs together or falls apart. Probably the one most crucial component you will learn about is the power of compounding. Other than that, each piece can be considered on its own merit.

One of the qualities that makes their Web site different from others is that its main function is financial planning. When they do deal with the process of investing, they put a strong focus on the planning part. What stocks, mutual funds, or bonds do you actually buy? It's the fifth step, but not the only step. There are important things you can do before you actually make the decision to buy.

Even if you simply choose a product such as a fixed income, CD, or a savings account, steps 1 through 4, which are savings techniques, are so powerful that you will really be far ahead of the game. If you only follow steps 1 to 4, you'll start saving regularly and putting money away for the long term. Then, when you are ready for step 5 to invest in the stock market, you're there.

If you just follow their advice and use index funds, 7 out of 10 times you'll make the right decision. Being in the market as a whole is a very valuable place to be. Virtually everything you do in investing involves looking at history and then projecting to the future.

Schiff and Gerlach also follow the rules of diversification, which makes an index fund choice so appropriate. When you diversify, you're essentially spreading risk, and that definitely can kill some of that exciting individual stock buzz—the U.S. dream of picking the next Microsoft, IBM, or Yahoo. There are great stories about people who invested in IBM, Sears & Roebuck, or Coca-Cola fifty years ago. But that's not too far from betting on the lottery. You're just hoping that a lot of things that are statistically against you will go your way.

They are launching a model portfolio as I am writing this book. It will be one-third S&P 500, which represents 70 percent of the publicly traded stock market; one-third in the Russell 2000, taking advantage of the phenomenon of the small company (which is that small companies gain faster than the average large cap); and one-third in the Morgan Stanley EFA, Europe–Australia–Far East Fund. They're making a bet there that the blue-chip stocks around the globe have value, are strategically important, and are growing. Historically, when it comes to diversification, that pays off. Investing in the large caps in the United States, especially the biggest, is practically like investing in a mutual fund.

Through their Web site, Schiff and Gerlach are trying to get more people to understand that investing is a psychological process. Why should anyone listen to these guys? The answer is, there is a certain amount of strength in numbers when it comes to investing. When people see other people doing it, they feel as if there must be some legitimacy to the style or the idea. You can actually see and meet the people who are doing it. You can talk to them. In particular, you can see how they're applying it in their own personal way. They address more life-style-oriented goals: sending kids to college and saving for retirement. And you can do this in the comfort of your own home.

The user becomes a member of the Armchair Millionaire Investor Club. An investing club is a great idea, and people who join clubs are having a great time. There are many people who don't have time to go to meetings, even once a month. The clubs bring you together for chats and message boards, special guests, special features, new tools, or special deals they've arranged with the sponsors—anything they think will help you better apply commonsense saving investment methodology. It takes 45 minutes to go through it once and get a sense of it, and it doesn't cost anything.

They have a message board called "There's No Such Thing as a Dumb Question." Why? Because everyone was a beginner when she or he started investing. And they know that you are going to have questions. They answer lots of questions on the site in the articles that are published and on the five steps.

The Web is seeing an explosion of women's participation on-line; a simple question has no gender associated with it, and the answers are given with respect and thoughtfulness from the users. Users don't know whether a person is tall, short, fat, skinny, male, or female. I think you will love this environment where they feel much freer to ask questions or to show how smart they are. There is no race, color, creed, or religion on the Internet. Armchair Millionaire is a Web site, but I think this site is the best place to be.

The theories you will learn at the site are not new, but the tools probably didn't actually exist to make them true until the Web came along. Even before the Web, Compuserve users were practicing this in a small, significant way. It's powerful. This is going to be a time which historians will look back on and say, "Something changed about investing in the middle of the 1990s." It has a lot to do with technology, the Web, and the sharing of information.

It's an environment where people are trying all sorts of things and learning so much so fast. This coincides with the rise of 401(k) programs in the United States and the sunset of the pension program and lifetime employment idea. It's a powerful movement taking place that has absolutely required that investors take on the responsibility and educate themselves.

DUE DILIGENCE

The way to do your due diligence is to educate yourself. Once you open an account with a brokerage firm, you can use the Internet for trading as well as research. After you log on with your account number, the on-line brokerage firm will give you a password. You can check your investments, and you can create a watch list of investments of your own. Don't worry about somebody stealing your money. Send a check to the brokerage firm—nothing gets invested until the money is safe in the bank. Investing on-line is covered by the same rules as regular investing. After you have opened an account, it's easy to bring up your portfolio on-line. It takes a matter of seconds to value your holdings. You could customize the look of your portfolio, and you could even have a message alert you when there's a news flash on one of your holdings.

For those of you who are delegators, or self-directed, you can now put several different brokerage firms or mutual fund families on the same screen and can potentially put all that information on one site. In less than five minutes, you can see how all your investments are doing.

On the Web, you are free to try many different suppliers, programs, services, and brokers. And you are free to change your mind. It's a new world, one in which public retailing, free trials, and competition among various investment software products and services will inevitably bring down prices.

Beware: There is a lot of free stuff for investors on the Internet. Some of it is wonderful, but you are probably not going to strike it rich just by picking up a hot stock tip from a news group or downloading some minimalist investment freeware. To make money, you need technology and a method, not just a tip.

ON-LINE TRADING

On-line trading has exploded over the past year as investors are becoming more self-sufficient and comfortable using their computers for investing. That's great for all the technically inclined folks, but is it right for you? It's great to be able to access your account information at a moment's notice and to place trades 24 hours per day. I like the idea of using an on-line brokerage account, but I also realize that some people prefer to deal with a real person when they are placing trades.

When shopping around for an on-line discount broker, you should ask plenty of questions about the customer service department. Sure, on-line brokerage accounts are becoming easier to use and are providing more and more information, but you need to know how to access your account information if you can't get on-line for some reason and need to make a transaction. Will a "live" broker be accessible to you if you need to place a trade?

If you're comfortable with your computer and you don't really need to hear that voice on the other end of the phone, we recommend that you go with a discount broker and trade on-line.

ON-LINE OFFERINGS

Wirehouses are beginning to offer on-line trading—albeit reluctantly—in order to retain clients. It should come as little surprise that in this era of do-it-yourself investing, Internet-based trading firms are flourishing. This new breed of brokerage, having grown from a mere handful a few years back to more than 70 brokerage firms today, has been luring a growing number of investors by drastically slashing the commissions that clients fork over to make transactions.

Fueled by the fear of losing valuable customers, some of the nation's largest wirehouses—PaineWebber, Prudential Securities, and Merrill Lynch—are planning to offer Internet trading in the near future.

Last year, the number of people in the United States investing over the Internet grew 120 percent, to 3.3 million, according to Credit Suisse First Boston. On-line transactions grew 181 percent, to 26 million.

The real challenge that full-service firms face is to offer on-line service to clients at competitive prices without angering their brokers. The average full-service commission for purchasing 3000 shares at $10 is $672.59—more than 4 times the average discount brokerage commission of $145.05 on the same trade, according to Credit Suisse First Boston.

Full-service firms can't offer $10 trades over the Internet, because their cost structure isn't set up to do that. They have to offer the convenience of on-line trading without creating internal warfare.

Despite these wirehouses' ventures into Internet trading, many analysts say their actions serve defensive purposes only. Major firms are not seeking to grab a share of the on-line firms' clients, analysts say, but are simply trying to keep their own clients.

Most of the people attracted to deep-discount trading left full-service brokerage firms a long time ago.

Here's a roundup of what's being offered in on-line trading at full-service brokerages:

PaineWebber

PaineWebber began a pilot test and is planning to offer on-line trading to all its clients shortly thereafter. The service will be offered in a fee-based structure, most likely through PaineWebber's wrap account, called Premier Asset Account. Fees for trading are based on a client's assets under management.

Merrill Lynch

Merrill Lynch is set to offer on-line trading as part of the Merrill Lynch Online account, which is slated for the fourth quarter of 1998. Still, Merrill has repeatedly stated that it will not discount commissions, and that on-line trading will be part of an account for which a customer must still utilize a broker. In fact, according to a company spokesperson, on-line transactions will be paid on the same grid and in the same manner as regular trades. As with many innovations in the brokerage industry, many of the brokerage firms are closely watching the reaction of Merrill brokers and clients to the new service, analysts say.

Salomon Smith Barney

Although Salomon Smith Barney continues to enhance the portfolio account access section of its Web site—providing charts, news, and commentary from analysts—insiders say the firm is far from entering into on-line trading. Industry observers predict that Salomon, ever the cautious firm, will watch how the other wirehouses fare with their offerings before making a move. A Salomon Smith Barney spokesperson says the firm is not commenting on any future plans regarding Internet trading.

Prudential Securities

Prudential Securities is currently beta-testing its new on-line trading service, called PruTrade, with approximately 200 investors. A company spokesperson says the firm is still looking at various price models. Prudential plans to offer the service fully to clients sometime later this year.

Morgan Stanley Dean Witter

Although MSDW offers discount on-line trading through its newly acquired Discover Brokerage Direct (formerly Lombard Brokerage), on-line trading is not available to MSDW retail clients. Insiders say the firm purchased the discounter to attract do-it-yourselfers not interested in full-service brokerage.

Brokers say that MSDW is planning to offer clients on-line trading eventually, but that the service is a long way off. In Fig. 16–2, you can see for yourself how on-line trading is taking off.

FIGURE 16–2   The Self-Serve Market Is Increasingly Becoming an On-Line Game

Active On-Line Accounts, May 1997 (Thousands)

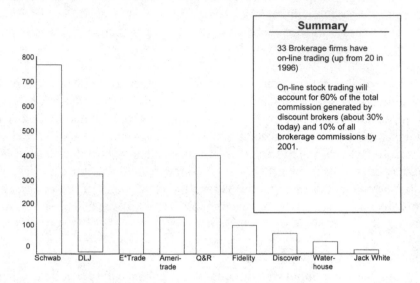

Summary

33 Brokerage firms have on-line trading (up from 20 in 1996)

On-line stock trading will account for 60% of the total commission generated by discount brokers (about 30% today) and 10% of all brokerage commissions by 2001.

ACTIVE ON-LINE WEB SITES

- Schwab, www.schwab.com. With over $160 billion in assets, it is by far the leader in on-line discount trading.
- Web Street Securities, www.webstreetsecurities.com
- E*Trade, www.etrade.com (This site also comes up fast.)
- Waterhouse, www.waterhouse.com (Great-looking site)
- Quick & Reilly, www.quick-reilly.com

ON-LINE DANGER

There are ads all over the Internet in which you can buy all the shares of stock you want for $6. If you do that three times in a year, you pay just as much as for a full-service broker. Statistically, studies show that you're going to lose money 90 percent of the time.

One idea is to track the odd lots and find out what they are doing, then go the opposite way. You will usually be right, because 90 percent of the time the small investor is wrong.

Most people don't keep their finances in perspective. They point, click, and sell; point, click, and buy; and try to trade on short-term profits—and we know that 90 percent of the people who do that are going to lose. But that is what Wall Street advertises: the perception that through trading, an investor makes big profits. How many trades do people make in a year on average? I've probably purchased two different classes in the last 12 months. The last time I sold anything was 10 years ago.

What you can do on the Internet, definitely and decisively, is to immerse yourself in the established subculture of computerized investing. You can learn what's available before purchasing packaged software or subscriptions, and you can see which techniques and services can help you win at your chosen game. Here are some good places to start:

THE ARMCHAIR MILLIONAIRE, www.armchairmillionaire.com
Summary. The five-step plan: pay yourself first; use dollar-cost averaging; understand compound interest; pay lower taxes; and build your plan.

BLOOMBERG, www.bloomberg.com
This is for news and updated market information (one of my personal favorites).

INVESTORAMA, www.investorama.com
This is a description of thousands of links to investor sites. How to build a million dollar portfolio. This links back to The Armchair Millionaire.

INVESTOOLS, www.investools.com
This site is free-sample heaven. It's great for reading investment resources such as investment newsletters, opinion pieces, helpful lists of money managers and advisors, and books and periodicals. Read a back issue or free-sample newsletter before deciding to subscribe. Ranked as one of the ten best Web sites by Barron's.
But beware: It is a very common and rather dangerous practice to collect free back issues of newsletters in order to heist the advisor's "hot list" of stocks in the recommended portfolio.

LOMBARD INSTITUTIONAL BROKERAGE, www.lombard.com
Without even opening an account, you can freely sample the range of services available on-line for this brokerage's customers. They are very good indeed and include delayed quotes and charts. Account holders can get real-time quotes, see displays of their portfolios and transactions, and of course place trades.
At this site, you can chart 7,000 stocks and 61,000 options, free of charge. The charts are excellent, although they are screen displays only. Nevertheless, it is an outstanding facility, and no doubt, option traders camp out at Lombard's Web site. It is currently one of the Net's top 5 percent most-visited sites.

THE MOTLEY FOOL, www.fool.com
> Go straight to a feature called the Fool Portfolio.
>
> This site is essentially an advertisement for the immensely popu-
> lar Motley Fool service on America Online. But the underlying phi-
> losophy is rock-solid and deeply conservative in tone. Fools or not,
> this is a good place to look for information on high-yielding Dow
> stocks. Take a look at the Dow Dividend Strategy.

PAWWS FINANCIAL NETWORK, www.pawws.com
> This is a no-nonsense site with a sampling of many different useful
> commercial services. I liked the coolly realistic and matter-of-fact
> tone of the site, which is essentially a multipage catalog. It covers a
> wide spectrum and will give you a good idea of the services available
> on the Web.
>
> PAWWS provides access to three affiliate brokers: National
> Discount Brokers (NDB), Jack White & Co., and Net Investor. Each
> offers special incentives to on-line traders. NDB will trade any NAS-
> DAQ stock for a flat fee of just $20. Jack White offers a 10 percent
> discount. Net Investor features a free package of on-line news,
> research, and analysis worth $50 per month.
>
> *Please note:* For security-sensitive investment services, such as
> stock trading through a broker and personal-portfolio displays over
> the Net, you should use "secure-aware" software. As of this writing,
> the security requirement is met only by Netscape.

SILICON INVESTOR, www.techstocks.com
> (Of course it would be fast! I love this site.)
>
> This is a big, well-focused site that concentrates on digital, elec-
> tronics, and communications technology. It has detailed data on near-
> ly 250 stocks and maintains indices on four of the technology groups:
> communications, software, computers and peripherals, and semicon-
> ductors.
>
> The service has quick-look fact sheets on individual stocks, news
> groups, detailed data, quotes, and charts. You can compare a stock's
> performance with that of its group, find out what other investors are
> thinking about it, and check the company's own news and news
> releases. Silicon Investor is a good place to learn what the day's big
> moves have been.

TIPNET, www.telescan.com
> This is a sampler of the full-blown financial software and services
> supermarket available via Telescan Investor's Platform, or TIP. It pre-

sents, in one place, the technical screening, portfolio, and quotes-retrieval software regarded by computerized investors as essential tools. Also TIPnet provides direct access to important services such as Zacks and Standard & Poor's MarketScope.

ZACKS INVESTMENT RESEARCH, zacks.com
   (It's News!)
      Probably the most powerful force driving the price of high-visibility stocks is this: the revisions in earnings estimates issued by the 2,500 analysts working at 210 brokerage firms. One could earnestly argue that earnings, not estimates, move stock prices. But the estimates are the earliest news the market gets, and wow, does it ever react to this news.

LET YOUR COMPUTER BE YOUR BROKER

Charles Schwab sells company reports for as little as $3. Services also give you an up-to-date picture of your holdings—some in so-called real time so you can find the last bid price on your Intel stock—and others are updated a few times a day.

   Still, no hacker can transfer assets out of your account—additional, off-line security procedures prevent it.

   Like full-service brokerage houses, the on-line trading companies carry Securities Investor Protection Corporation (SIPC) coverage, which will replace up to $500,000 in losses, including up to $100,000 cash, if the brokerage goes bankrupt.

   Pay a visit to the Gómez Advisors Web site (www.gomezadvisors.com). This Boston firm ranks on-line trading services according to cost, ease of use, customer confidence, on-site resources (quotes, news, advice, recommendations, and screening tools). Gómez also scores the firms according to their appropriateness for four kinds of investors: life goal planner, serious investor, hyperactive trader, and one-stop shopper. From the Gómez site, you can visit other sites.

FINANCIAL MANAGEMENT SOFTWARE

Financial management software can help you get organized while letting you indulge your passion for computing.

   Microsoft, Intuit, and Meca Software, the companies that make the most popular financial planning programs, are all offering brand-new editions. They automatically update your portfolio, balance your checkbook, and sort your spending into categories.

Microsoft Money '98 Financial Suite ($29.95; $54.95 for the deluxe version) includes a goal planner that allows you to monitor your progress toward long-term goals, say, retirement in Provence. You can also use the program to connect to the Microsoft Investor Web site.

Intuit's Quicken ($39.95 basic; $59.95 deluxe; and $89.95 for Suite '98, a program that includes a special retirement planner) gives you a jazzier version of the goal planner. It automatically calculates how quickly your savings program will get you to Provence. The deluxe version lets you connect to Quicken's Web site (www.quicken.com).

FINANCIAL PLANNING

Deloitte & Touche (www.dtonline.com), the accounting firm, provides financial planning and retirement advice. They have been selected by the Ministry of Finance of the People's Republic of China to play a key role in Chinese government modernization of its tax system. Not bad!

Fidelity Investments (www.fidelity.com) recommends Fidelity products to use for a variety of financial problems.

FinanCenter/Smartcalc (www.financenter.com) will calculate your car and mortgage payments and show you how much you need to save in order to retire.

Intuit (www.intuit.com) offers samples of its financial management software programs Quicken and TurboTax.

INVESTING

Among general information sites providing research, tips, and market updates are a few of our favorites:

Morningstar, Inc. (www.morningstar.net), the Chicago mutual funds research company, offers one of the most useful sites on the Web, including exhaustive information on more than 6,500 individual mutual funds as well as financial news and columns. (This is an excellent Web site. Go here first.)

The Street.com (www.thestreet.com) provides quirky commentary on stocks, interest rates, and the economy. After a two-week free trial, subscriptions cost $9.95 per month for access to the Web site and a daily morning bulletin. (This site has everything.)

IBC Financial Data (www.ibcdata.com) lists money market funds and bond funds with data on their historic performance.

Microsoft Investor (www.investor.msn.com) contains data on thousands of
individual stocks and mutual funds and makes recommendations.
Subscription costs $9.95 per month.

Nest Egg (www.nestegg.com), sponsored by Investment Dealer's Digest,
provides news on mutual funds and stocks and can help you calculate
your ideal rate of retirement saving.

TAX HELP (WWW.MACINTAX, COM)

The two most popular tax software offerings are *TurboTax* and its Macintosh
cousin *MacinTax* by Intuit, and Kiplinger Tax Cut by Block Financial
Software. In addition to their other features, both allow you to transfer data
from other financial management software into relevant tax-deduction or
expense categories.

TurboTax (www.turbotax.com) ($35; $50 for the deluxe version) takes
you through an interview process that includes a "refund monitor" that automatically changes your bottom line every time you make an entry. You don't
have to look at intimidating forms because the program enters the data in the
proper categories and does the calculations for you. After the interview,
TurboTax checks for omissions and flags deductions that you may have for-
gotten. You can see for yourself whether you've gone overboard in making
claims. When it finishes, it pumps out tax forms—or submits them electronically to the IRS.

Kiplinger Tax Cut (www.kiplinger, com) ($20; $25 for a state version)
does everything TurboTax does and also displays lines of the tax form as
you answer its questions. It prints or files electronically. Plus, you get news
of the day.

Summary

There are currently over 200 mutual fund sites on the World Wide Web; and
because this is an advantage for mutual fund companies, it's growing rapidly. The Web offers cost savings in the distribution of information and the
handling of transactions. For the first time investor, the Web offers convenient up-to-the-minute information and account security. Just keep in mind
that the fund families with the highest level of assets under management
compose the bulk of Web sites.

17

YOUR INVESTMENT PLAN

BEFORE YOU CONSIDER HIRING SOMEONE to assist you, take some time and write out an investment plan. Or if that's too great an effort, use the Six Step program below as a guide. It will enable you to clearly communicate your long-term financial goals and objectives and will serve as a guideline to help implement the investment strategy. An advisor will call this an *investment policy statement,* but it's the same thing.

This plan will give you a way of evaluating how you and your advisor are doing. You need a way to assess if you are on track with your investments. It also protects you from seat-of-the-pants revisions to an otherwise sound investment plan. This document will help you create a set of expectations. You might compare this to a business plan. Very few successful businesses have started and succeeded without one.

Having and using this plan in written form compels you to become more disciplined and systematic, increasing your probability of success.

SIX STEPS TO WRITING YOUR OWN INVESTMENT PLAN

1. Set long-term finanical goals and objectives. Long-term goals can be anything from early retirement to purchasing a new home. One of the most common goals I see is to be financially independent. What that often

---

means to most first time investors is that their investment portfolio will provide them with the income necessary to maintain their quality of life. This is just as important for those who are still working as those already retired.

Your goals:

_____

_____

_____

2. Establish your expected time horizon. You have to determine your investment period. The minimum expected investment period must be at least 5 years for any portfolio containing equity securities. For any portfolio with less than a 5-year time horizon, your portfolio should be in a core savings or comprised predominantly of fixed investments. This 5-year minimum investment period is critical. The investment process must be viewed as a long-term plan for achieving the desired results. One-year volatility can be significant for many equity asset classes. However, over a 5-year period, the range of returns is greatly reduced.

Your time period: _____

3. Determine the rate-of-return objective. In getting started, you should write down a range of returns that would be acceptable.

In John Bowen's *The Prudent Investor's Guide to Beating the Market* (McGraw-Hill, 1998), the author has identified the specific return risk profiles of each optimized model portfolio. We have reproduced these in Fig. 17–1. You can use these ranges of returns for each risk level as the framework to determine your return expectation and standard deviation for your portfolio as well as the component asset classes.

The range should be consistent with the weighted-average expected rate of return of your prospect's portfolio asset classes over the last 20 years. Don't just look at the last 5 years. That is likely to be an unusual period. You also want to examine some difficult market periods such as the 1973–1974 time frame to see if your prospect can stay the course.

Your return expectation: _____

4. Define the level of risk you are willing to accept. Along the road to reaching your financial goals, there are going to be bumps caused by the downturn in various markets. It is important for you to understand the amount of risk you are willing to tolerate during the investment period. In designing a portfolio, you must determine the absolute loss you will accept in any 1-year period without terminating the investment program.

The level of risk you are willing to accept (standard deviation):

_____

5. Select the asset classes to be utilized to build your prospect's portfolio. In Part Three, you will find the list of all the different asset classes that you might want to consider in your portfolio.
Asset classes:

_____

_____

_____

6. Rebalancing. A financial advisor can help you create a measuring benchmark to review investment portfolio performance. If goals and objectives have been clearly defined, it becomes much easier to determine how the portfolio is performing relative to these goals and objectives.

You should familiarize your investment advisor with this plan and see if this is an area which she or he can assist you in the implementation. The written plan will enable you to better define your investment expectations and put you in a position to decide how best to implement an asset class portfolio.

Are you a trustee of a retirement plan? This investment plan can assist you. If you have no interest in this, skip to the next section.

If you are a trustee and subject to the following guidelines, the written investment policy statement creates a road map for plan fiduciaries to meet the legal requirements of the "prudent investor" rules. The written plan also provides standards against which the trustee can be judged. The written investment policy statement must be clear and specific enough to be a working doc-

FIGURE 17–1 Expected Returns/Standard Deviation

Asset Class	Expected Return	Standard Deviation
Money Market	4.90%	3.30%
Fixed Income	6.70%	3.90%
U.S. Large	13.60%	20.30%
U.S. Small	19.40%	38.50%
International Large	13.60%	20.30%
International Small	19.40%	38.50%
Emerging Markets	16.00%	29.00%

ument. Broad-based generalities will not serve as investment objectives. Being specific is the key to providing a proper working investment plan.

The American Law Institute, Restatement of the Law Third, Prudent Investor Rules, instructs trustees and courts that

1. Sound diversification is fundamental to risk management and is therefore ordinarily required of trustees.

2. Risk and returns are so directly related that trustees have a duty to analyze and make conscious decisions concerning the level of risk appropriate to the purposes, requirements, and circumstances of the trust.

3. Trustees have a duty to avoid fees, transaction costs, and other expenses that are not justified by needs and realistic objectives of the trust's investment program.

4. Fiduciary duty of impartiality requires a balancing of elements of return between current income and the protection of purchasing power.

5. Trustees may have the duty as well as the authority to delegate as prudent investors would.

CORPORATE QUALIFIED PLAN REQUIREMENTS

If you represent a corporate pension plan or other plan governed by the Employee Retirement and Income Securities Act (ERISA), you must diversify your plan's assets unless it is clearly prudent not to do so. Asset class investing clearly complies with the state recommendations. The Department of Labor states that a fiduciary can be held personally liable for breach of violation of these responsibilities, even to the extent of having to restore lost profits to the plan. ERISA was enacted to protect the interests of participants in employee benefit plans from abuses and discriminatory practices.

The scope and complexity of ERISA have led to a widespread lack of understanding of its basic principles and a commensurate lack of understanding of liabilities that trustees may be subject to. Compliance with the ERISA rules has been a major concern of trustees and plan sponsors since this landmark legislation was passed in 1974. These rules, governed by the Department of Labor (DOL), impose heavy responsibilities on any persons involved in the management of employee benefit plans. Unfortunately, many trustees and advisors are not aware of the responsibilities, liabilities, and penalties under ERISA until they find themselves in violation of the act.

ERISA provides a federal standard of conduct to be followed and observed concerning the management of retirement fund assets. A fiduciary not acting in accordance with the precepts of ERISA can not only be subjected to personal liability, but could subject the plan under management to loss of its tax-free status.

A trustee has a duty not only to become familiarized with and follow standards set in ERISA, but also to seek outside assistance when appropriate. The scope of fiduciary responsibility is much wider than generally recognized because the definition of *fiduciary* is so broad. To be considered a fiduciary, one must have an element of authority or control over the plan, including plan management, administration, or disposition of assets.

To the extent that plan sponsors, consultants, and/or advisors influence or maintain discretionary authority over plan management or investments, they are also fiduciaries. *Named* fiduciaries are those listed in the plan documents as having responsibility for plan management. Obviously, trustees, plan officers, and plan directors fall under this definition, but so do persons who are delegated duties by named fiduciaries. Others, such as corporate officers, directors, and shareholders, also exert enough control to be deemed fiduciaries.

It is important to note that if trustees or named fiduciaries properly select and appoint a qualified money manager, they will not have a cofiduciary responsibility for acts and omissions of the advisor, unless they knowingly participate in or try to conceal any such acts or omissions.

ERISA outlines the following broad areas which set the standards of fiduciary conduct in administering a plan. In essence, anyone who exercises any authority over management, administration, or disposition of assets, or renders advice, will be held as a fiduciary.[1]

The fiduciary's duties must be discharged solely in the interest of plan participants and their beneficiaries. The prudent expert rule defines the standard of competence to which a fiduciary will be held responsible with respect to plan investment decisions. ERISA states that a fiduciary must discharge her or his duties "with the care, skill, prudence and diligence under the circumstances then prevailing that a prudent person acting in a like capacity and familiar with such matters would use in the conduct of an enterprise of a like character with like aims." In other words, fiduciaries can be held to the same level of skill as a professional money manager in making investment decisions. It is important to remember that pension dollars belong to employees and beneficiaries, not the sponsoring company. Hence, ERISA holds fiduciaries to as high a standard as that of a professional investment expert.

---

[1] Section 404(a)(1)(b) of the Internal Revenue Code.

Penalties may be imposed for up to 6 years after the fiduciary violation, or 3 years after the party bringing suit had knowledge of the breach. A willful violation carries personal criminal penalties of up to $5,000 ($100,000 for corporations) and up to 1 year in prison.

Civil actions can be initiated by plan participants, beneficiaries, other fiduciaries, and the Department of Labor. Losses to the plan as well as profits made from the improper use of plan assets must be restored to the plan. Failure to disclose information to plan participants can result in a daily penalty of $100. The Department of Labor which oversees ERISA can also remove the fiduciary and take control over plan assets.

It is critical to bear in mind that the fiduciary's responsibilities are ongoing, and liability exists even when professional advisors are hired and subsequently breach their fiduciary duties or fail to meet plan goals. In other words, delegation alone will not protect a fiduciary; a system of delegation and oversight will. The process of monitoring should mirror the plan's funding and investment objectives. Asset class investing will assist you in effectively meeting your responsibilities as a fiduciary.

18

SELECTING AN INVESTMENT ADVISOR

MANY FIRST TIME INVESTORS feel uncomfortable dealing with the financial services industry due to the transactional nature of the broker's or advisor's compensation. Many feel that the recommendations they receive are suspect due to the inherent conflict of interest in a commission sale. Many investors also are unsure how to discern how well their portfolios are performing, and their monthly brokerage statements are intimidating. Tracking performance can be especially troublesome if there is more than one brokerage account involved. There is just so much information to ingest that the potential first time investor often doesn't feel comfortable taking any action at all.

Most first time investors feel they need an effective filter, so they subscribe to such publications as *Money, Forbes, Fortune, Business Week,* or *The Wall Street Journal.* Frequently these periodicals contain conflicting recommendations, even though they draw from the same data. In today's information age, one huge challenge is to deal with information effectively and use it to advantage.

The difference between working with a good versus merely an average financial advisor can be seen in your success. Let's look at a recent study completed by Dalbar Financial Services, Inc., to see how big this difference can be.

The following study shows how individual investors did on their own compared to when working with a financial advisor. There is a significant difference in returns realized by working with a qualified financial advisor.

The study measured the total returns over the past 10 years earned by investors who purchased directly marketed investment products versus returns earned by investors who used the services of a financial advisor. Although using a financial advisor did improve overall returns compared to do-it-yourself investing, it added value in only one dimension. See Fig. 18–1. From January 1983 through September 1993, equity investors using a financial advisor realized total returns of 90.21 percent versus a total return of 70.23 percent for the do-it-yourself investors. The study concluded that individuals who go it alone are more likely to try to time markets than to hold assets long-term. If you used the services of a financial advisor, you would have increased your returns 20 percent on average over time. That builds a pretty good case for working with an advisor. Why? Individuals who manage their own money unwittingly become market timers.

Let's take it a step further. During the same time period, Dalbar reports that the total return from the unmanaged S&P 500 Index was 293.44 percent, and the total return from the unmanaged Shearson Lehman Corporate Bond Index was 274.12 percent. I rest my case.

"But you told me earlier to get a financial coach!" I know I did. When I said financial coach, I meant someone who truly understands asset class investing and modern portfolio theory. My fear is that you will walk into the office of a broker or financial advisor, and the next thing you know, you will be investing in both the advising firm's fully loaded growth mutual fund and value fund. Your new advisor has just put your money in the same asset class within those two investments, and he doesn't even know it. Ouch! My job here is to help you avoid that.

FIGURE 18–1   Summarizes of Total Returns for Each

Dalbar Results / Model Portfolio	Total Return Jan 1983 - Sept. 1993
Investors on their Own	70.23
Investors with Advisors	90.21
S&P 500	293.44
Shearson Lehman Corporate Bond Index	274.12

Many stockbrokers, planners, and financial advisors make the language about investing much more complex than it needs to be. This just creates noise and confusion. Many professionals unconsciously (or consciously) change their voices when speaking to a client, literally becoming "the voice of authority." The timber in their voices deepens, and their stories are well rehearsed. But just because someone sounds authentic, that doesn't mean he or she knows much.

A recent UCLA study[1] revealed that the words we use contribute only 7 percent to the decision-making process. Thirty-eight percent was attributed to voice quality—tone, timber, and tempo—and 55 percent to body physiology—facial expression, body positioning, and physical gestures. The listener's brain discerns if the words match the body language. If they do, he or she makes a decision in favor of investing, buying, or whatever. In other words, the audience will buy a good story. But that doesn't ensure that the story is a true or valid story. Your job as an investor is to separate the information from the noise. Chapter twenty on asset class investing will help you do this. My promise was that as a result of reading this book, you would know more than 90 percent of what professional finanical advisors know—and by now you do. Use this knowledge in your interview process.

THE ADVICE GIVERS

Think of all the various professionals out there selling investments as being like different divisions of the armed services. There is the Army, Navy, Marine Corps, and Air Force. All have a similar objective and often even use the same type of equipment; they just carry out their missions differently. To the public, this can be confusing, and cross rivalries can result. The New York firm stockbrokers think they are at the top of the pecking order; bank representatives believe they sell on hallowed ground; and independent fee-only financial advisors sense they are close to nirvana. Yet they all may be selling the exact same investment product or offering the same service. The joint mission they all share, however, is to provide a service to the public. Unfortunately not all advisors share this sense of mission. In fact, some have changed their titles to *financial planner* simply to gain a marketing advantage. Often these individuals want to sell you a product, not assist you.

STOCKBROKERS

Most investors have a good relationship with their traditional Wall Street brokers; in surveys these brokers score high marks. People feel secure when they

---

[1] 1998 Robbins Research International, Inc. refers to the UCLA study in their communication courses.

see the plush offices, dark wood paneling, and concentrated activity. They don't realize that much of that activity revolves around cold calling and sales.

Most stockbrokers attempt to add value by following traditional investment strategies such as trying to pick exceptional securities, stocks, or mutual funds—or even worse, predicting which way the market's going. All academic studies, however, conclude that these two strategies—stock picking and market timing—over the long run don't work.

These active strategies entail investigation and analysis expenses, increase general transaction costs, and involve capital gains taxation. These judgment calls may also involve the acceptance of a relatively high degree of diversifiable risk. The extra costs and risks can be substantial and must be justified by realistically evaluated return expectations.

Most of the big firms also have their brokers sell *proprietary mutual funds*. This is just their in-house packed version of an already available investment product—but now the firm is biased toward this product over others. One firm, Prudential Securities, recently allegedly began restricting access by its brokers to outside mutual fund vendors in an effort to increase sales of its proprietary mutual funds.

According to insiders, Prudential regional managers aim for brokers to reach a minimum sales ratio of 40 percent proprietary funds to 60 percent outside funds. Currently, proprietary funds account for only about 20 percent of Prudential's mutual fund sales.

To help push in-house funds, Prudential recently targeted those branches below the minimum ratio and sent them a restricted list of outside fund vendors allowed into those branches. Although Prudential brokers are compensated equally for selling in-house and outside funds, brokers say the pressure to sell the firm's funds has been immense.

While many brokers resent the pressure to sell in-house funds, industry observers say Prudential's target ratio is far below that of other major wirehouses. At Merrill Lynch, proprietary funds constitute about 50 percent of mutual fund sales. And at Morgan Stanley Dean Witter, branch managers are required to maintain a minimum sales ratio of 75 percent proprietary funds to 25 percent outside funds. MSDW is also the only major wirehouse that continues to compensate its brokers more for selling in-house products, paying them 20 percent less for selling outside funds.

DIFFERENCES BETWEEN WALL STREET BROKERAGE FIRMS AND DISCOUNT FIRMS

The big Wall Street firms are also called *full-service,* meaning they offer a wider variety of financial products than discount brokerages while charging considerably higher fees. Products they offer include stocks, bonds, deriv atives, annuities, and insurance. A full-service stockbroker solicits business and is paid mostly by commissions. These houses also offer investment advice and research.

A recent study by Prophet Market Research and Consulting in San Francisco shows that brokers continue to suggest investments without knowledge of investors' financial backgrounds or objectives. Of the 300 brokers audited from 21 of the nation's largest full-service firms, 42 percent made investment recommendations without learning the potential investors' tax situations; 32 percent without knowing their financial status; 25 percent without knowing what securities they held; and 21 percent without knowing what the investors' financial objectives were. Furthermore, 9 percent of brokers studied from regional firms and 5 percent of brokers from national firms made recommendations without uncovering *any* qualifiers. In other words, they were there for one thing and one thing only: to sell stock.

Discount brokerages usually don't offer the full range of services provided by full-service brokers. They do not offer any advice or research—they simply transact trades, no frills. Because they manage fewer products than their full-service counterparts, discounters charge considerably lower fees. Discounters also often offer on-line computer order entry services. Those that have live brokers generally pay them a set salary to execute trades. The brokers don't solicit and aren't paid commissions. Discount brokerages make money by doing business in volume, competing mostly on price and "reliability" of the service. If they have the lowest prices and the best service, they get the most trades.

Which broker should you choose? You need to determine what types of services you need. If you need lots of research backup and advice, you should go to a full-service broker. If you are happy doing your own homework and don't need the advice, a discount broker is preferable.

INVESTMENT CONSULTANTS

Investment consultants normally work for Wall Street firms but specialize in consulting with investors about their investments, and they charge fees for services rather than commissions on transactions. Consultants are going to make more money only if you make more money—so you're on the same side of the fence. You also know in advance what your costs are going to be.

Investment consultants specialize not only in consulting but also in helping to educate investors about the capital markets. They take a much broader approach and maintain a macro perspective of global, small-cap, and large-cap equities. They provide educational materials and attend training sessions. They help investors set financial goals and come up with comprehensive plans, rather than simply try to sell particular investments.

BANK INVESTMENT REPRESENTATIVES—
A BROKER-IN-THE-BANK

For decades, consumers have listed banks as the most trusted source of financial products and advice. The primary reason is that bank savings and CDs are backed by the Federal Deposit Insurance Corporation (FDIC). Traditional bankers, however, knew little about investments, financial planning, or diversification; bank employees were basically trained in making loans, taking deposits, and issuing credit cards. Then a few years ago, banks decided to cross over the line and offer investments as well as savings. After all, banks already had the customers, so it was natural to hire and train brokers and advisors and to offer investment products. These bank advisors have the same securities licenses as other brokers, and many have gone through traditional Wall Street training programs. What I don't like is that banks use mostly third-party investment products, meaning investments manufactured outside the bank which utilize active investment management strategies and market timing. See Fig. 18–2.

INDEPENDENT FEE-ONLY FINANCIAL ADVISORS

There are many types of advisors, and many are very good, but if you want someone without a built-in conflict of interest, find a fee-only advisor or planner. These advisors have no incentive to sell you a financial product for the commission they'll personally gain. They still have access to all the mutual fund vendors and meet with representatives of many mutual fund companies. The main difference lies in how they are paid. The next step is to find one who understands and uses asset class investing. Here's a list of questions to ask and what you should be looking for:

What You Need to Know to Pick an Advisor

1. Education, any certifications with independent associations.
2. What percentage of their clients are fee-based? Sixty to 70 percent or more is favorable.
3. What investment vehicles do they offer—mutual funds, individually managed accounts, and/or annuities?
4. Three references to call. Fee-based advisors generally don't mind at all if you ask for references of existing clients.
5. Where do they get their research? Who's their provider?
6. Do they use asset class mutual funds?
7. Do they rebalance?

FIGURE 18–2 Summary of Bank Investment Programs

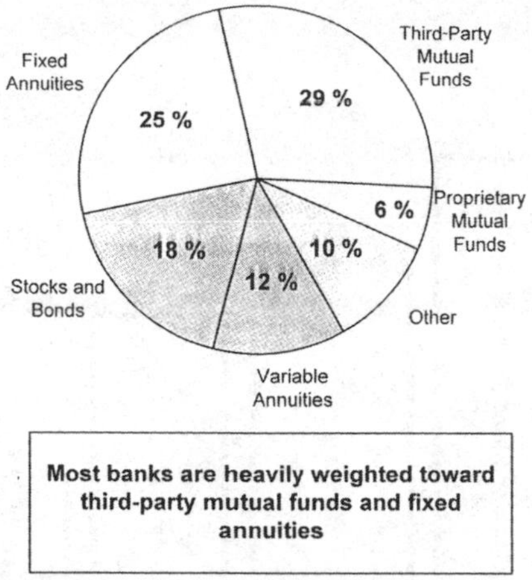
Fixed Annuities
25 %
Third-Party Mutual Funds
29 %
Proprietary Mutual Funds
6 %
Other
10 %
Variable Annuities
12 %
Stocks and Bonds
18 %
Most banks are heavily weighted toward third-party mutual funds and fixed annuities

Reprinted with permission by Russ Prince & Associates.

The professional designations in Fig. 18–3 confer some assurance of thorough training and high standards of conduct; but these designations only tell you the consultant has had some extra training. It's still up to you to do your own homework.

FINANCIAL PLANNING

Figure 18–3 presents the results of a survey of 4,212 consumers who were asked which type(s) of financial advisors they consider reliable for investment advice. Consumers considered financial planners most reliable for this type of advice in nearly all demographic segments, while insurance agents were considered least reliable.

You still need to be aware that more than 200,000 women and men call themselves financial planners, including accountants, attorneys, stockbrokers, insurance agents, self-styled money managers, credit counselors, and the Internet junkie down the street. But only a small number are registered certified financial planners,[2] a designation that guarantees a person has passed a rigorous set of tests in all parts of personal finance (investing, retirement and estate planning, taxes, insurance, and more) and has at least 3 years of experience in the field. This still doesn't mean the person understands modern portfolio management.

[2] Certified Financial Planners lists financial planners with a CFP designation. Call (303) 759-4900.

FIGURE 18–3   Most Reliable Source of Financial Advice

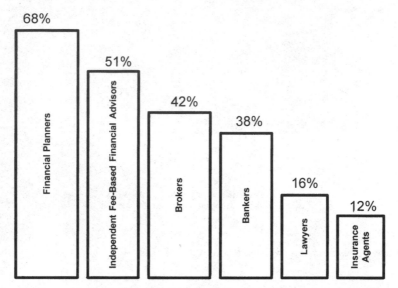

Reprinted with permission by Russ Prince & Associates.

Whatever the designation, many advisors get the bulk of their compensation through the commissions clients pay on the investments they purchase as a result of the planner's advice—just as stockbrokers do. This sets up a potential conflict of interest for them and a proceed-with-caution sign for you: Since the advisor or planner will profit most from high-load and high-commission items, it's tempting to recommend those items to you, regardless of whether they best suit your pocketbook and goals. It's best to derail the profit motive and pay a set fee for a planner's advice. If any potential advisor asks only how much you have or want to invest, head for the door.

- CFP (certified financial planner): designated by the Certified Financial Planner Board of Standards (based in Denver, Colorado), to those who complete an approved course, pass an examination, and meet work experience requirements.
- CPA/PFS (certified public accountant/personal financial specialist): designated by the American Institute of Certified Public Accountants (based in New York City) to CPAs who pass an examination and meet work experience requirements.
- CFC (chartered financial consultant): designated by the American College (Bryn Mawr, Pennsylvania) to those who complete a 10-part course of study.

Investment Analysis

- CFA (chartered financial analyst): Designated by the Association for Investment Management and Research (based in Charlottesville, Virginia) to those who pass a rigorous three-level examination (levels of examinations must be taken 1 year apart), each administered by the association and covering investment principles, asset valuation, and portfolio management. Candidates must also have 3 years of investment management experience.

- CIC (chartered investment counselor): designated by the Investment Counsel Association of America (based in Washington, District of Columbia) to those holding CFAs and currently working as investment counselors.

Investment Consulting

- CIMC (certified investment management consultant): designated by the Institute for Investment Management Consultants (based in Washington, District of Columbia, and Phoenix, Arizona), to Institute members who pass an examination and have at least 3 years' professional consulting financial experience.

- CIMS (certified investment management specialist): designated by the Institute for Investment Management Consultants to associate members who pass an examination and meet financial service work experience requirements.

Where to Turn

These professional organizations will provide you with select lists of financial planners in your area.

- For names of leading advisors around the country, contact RWB Advisory Services, Inc. at 1-800-366-7266 or email jbowen@rwb.com.

- The Institute of Certified Financial Planners lists financial planners with a CFP designation. Call (303) 759-4900.

- LINC (Licensed Independent Network of CPA Financial Planners) lists members who are CPSA/PFS fee-only planners in public accounting firms. Call (800) 737-2727.

The exact role that an advisor plays is up to you. The more hands-on help you want, the more you may end up paying in fees and commissions. You may opt for an advisor who analyzes your financial condition, strategizes with you on the best route forward, and sends you on your way—in other words, who empowers you to take action on your own.

One of the advantages of being a financial trade writer is that I get to read these investment trade journals and see these studies. The following is a list of my favorite investment trade magazines. I suggest reading one. They could help you find reliable information rather than just noise.

These are magazines that brokers and advisors read.

On Wall Street
Securities Data Publishing
40 West 57th Street 11th floor
New York, NY 10019
(800) 455-5845

Financial Planning
Subscription Department
PO Box 5186
Pittsfield, MA 01203-9622
$79 per year

Registered Representative
Subscription Department
PO Box 3270
Northbrook, IL 60065-9566
(949) 851-2220 ext. 220

Investment News
Subscription Department
PO Box 07944
Detroit, MI 48207-9923
(800) 678-9595

Financial Advisory Practice
RIA Group
31 St. James Ave.
Boston, MA 02116-4112
$145 per year

The Journal of Investing
Subscription Department
488 Madison Avenue
New York, NY 10126-0796
$160 per year (212) 303-3300

19

HOW TO ANALYZE AN INVESTMENT

The fastest way to lose your money is to follow a trend.

I HAVE BEEN SAYING THROUGHOUT THIS BOOK that you can't beat the stock market by buying and selling hot stock picks. I don't want to discourage you from buying and holding an individual stock long-term, especially stock in the company you work for. But your core investment strategy shouldn't include the growth of that stock. You might invest in an individual company and hold it for years, and the company could go bankrupt. No one can predict the future, but if you built your core investment program with asset class mutual funds, your program would still be in place.

THE STOCK MARKET
Okay, if you still insist on wanting something to watch, let me give you an indicator I pay attention to.

In trying to guess what the stock market's going to do, most investors don't look past short-term indicators. But as you've been reading, consistent results come from a long-term holding strategy. So what can you watch that may indicate the future of the stock market? Well, nothing gives you a better long-term indicator of economic health than the relationship of a country's spending patterns to its deficit.

The national deficit is one of the least understood economic concepts, yet it's one of the best indicators of long-term economic health. You may be wondering, *Who owns the national debt?* The media have led many to believe that the Japanese do. *Wrong!* According to Dr. Bob Goodman, senior economic advisor for Putnam Investments, over 80 percent of the total outstanding national debt is owned by people in the United States in the form of bonds. People in the United States consider the bonds they buy as assets, not liabilities—and 80 percent of the interest on the national debt goes right back to U.S. taxpayers as income.

The next concern is the size of the deficit. It's not so much the actual size of the debt that is critical, but rather whether our economy is growing faster than the debt is accumulating. That's what you want to focus on. Think in terms of your own income. As long as your income is growing faster than your debt, you're going to come out ahead even if your debt grows.

The total government debt just after World War II, 60 years ago, was around $120 billion, while our annual gross domestic product (GDP) was $100 billion. Our government, therefore, owed 1.2 years' worth of GDP. Today our debt is $5 trillion, 40 times higher than after World War II, but our GDP is now over $7 trillion, so the national debt represents only 70 percent of the GDP. That's only 70 percent of a year's income versus 120 percent back in 1946. It's important to watch where the ratios are and if they're going down—which they have been.

Today our government is taking in more than it's spending. Recently the Congressional Budget Office estimated that the total federal budget surplus should amount to around $1.55 trillion over the next decade. That's how much more the government expects to take in from taxes than it expects to spend on government services. That's an annual surplus of over $60 billion. While that money may burn a hole in the government's pocket, one way or another, it's a good long-term indicator to watch.

The general trend in the stock market for the past 60 years has been upward and is likely to continue to climb. At times during that upward march there will be downturns—and that's inevitable and normal. A 200-point drop on the Dow, today at 8,000, is a drop less than 2 percent, and that shouldn't scare anyone into selling funds. Instead of panicking when the stock market drops, you should hold on for the long term. Take advantage of the dips by adding to your holdings.

For more information, read John Maynard Keynes' 1936 book *The General Theory of Employment, Interest and Money,* Prometheus Bound.

I once placed a huge order of an individual stock. It was General Electric, 55,000 shares, and it amounted to over $3 million. The stock was part of an estate left to the university I was working with. What was amazing was that the person who left it was not part of a rich family or the head of a company, but a secretary to a bank president. Years ago, her employer gave her shares of Utah Construction Company as part of her bonus and told her to hold onto it. She kept accumulating the shares, and the stock split more than 1,200 times before General Electric bought the company.

There are three basic concepts that Wall Street uses to analyze an investment—technical, fundamental, and trend analysis.

Technical analysis is essentially the making and interpreting of stock charts. Technical analysis basically ignores the fundamentals. The people who swear by technical analysis are often referred to as *technicians* or *chartists*. The chartists believe that the market is only 10 percent logical and 90 percent psychological, so the charts are like a crystal ball to them. But 90 percent of Wall Street security analysts consider themselves fundamentalists, and chartists are not very accurate.

Technicians deal with charts and patterns from the past. They analyze current price movements and chart patterns, then relate them to price movements and patterns from the past. By applying mathematical charting methods from the past to the present, they draw conclusions about future buying and selling. The problem with technical analysis is that it is too technical and ignores the all-important cultural factors. If human activities really could be reduced to mathematical patterns, I'd be writing a book about technical analysis. But of course, they can't, so I'm not.

Fundamental analysis looks at all the known facts about a particular investment, including external factors that technical analysis often overlooks. These external factors include cultural and political trends, general investment areas and industry groups, the future of inflation and interest rates, and investment cycles. Internal factors include earnings per share, the track record of management, the price/earnings ratio, any new technical breakthroughs, cost of production, valuable contracts, and worker morale.

Few investors ever bother to perform an independent investigation of a company, although fundamental analysis can be a very useful tool.

Here are the basic points of fundamental analysis:

1. *Management.* One of the key factors that doesn't appear in all the dense small print of a prospectus—but is a proper study for fundamental analysis—is the ability and integrity of a company's management. In the last chapter, we suggested that you get in touch with the people whom the managers have supplied as references.

     a. Do the managers own stock in the company they are managing—
if so, how much? If they don't invest in their own offering, you'd
be foolish to do so. (Be wary of *dilution.* You can find information about dilution in the prospectus under the heading "Dilution."
If you find dilution, it might be wise to investigate further. Dilution
is not evidence of fraud or wrong-doing, but it is a red flag. A
high degree of dilution is almost always a bad sign.)

     b. *Management compensation.* Compare to that in similar com-
panies. Some U.S. American managers tend to be grossly over-
paid in comparison to their foreign counterparts.

     c. *Experience.* In general, you should look for management with
at least 10 years' experience in the business.

2. *Size.* Look at the size of the company. This appears in the balance
sheet. The smaller the size, the greater the risk involved.

3. *Good balance sheet.* Look at the company's debt. This is also in the
balance sheet. Preferred stocks and debentures—"senior" securities—are just another form of debt, so be on the lookout for them.
In the 1980s, with seemingly unlimited credit available, many companies were restructured. Some of these companies, with their atten-
dant heavy debt loads, will be at a competitive disadvantage against
high-quality growth companies carrying relatively light debt. Those
companies with sizable debt service obligations will be focused on
short-term cash flow (profits, rather than market share gain). A focus
on short-term cash flow can be inimical to strategic planning.

4. *Dominance.* Look for companies with limited competition.

5. *Return on equity.* The return on equity tells an investor how efficiently her or his money is being used. A minimum of 15 percent is
recommended.

6. *Reasonable price/earnings ratio.* The higher the P/E ratio, the higher the risk. We recommend companies with a P/E ratio at, or below,
the current market multiple. A good benchmark is the S&P 500,
which carries a P/E ratio of 13 times.

7. *Simplified annual report.* The simpler the better. No CPA gobbledy-
gook.

I'm going to skip trend analysis, since it is really a big waste of your time.
Suffice it to say it's really just another form of market timing.

Since we are on the subject of individual securities, let's look at other
kinds of investments and how they work. I'm not recommending them, you
just need to understand them.

CHAPTER 20

OTHER TYPES
OF ASSETS

I AM NOT SUGGESTING these assets for the first time investor, but you should know what they are and how they work.

What are *hard assets?* Hard assets are sold as defensive-type investments and would do best during bear markets or during times of high inflation, neither of which holds now. They are also not liquid, which means you may have a hard time getting your money out if you need it.

All tangibles are inflation hedges. Their value tends to flourish during times of soaring inflation, and volatile interest rates languish when the economy is stable. Owners can make money on their investments only when they sell, with some exceptions in real estate. Investors should plan to hold their assets for the long term, sometimes as long as 10 to 20 years. However, to compensate for their illiquidity, tangibles appreciate tax-free during the years you hold them.

Each tangible investment offers some advantages and disadvantages. Real estate is good for the investor who wants to build personal financial security while curbing the tax bite; or for the investor who has little or no capital and who is seeking a tax-deductible shelter for other income. It's generally a safe, conservative investment, and one on which banks will often lend up to 95 percent of its value.

REAL ESTATE

During the 1970s, when inflation was rampaging in a way the United States had never before experienced, real estate investment became the darling of investors and speculators alike. Interest rates lagged behind the inflationary upticks, mortgage money was available, and repayment could be made in ever-cheaper dollars. In fact, tax savings subsidized out-of-pocket costs.

Euphoric investors caught the scent of fast profits and snapped up properties regardless of costs, and often regardless of quality. The prevailing wisdom dictated that inflation would inevitably push prices higher, and another investor would willingly pay an even fatter price later on. This delivered nice capital gains to countless sellers. In those glorious days, everyone investing in real estate became an instant financial genius.

Of course, the bubble burst, as it always does. The real estate frenzy slowed to a crawl in the early 1990s, as inflation fell. Prices remained high, but there were precious few buyers.

REAL ESTATE SYNDICATION

On the surface, real estate syndication looks like an ideal vehicle for those who'd like to join the parade but don't care for hands-on exposure. Such deals *need* inflationary pressures to boost profits at resale. Most never pan out.

The syndicator generally assumes the role of general partner, meaning he or she manages the properties, collects rent, and eventually sells them. Theoretically, the general partner's risk is unlimited, but the general partner usually puts no cash into the project and receives an acquisition fee, often a management fee, a share of the cash flow from the properties, and a share of any capital gains realized at sale. Real estate is subject to cyclical swings. I would avoid this type of investment.

Real Estate Investment Trusts

Real estate investment trusts (REITs) are like a mutual fund of real estate investments. A typical REIT invests in different types of property, such as shopping centers, apartments, and other rental buildings.

REITs are a specialized form of equity that allows investors to own a portion of a group of real estate properties, although most investors think of them as an alternative to bonds. REITs have become increasingly popular over the past decade. Granted special tax status by the Internal Revenue Service, REITs pay out at least 95 percent of their earnings in the form of dividends to shareholders, often offering healthy dividend yields of the same magnitude as bonds. Even better, as REITs acquire more property and increase the value of the properties they own, the value of the equity increases as well, providing a nice total return.

REITs trade as securities on the major stock exchanges. You can research and purchase individual REITs. Even better is to buy a mutual fund that invests in a diversified mixture of REITs. Some real estate writers have criticized REITs. REITs are a good alternative for people who want to invest in real estate without all the hassles and headaches that come with directly owning and managing rental property. You can easily buy REITs in a retirement account investment (you can't do so with rental properties). For more information on REITs, check the Web site of the National Association of REITs (NAREIT).

FUTURES
Most futures transactions involve exchange of contracts on goods not yet produced. Originally, all commodities were agricultural products. Today, they include currencies, petroleum, metals, cotton, and lumber.

STOCK DERIVATIVES—OPTIONS AND FUTURES
Options and futures are *derivative* securities, meaning their value is derived from that of another security or commodity. Options and futures both are very risky because they often carry an incredible amount of leverage. For instance, each options contract on an individual stock controls 100 shares of that stock for a fraction of the stock's current value. This can make for huge upward moves, but this is offset by the risk of losing 100 percent of the money put into the option. If an investor owns an option and the underlying stock is not within the given price range within the given time period, the option expires, worthless.

COLLECTIBLES, ART, AND ANTIQUES
Art, antiques, and collectibles constitute a rather difficult sector of the investment world—difficult because of the lack of liquidity and the subjective nature of this type of investment. The best advice is to buy art you enjoy and keep it out of your investment planning.

INVESTMENT GEMSTONES
To look at a gem is to know its worth. For centuries, people have understood that the beauty and rarity that separate precious stones from mere rocks also make them real stores of value. Boasting a track record of appreciation that spans all recorded history, gems have been a "given," set against the variable of myriad failed get-rich-quick investment vehicles. The time-tested appeal of precious stones virtually guarantees future worth, regardless of the ravages of short-term market swings.

Investment-grade gemstones may be diamonds, other precious stones such as emeralds or rubies, or semiprecious stones, perhaps topaz or tourmaline. These stones will always have some intrinsic worth, but that does not mean that the changing demands of the marketplace will not influence their price. The market for both diamonds and colored stones can and does fluctuate dramatically, following swings in the overall economy and the weighting of supply and demand. Like most tangibles, gems tend to flourish during periods of soaring inflation and volatile interest rates, and languish in stability.

The effects of this kind of speculative fever took center stage during the last bout with inflation during the late 1970s and early 1980s. Investors scurrying to find investments capable of retaining their worth sent the price of a one-carat flawless diamond from $20,000 in 1979 to more than $60,000 by 1980. By 1981, when inflation began to cool, the same stone commanded only $16,000. The 16.9 percent compounded annual rate of return generated by diamonds during the high-flying inflationary years from 1976 to 1980 plummeted to zero during the disinflation of 1982 to 1984.

These blips in the performance of gems cannot detract from their long-term potential—and that is what the investor must keep in view. For example, even with these sharp declines, certain diamonds enjoyed a price increase of 1,100 percent from 1970 to 1983, while rubies rose 650 percent during the same period and blue sapphires advanced 300 percent.

By definition, a mineral must possess beauty, rarity, and durability and must be in demand in order to be considered a gem. While rarity and durability are fairly easy to determine, judgments about beauty and demand are much more arbitrary. Discovery of new gem deposits also influences the market. As a result, gems are subject to fads and tend to rise and fall according to the current vogue.

Diamonds account for about 80 percent of all gemstones sold today. For that reason, they remain the blue-chip investment among precious stones. The problem, again, is that there is no efficient market for diamonds. I have a hard time with any investment that has four or five different prices—retail, wholesale, below wholesale, and investment wholesale. *Warning!* This whole area requires a lot of study and should be at the top of your investment pyramid.

NUMISMATIC COINS

These are defensive instruments. Coin profits usually run higher during periods of inflation, but don't try to sell them when the market drops. If you buy coins, buy them because you love to collect them.

SUGGESTED READING

- *Gemstone Investing Fact Sheet,* Federal Trade Commission (free), Room 130, Sixth St. and Pennsylvania, N.W., Washington, DC 20580.
- *How to Buy and Sell Gems,* by Benjamin Zucker, Times Books, Three Park Ave., New York, NY 10016. (This book is available in most libraries, but is now out of print.)
- *Colored Stone Aesthetics,* by John Rouse, Ge-Odyssey Gem Publications, 7271 Garden Grove Blvd., Garden Grove, CA 92641.
- *The Gemstone Identifier,* by Walter Greenbaum, Acro Publishing, 215 Park Ave. South, New York, NY 10003.

Tangibles have risks, as do all investments. Unless you choose to speculate on a high-flying fad, you risk only that your investment will underperform the overall economy. The main point to remember about tangible investments is that they are risky and may not be a wise choice for the first time investor.

21

HOW TO READ
A PROSPECTUS

A JARGON-FILLED MUTUAL FUND PROSPECTUS may not be enthralling, but it's a must-read for would-be first time investors. It describes investment objectives, strategies, and risks, and it's required by the federal government as a protection for investors. Any misstatements or omissions can lead to stiff penalties, thus the tendency for legalese.

Start by identifying the type of asset class mutual fund you are interested in, and request a prospectus by calling or writing the fund or asking a broker or financial planner. When you get it, check the date to make sure it is current—such documents must be updated at least once per year.

Here's what to look for in a mutual fund prospectus:

Minimums. If the minimum amount required to open an account is too high for you, read no further.

Investment objective. At the core of the prospectus is a description of the fund's investments and the portfolio manager's philosophy. The objective should outline what types of securities the fund buys and the policies regarding the quality of those investments. If the fund has more than 25 percent of its assets in one industry or holds bonds rated below investment quality, these policies must be included in the prospectus.

A global equity fund, e.g., earns a high level of total return through investments in world capital markets. A typical balanced fund strives to obtain income equally with capital growth, while the investment objective of a long-term municipal bond fund is to preserve capital by seeking a high level of interest income exempt from federal income tax.

Performance. This bottom-line information on how funds have fared over the last decade shows you what you would have earned in per-share dividends and capital gains distributions, and any increase or decrease in the value of that share during the year. The portfolio turnover rate reveals how actively the fund trades securities. The higher the turnover, the greater the fund's brokerage costs.

Risk. Different investors can tolerate various risk levels. In this section of the prospectus, the fund should describe the potential for risk. For instance, a fund that invests in only one portion of the economy may offer greater risk than a highly diversified fund, while a fund that invests in well-established companies may be less risky than one that favors start-up companies.

Other risks are associated with certain types of funds or securities. Bond funds are susceptible to interest rate changes, while fixed-income savings and investment vehicles are subject to inflation risks.

Fees. Management and accounting fees and the cost of printing and mailing reports to shareholders are internal charges that should be evaluated. Generally, a company that keeps its expenses—excluding sales fees—at 1 percent or less of its assets is considered a low-cost fund. A fund whose expenses are above 1.5 percent of its assets is viewed as high-cost.

Fees are required to be summarized in a table in the front of the prospectus. Other charges to consider are minimum fees for subsequent investments or fees for switching from one fund to another in the same family.

This section will tell you if features such as check writing or automatic investing are available.

Management. When you're putting money in a mutual fund, you're paying for professional management. Evaluate investment philosophy and to find out whether the portfolio is managed by an individual or committee.

Buying or selling shares. This information details how to get in and out of a fund and whether there's a charge for redeeming shares.

Additional information, such as securities in the fund's portfolio at the end of its fiscal year, is included in a Statement of Additional Information, also called part B of the prospectus. Funds must provide this information free on request.

Other tools to evaluate mutual funds include news accounts and the fund's annual report. Make sure you are comparing *apples to apples*. Magazines measure funds during different time periods and use different criteria, which could affect a fund's ranking.

The good news is that a movement is afoot to simplify the language used in prospectuses. The Securities and Exchange Commission (SEC) is recommending the creation of a clearly written one-page summary to accompany these documents. The SEC is demanding the use of plain English. The new rules are going to target the fund booklets. Hopefully, by the time you're reading this book, the Securities and Exchange Commission and the mutual fund companies will have adopted their new language, called *plain English*. The SEC has adopted rules that will force mutual funds to ditch the legalese and translate their prospectuses—the disclosure booklets most people toss in the trash unread—into easily understood language.

Also, fund companies may distribute a streamlined profile that includes a mutual fund's vital statistics. This is a victory for consumers, at least for those who care enough to follow through and do their homework. Both documents will contain a 10-year bar chart, a fund performance, a table comparing performance to market index, and a description of the risk involved in the investment. A three- to six-page profile also will summarize the fund's fees, risks, and investment objectives at the beginning of the document.

There's one significant difference between the two new documents. Fund companies must begin distributing the plain English prospectuses in 1998, which is good news. With more than the estimated 6,000 mutual funds to choose from, many investors feel overwhelmed when comparing possible investments, particularly when they have to wade through prospectuses that make no sense.

A survey by the Investment Company Institute, the mutual fund industry's trade group, discovered that only one-half of the fund shareholders consult a prospectus before investing. The SEC is going to coach the writers on how to translate common jargon, spot when they're writing in a passive voice, and find a strong verb that lies hidden in the text.

Now, for you Internet investors whose printers have been clogged after trying to download a 20-page prospectus, this should be a relief. Soon you will be able to make side-by-side comparisons of different funds. Information will be more visible in a shorter document available on-line.

22

HOW TO PAY FOR YOUR CHILDREN'S COLLEGE!

THE BEST WAY TO PAY FOR COLLEGE is to motivate your kids to achieve a high grade-point average for scholarship eligibility. Begin searching the Internet for grants and scholarships when your children first start high school. Find an advocate or counselor at their school who can alert and steer them toward scholarships. I found that many states have *college fee waiver programs* for children and dependents of service-connected or service-related disabled veterans. Because of the Purple Heart I earned in Vietnam, both my children can attend any of the California universities or state colleges for free. That's a major savings. Most of these college fee waiver programs are not public knowledge, so it takes a little research that is well worth it. Check with your state Veterans' Affairs office if you believe you may be eligible.

In addition to scholarships, grants, or waivers, you may still need extra money. And providing a college education today (and even more so tomorrow) can cost as much as buying a house. It's going to require some careful advance planning. [For more information, call the Federal Student Aid Information Center, (800) 333-4636.] See Fig. 22–1 to look at the value of education.

There has been a shift in the balance in federal student aid (see Fig. 22–2). This trend does not seem likely to reverse anytime soon. Moreover, with government assistance to higher education being cut back and current

FIGURE 22–1   The Value of Education

Median Weekly Earnings of Full-Time Wage and Salary Workers 25 Years and Over, by Educational Attainment

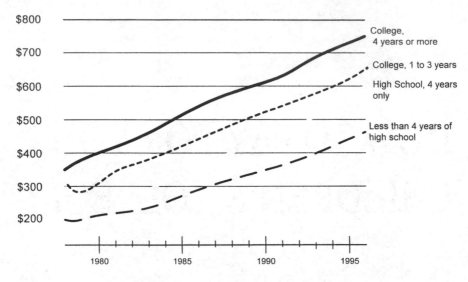

Year	Less than 4 years of high school*	High school, 4 years only*	College, 1 to 3 years*	College, 4 years or more*
1980	$222	$266	$304	$376
1982	248	302	351	438
1984	263	323	382	486
1986	278	344	409	525
1988	288	368	430	585
1990	304	386	476	639
1992	312	404	485	697
1994	307	421	499	733
1995	309	432	508	747
1996	317	443	518	758

- *Since 1992, data on educational attainment have been based on the 'highest diploma or degree received' rather than the 'number of years of school completed.' Data for 1994 and beyond are not directly comparable with data from earlier years.

Source: U.S. Bureau of Labor Statistics

tax law changes, it will become increasingly difficult for schools to raise money from private sources. Thus, planning for college costs means planning to hit an even higher target.

I have provided a college cost worksheet (Fig. 22–6) later that is designed to help you set up a personalized action plan for meeting your family's edu-

FIGURE 22–2   The Shifting Balance of Federal Student Aid, 1975 to 1995

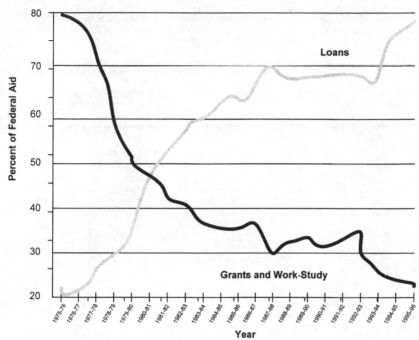

Source: U.S. Bureau of Labor Statistics.

cational costs. When you complete it, you will have the basic information you will need to plot your course.

HOW TO MEET THE COST
Step 1
Estimate how much you will need. To estimate total college costs (see Fig. 22–3), complete step 1 of the worksheet. The annual average increase in school costs may turn out to be higher or lower than the 6 percent projected.

Step 2
Find the future value of your current savings. To estimate how compounding can increase the value of your current savings by the time your child enters college, complete step 2 of the worksheet.

Step 3
Before you become unduly alarmed over the gap between your savings and the amount of money you will need, remember that there are a wide variety of financial and student aid programs available. Each school has its own

FIGURE 22–3   Projected Total Four-Year Costs of Attending College

To determine the four-year cost of attending college, find the year your student will be starting college in the left column. Then read across the column to find the projected total costs (including tuition, room and board, books and other expenses) for a student entering college in that year.

Chart assumes 6% annual increases of college costs. The savings compounding factor and monthly investment factor assume 8% pre-tax return on all investments. Based on 1998-99 costs projected by The American Council on Education.

Year Student Will Begin College	Public College	Private College	Savings Compounding Factor (See Step2)	Monthly Investment Factor (See Step 4)
1998	$48,377	$98,015	2.00	158.48
1999	$51,279	$103,895	2.16	184.17
2000	$54,356	$110,129	2.33	211.98
2001	$57,617	$116,737	2.52	242.11
2002	$61,074	$123,741	2.72	274.74
2003	$64,739	$131,166	2.94	310.08
2004	$68,623	$139,036	3.17	348.35
2005	$72,741	$147,378	3.43	389.79
2006	$77,105	$156,220	3.70	434.68
2007	$81,731	$165,594	4.00	483.29
2008				
2009				
2010				
2011				
2012				
2013				
2014				
2015				

Source: T. Rowe Price Associates, Inc.

way of deciding whether a student qualifies for aid, and the federal government has its own criteria for rewarding federal grants.

Figure 22–4 will give you a rough idea how much help you might be eligible for today. If you expect to finance some of your educational costs through outside sources, complete step 3 of the worksheet.

Step 4
Complete steps 1 through 3 of the worksheet. If line 10 shows that you will have expenses which won't be covered either by your current savings or by outside aid, then you will need to add to your savings between now and when your child enters school. To estimate how much you will need to save each month to reach your target amount, complete step 4 of the worksheet.

Step 5
Now you know how much money you will need to invest. But which investment should you choose? Your time horizon, more than any other factor, should dictate your choice because it is intimately linked to investment risk and return. Figure 22–5 shows appropriate investment strategies based on your time horizon.

FIGURE 22–4   How Much Will Financial Aid Cover Today?

Estimated percentage of average 1998-99 private college costs paid for by financial aid.

		Annual Family Pre-Tax Income	
Total Family Assets*	**$20,000**	**$40,000**	**$60,000**
$40,000	94%	61%	15%
60,000	90%	52%	6%
80,000	86%	43%	0%
100,000	81%	34%	0%

*Includes equity in home (estimated value of home less unpaid mortgage).

Note: The percentages of college costs covered by financial aid are based on approximate expected parental contributions toward 1998-99 college expenses (for a family of four) from *Peterson's College Money Handbook,* and assume an average 1998-99 private college cost of $12,500.

Source: T. Rowe Price Associates, Inc.

FIGURE 22–5   Timing is the Key to Your Investment Strategy

Years Until Student Begins School	Appropriate Risk/Reward Level	Investment Strategy
More than 5	High	Invest in an index mutual fund to build maximum assets and outpace inflation of educational costs. Don't worry now about short-term ups and downs – time will tend to smooth them out. Long-term growth should be your primary goal, and the longer your time horizon, the more aggressive you can be.
3-5	Moderate	Choose a more conservative growth and income stock fund or higher yield bond fund to continue building assets while reducing overall price volatility.
0-2	Low	Switch to a taxable or tax-exempt money market or short-term bond fund which earns safe, steady income and will provide easy access to your money when you need it.

Source: T. Rowe Price Associates, Inc.

The College Board publishes the latest cost figures each fall in *College Cost Book.* To obtain a current catalog or more information, call (212) 713-8150 or write to College Board Publications, P.O. Box 886, New York, NY 10101-0886.

Two other excellent sources on financial aid are

● *Don't Miss Out, The Ambitious Student's Guide to Financial Aid,* published by Octameron Press, P.O. Box 3437, Alexandria, VA 22302, or call (703) 828-1882

● Peterson's *1989 College Money Handbook,* Petersons Guide, 1997, 760 pp, available at your local bookstore. Or, for a free copy of T. Rowe Price's *Asset Mix Worksheet* call (800) 638-5660.

The best way to pay for college is to start now teaching your kids how to invest and get motivated and to help them find scholarships, college aid,

FIGURE 22–6   College Cost Worksheet

Facts You Will Need	Student Data	Special Instructions
Step 1 1. Student's name. 2. Year student will start college. 3. Student's total 4-year college expenses.	1. _____ 2. _____ 3. _____	(3) On Fig. 22–3, find the year student will start college, the read across to find corresponding cost figure.
Step 2 4. Amount you have already saved for college expenses. 5. Savings Compounding. 6. Estimated value of your savings by the time student starts college. 7. Remaining expenses not covered by your current savings.	4. _____ 5. _____ 6. _____ 7. _____	(5) On Fig. 22–3, read across from the year the student will start college to find the appropriate Savings Compounding Factor. This multiplier estimates how much your savings could grow by the time the student enters college. (6) Multiply Line 4 by Line 5. (7) Subtract Line 6 from Line 5. If you have no current savings, enter amount from Line 3.
Step 3 8. Amount of total expenses (Line 3) which may be met through financial aid and/or loans, gifts, or other outside sources. 9. Estimated total dollar amount you expect from all outside sources. 10. Net expenses not covered by current savings or outside sources.	8. _____ 8b. _____ 9. _____ 10. _____	(8) Use Fig. 22–4 to estimate the percent of financial aid you could expect today, based on your current income and assets. Multiply this percent by Line 3, and enter result on Line 8a. (8b) Enter dollar amount of any loans, gifts, or other outside sources on Line 8b. (9) Add Line 8a to Line 8b. (Enter zero on Line 9 if you do not expect help from any outside sources.) (10) Subtract Line 9 from Line 7.
Step 4 11. Monthly Investment Factor. This will help you estimate how much you will need to put away in equal monthly installments to meet total expenses. 12. Amount you should invest each month until September of the year this student starts college.	11. _____ 12. _____	(11) On Fig. 22–3, read from the year the student will start college to find the appropriate Monthly Investment Factor. (12) Divide Line 10 by Line 11.

Source: T. Rowe Price Associates, Inc.

and grants. Use the new educational IRA. One easy way to make contributions is through an automatic investment plan. Investments grow tax-deferred. Earnings are withdrawn tax-free if they are used to pay for college costs, and the beneficiary has until age 30 to do so. Anyone, including nonrelatives, can invest money for a child. The only drawbacks are that contributions are not tax-deductible and educational IRAs are not available to high-income individuals or couples. And there is a 10 percent penalty if the child doesn't go to college. The good news is you can transfer the account to a younger sibling who will.

23

PUTTING IT
ALL TOGETHER

BY NOW, YOU MUST REALIZE investing doesn't require a master's degree or five undisturbed hours in a brokerage firm and a lot of money. The idea of investing has become a lot less mysterious and intimidating. It's just a process to follow. You now have the knowledge that will enable you to achieve your financial goals.

Following is my quick-start plan to get you going—safely and intelligently.

PRINCIPLE 1—PAY YOURSELF FIRST AND ELIMINATE DEBT

Pay yourself before anybody else! As selfish as that might sound, it is a *sound* approach. Perhaps the most important piece of advice is to pay down your consumer debt and then pay the equivalent of those monthly interest payments to your investment program.

PRINCIPLE 2—GET STARTED NOW AND BUILD A CORE "SAVING" PROGRAM

Overcome the hurdle of getting started. Start small, but be consistent. Put the money into a savings vehicle where you can't spend it. You'll be encouraged by how quickly your weekly or monthly contributions add up. Challenge yourself to increase the amount frequently. Become a saver first, then build that savings into an investment program.

If you think you can't find a large amount of money to invest, you can start out by saving just $6 per day. Take just $6 per day (the cost of lunch), invest, and reinvest it in a no-load index fund compounding over time at 16 percent. In 5 years, this account would be worth $19,000; in 10 years, $60,000; in 15 years, $150,000; in 20 years, $350,000. And in 25 years, this account would be worth just under $1 million.

PRINCIPLE 3—EVALUATE YOUR FUTURE NEEDS
Determine your financial and personal needs and time frames. The most important thing is to match your investment program to your own personality and implement a clear plan. Define them in writing.

PRINCIPLE 4—BUILD YOUR INVESTMENT PROGRAM
During the 1990s, we experienced an explosive advance in bond and stock prices, perhaps unprecedented in this century. Almost every investment method and recommendation made money. But for a sustained investing experience, copy the investment masters. Follow the principles developed in modern portfolio theory. Now taught in virtually every graduate business school in the country, modern portfolio theory instructs investors, no matter what size their wealth, how to achieve higher returns through asset allocation while minimizing risk by diversifying investments.

PRINCIPLE 5—ELIMINATE INVESTMENT NOISE
Look past all the hype and maintain realistic expectations. Don't panic and sell if your mutual fund prices go down. In fact, it's wise to expect fluctuations and ride them out. Use a drop in the stock market as an opportunity to average your cost downward (dollar cost averaging). Upgrade your knowledge about investing. Education is the key to simplifying all the investment advice and products available and to knowing how to apply them to the investor's personal situation.

PRINCIPLE 6—ADD TIME!
Become a long-term investor. Lengthen time horizons for investments. The problem is that every investor has expectations of having immediate performance, and those expectations are not compatible with being a long-term investor. Instead of running down the road in hopes of finding the pot of gold at the end of a rainbow, why not be standing where the next rainbow appears?

PRINCIPLE 7—DIVERSIFY
Diversification enhances returns. To the extent that you take advantage of effective diversification, you will increase the expected rate of return of your

portfolio over time. We learned from Harry Markowitz, a Nobel Prize winner in economics, that while almost all diversification is good, there is effective diversification and ineffective diversification. If your investments move together, then this is ineffective diversification. It's as if you didn't diversify. If your investments do not move in tandem, you can accomplish effective diversification of your portfolio. This is accomplished because the overall risk of the portfolio can be less than the average risk of its components.

PRINCIPLE 8—TEACH YOUR FAMILY ABOUT INVESTING
Providing for family is at the heart of everyone's financial concerns. But who said it was up to you alone? Don't operate in a vacuum, leaving those you care about in the dark. There is no better way to provide for your loved ones' future than to teach them to help themselves. Not only does this enpower them as participants, but also it gives them a better appreciation of your efforts.

PRINCIPLE 9—BUILD ASSET CLASS PORTFOLIOS, ONE ASSET CLASS AT A TIME
Most investors utilize active management and do not stay invested for the long term. When you compare what the average investor might have experienced from 1976 through 1993 with the results if that person had utilized the asset class lessons in this book, it will provide an effective starting point to see how the asset class strategy can add value to your portfolio. See Fig. 23-1.

GETTING A QUICK START ON YOUR OWN ASSET CLASS PORTFOLIO

1. *Identify how much money* you can leave untouched for 5 years in an investment portfolio except for emergencies or income needs. This is the dollar amount you should start with.
2. *Consider using one of the model portfolios* that most closely aligns with the risk you want to take as your target investment allocation.
3. *Select the asset class mutual funds* that best incorporate the concepts that we have discussed on a cost-effective basis. In Part Two, I've listed many of the currently available retail asset class funds.
4. *Global diversification.* It does no good to have all your money in a single country's equity market because those investments on average will tend to move together. When the U.S. market periodically moves down, it tends to take most investors with it. With the introduction of international asset classes, you can provide for greater protection against risk than with an efficient all-U.S. portfolio and increase expected returns.

FIGURE 23-1   Asset Class Combining

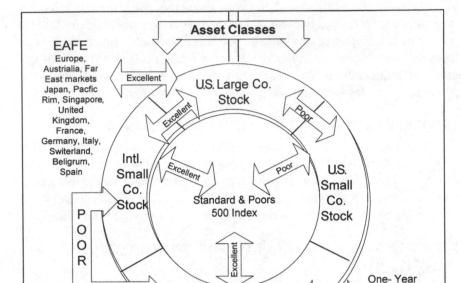

5. *Find an investment advisor who understands asset class investing.* It
    is unlikely that one mutual fund family will have all the asset class
    mutual funds that you will need for your portfolio. For many
    investors, having a qualified investment advisor on their financial
    team, to make sure they stay on track, will add substantial value.
    Financial planners, brokers, or finanical advisors will make rebal-
    ancing much easier to complete.

6. *Rebalance at least annually.* By systematically rebalancing your
    original portfolio at least annually, you will gradually sell those
    asset classes that have gone up while buying those that currently
    have lower returns. This approach eliminates the negative results of
    being driven by emotions.

There we are, we're done. Some parts of the book were very difficult to write without getting into the mathematics and deeper explanations, but the idea was to expose you to these new concepts and get you thinking that you can win at this investing game. Use these steps to build a secure retirement.

So that's it. We've covered the basics of being a first time investor, but really we've taken you to a much higher level. We're trying to get through the noise and make it as easy and simple as possible, as well as easy to understand. See Figure 23-2, a calendar with important dates and the investment steps I put together to keep you on track. Best of luck!

FIGURE 23-2   Here's Your Investment Calendar

TO DO:

Pay for holiday gifts by check or cash. That way, you'll spend only what you have on hand and slash your finance charges, which can cost between 12 percent and 18 percent annually.

Open a Keogh by December 31 if you have self-employment income. Contribute 25 percent or up to $30,000 of adjusted self-employment earnings, whichever is less.

✓ **Donate appreciated securities instead of cash.** You'll get the full value of your charitable tax deduction without taking a capital gain.

Step One. Start Your Core Savings Plan. Identify how much money you can leave untouched except for emergencies or income needs.

TO DO:

✓ **Draw up a budget plan for the new year.**

✓ **Pay off consumer debt.** Pay yourself first.

✓ **Use a large manila envelope for saving your 1099 and W-2 forms** and other tax documents as they arrive in the mail. The more orderly your preparations, the more likely that you (or your accountant) will find all your deductions.

✓ **File your quarterly estimated tax** due January 15, using Form 1040-ES.

✓ **Step Two: Start Your Investing Program.** Identify how much money you can leave untouched for 5 years in an investment portfolio. This amount is the dollar amount you should get started with.

TO DO:

Step Three: Decide The Risk You Are Willing To Take. You should decide on what risk you are willing to take, based on the assumption that the next 2 years could be the same as the 1973-1974 period.

✓ **Reduce your withholding tax.** Refile Form W-4 with your employer and take all possible exemptions and deductions; the goal is to pay your exact tax in 1999 and not get a refund, which is simply an interest-free loan to the federal government. Invest the additional income on a monthly basis all year long.

TO DO:

Step Four: Select Asset Class Mutual Funds. Select the asset class mutual funds that best Incorporate the concepts that we have discussed on a cost-effective basis. In chapter 10, you will find a list of many of the currently available retail asset class funds.

Step Five: Select a brokerage firm or broker. Find one who is knowledgeable with asset class investing and modern investment theory. Custodians, such as investment advisors or discount brokers, will make rebalancing much easier to complete.

(continued)

FIGURE 23-2   *Continued*

TO DO:

Step Four: Open An Account at one of the discount or full service brokerage firms. It is unlikely that one mutual fund family will have all the asset class mutual funds that you will need for your portfolio.

✓ Fund your IRA ($2,000), SEP or Keogh to the max to reap multiple tax benefits.

✓ Pay your IRA trustee or custodial fee with a separate check, so it is tax deductible.

✓ File on April 15.
✓ If you can't, get a four-month filing extension.

✓ Tele Tax at 800-829-4477. To contact the IRS on-line, click www.irs.ustreas.gov.

TO DO:

✓ Make spring cleaning pay off. Take an inventory of your household possessions and update insurance coverage.

✓ Moving? Do it before June, July, or August, the most popular, expensive months to move. If the move is job related, expenses may be deductible; save receipts and consult IRS publication #521, "Moving Expenses." Call 800-829-3676.

TO DO:

✓ Make A Semi-Annual Review Of Your Investments. Consult your financial plan; then call your advisor and decide which stocks, bonds, and mutual funds to hold and which to sell.

✓ Trade in low-yielding cash-like investments. Call your nearest Federal Reserve Bank or the Bureau of the Public Debt at 202-874-4000.

✓ Pay your quarterly estimated tax. Second installment (first was due April 15) is due on June 15. File Form 1040-ES.

TO DO:

✓ Save patriotically. EE U.S. Savings Bonds, tops in safety, are sold at local banks for as little as $50. Call 800-US-BONDS.

✓ Call your health insurance provider to confirm your coverage when traveling outside the U.S. If you need additional coverage, call Travel Guard International at 800-826-1300, TravMed at 800-732-5309 or U.S. Assist at 800-756-5900.

✓ Help your child open an IRA. Summer wages up to $2,000 can be used to fund it.

FIGURE 23-2   *Concluded*

TO DO:

✓ **File your tax return** if you applied for a four-month extension in April. Your return is due August 15.

✓ **Draw up a school-year budget** for and with children going away to secondary school or college. Set a monthly stipend. Agree on a policy for credit card use: for entertainment expenses? For emergencies only?

✓ **Look for good deals this month** on lawn and patio furniture, bathing suits, lawnmowers, barbecues.

TO DO:

✓ **Figure out what your child earned** from a summer job. A tax return must be filed for any dependent child who earns more than $4,150 a year. Failure to file may result in a penalty. For a free copy of IRS publication #4, "Student's Guide to Federal Income Tax," call 800-829-3676.

✓ **Pay the third installment of your estimated quarterly income taxes.** They're due by the 15th. Use Form 1040-ES.

TO DO:

✓ **Organize your financial documents before year's end.** This is the best way to avoid automatically renewing expensive insurance policies, overlooking valuable tax deductions and holding on to stocks, bonds, or mutual funds that have declined in value.

The Financial Planning Organizer Kit includes plastic-coated file dividers and a 48-page handbook ($19.95 plus $4.25 shipping). Call Financial Advantage at 800-695-3453.

✓ **Start saving for holiday gifts.** Open a money market account, fund it with the amount you plan to spend.

Call insurance carriers to confirm or extend coverage for a child away from home at school.

TO DO:

Step Six: Rebalance at least annually.
✓ By systematically rebalancing to the original model portfolio at least annually, you will gradually sell those asset classes that have gone up while buying those that currently have lower returns. This approach eliminates the negative results of being driven by emotions.

✓ **Review your employment benefits package.** October and November are benefits sign-up periods at many companies.

Visit your corporate benefits office. November is the month when most companies let employees revise job-benefits packages. Consider upping your 401(k) contribution.

SOURCES

For some of the best books around for anything you need, consult these.

1. Jane Bryant Quinn, *Making the Most of Your Money.* Simon & Schuster, 1997.

2. Just about anything from Peter Lynch.

3. *Personal Finance for Dummies* by Eric Tyson is excellent. I.DG Books worldwide, 1996.

4. Matt Seto and Steven Levingstone, *Whiz Kids of Wall Street, Investment Guide.* William Morrow & Co., 1997.

5. *The Intelligent Investor* by Benjamin Graham; *The Battle for Investment* by Gerald Lobe. HarperCollins, 1997.

6. *A Random Walk Down Wall Street* by Michael Burton G Malkiel. W.W. Norton & Co., 1996.

7. Charles Schwab, *Guide to Financial Independence.* Crown, 1998.

8. *Independently Wealthy—How to Build Financial Security in the New Economic Era,* by Dr. Robert Goodman. Irwin, 1996. Goodman is the senior economic advisor for Putnam Investments and the author of a new book, published by John Wiley & Sons, New York, 1997.

9. *The 9 Steps to Financial Freedom,* Crown, 1997.

10. *The Roaring 2000s,* Harry S. Dent, Simon & Schuster, 1998.

11. *Money Doesn't Grow on Trees,* Neale Godfrey Fireside, 1994.

12. *Best Practices for Financial Advisors,* Mary Rowland, Bloomberg, 1997.

Recommended Reading about Asset Class Investing

John J. Bowen, Jr. and Dan Goldie, *The Prudent Investor's Guide to Beating Wall Street at Its Own Game,* Second Edition hardcover; $24.95, McGraw-Hill, 1998.

For asset allocation see Roger C. Gibson, *Balancing Financial Risk,* hardcover; $45.00, Irwin, 1996.

For information on mutual funds, *Morningstar Mutual Funds* is the absolute best—it costs about $400+ per year. For more information, call (800) 735-0700, or you can write to Morningstar at 225 West Wacker Drive, Chicago, IL 60606; or visit their site: www.morningstar.net.com. It is published every 2 weeks, and it itemizes each mutual fund, performance, risk, portfolio operating history, and distribution information. It offers interviews with fund managers and gives advice on buying or avoiding particular funds.

Standard & Poor's *Stock Guide for Quick Review* used to belong on every broker's desk. It comes out weekly and is a 12-page publication called *Outlook.* It gives a ranking of the major companies' potential quality. An annual subscription to *Outlook* costs about $300. You can reach Standard & Poor's at (800) 221-5277, 65 Broadway, New York, NY 10006, or on-line at www.stockinfo.standard&poor.com.

For those who want to start or join an investment club, you can contact the National Association of Investment Corporations (NAIC), 71 W. 13 Mile Road, Madison Heights, MI 48071, telephone (248) 583-6242.

GLOSSARY

Accumulated Value: The value of all amounts accumulated under the contract prior to the annuity date.

Accumulation Unit: A measure of your ownership interest in the contract prior to the annuity date.

Administrative Fee: An annual fee, usually 0.15 percent or less of the daily subaccount asset value, charged to reimburse administrative expenses.

Advisor: One who gives investment advice in return for compensation.

Aggressive Growth: High-risk/reward investments, funds, or securities classes.

Analysis: Process of evaluating individual financial instruments (often stock) to determine whether they are an appropriate purchase.

Analysts: Those on Wall Street who study and recommend securities.

Annual Insurance Company Expenses: Charges for insurance companies' annual expenses included in annuity contracts. In addition to the asset management fees, there are three other annual charges: annual policy fee, mortality and expense risk, and administrative.

Annual Interest Income: The annual dollar income for a bond or savings account, calculated by multiplying the bond's coupon rate by its face value.

Annual Policy Fee (Maintenance Fee): An annual fee, usually $50 or less, charged for the maintenance of the annuity records. The fee pays accounting, customer reporting, and other general expenses associated with financial record-keeping requirements.

Annualized Return: The total return on an investment or portfolio over a period other than 1 year, restated as an equivalent return for a 1-year period.

Annuitant: The person whose life is used to determine the duration of any annuity payments and upon whose death, prior to the annuity date, benefits under the contract are paid. The recipient of annuity benefits; usually, but not always, the contract owner.

Annuitant's Beneficiary: The person(s) to whom any benefits are due upon the annuitant's death prior to the annuity date.

Annuity: A contract between an insurer and a recipient (annuitant) whereby the insurer guarantees to pay the recipient a stream of income in exchange for premium payment(s).

Annuity Date: The date on which annuity payments begin. The annuity date is always the first day of the month you specify.

Annuity Payment: One of a series of payments made under an annuity payment option.

Annuity Payment Option: One of several ways in which withdrawals from the contract may be made. Under a fixed annuity option, the dollar amount of each annuity payment does not change over time. Under a variable annuity option, the dollar amount of each annuity payment may change over time, depending upon the investment experience of the portfolio or portfolios you choose. Annuity payments are based on the contract's accumulated value as of 10 business days prior to the annuity date.

Annuity Unit Value: The value of each annuity unit, which is calculated each valuation period.

Asset Allocation: The decision as to how a customer should be invested among major asset classes in order to increase expected risk-adjusted return. Asset allocation may be two-way (stocks and bonds), three-way (stocks, bonds, and cash), or many-way (i.e., value mutual funds, growth mutual funds, small mutual funds, cash, foreign mutual funds, foreign bonds, real estate, and venture capital).

Asset Class: Group of assets composed of financial instruments with similar characteristics.

Asset Class Funds: Funds composed of financial instruments with similar characteristics. Unlike managers of index funds, asset fund managers actively manage costs when buying and selling for funds.

Asset Class Investing: The disciplined purchase of groups of securities with similar risk/reward profiles. This strategy is based on valid academic research, and its results are predictable rather than random.

Asset Mix: Combination of investable asset classes within a portfolio.

Average Daily Trading: The number of shares of stock traded in the preceding calendar month, multiplied by the current price and divided by 20 trading days.

Average Return: The measure of price of an asset, along with its income or yield on average over a specific period. The arithmetic mean is the simple average of the returns in a series. The arithmetic mean is the appropriate measure of typical performance for a single period.

Back-End Load: A fee charged at redemption by a mutual fund or a variable annuity to a buyer of shares.

Bailout Rate: Feature offered on some annuities that allows the customer to surrender the annuity with no penalty if the interest rate falls below a certain floor.

Balanced Index: A market index that serves as a basis of comparison for balanced portfolios. The balanced index used in the *Monitor* is comprised of a 60 percent weighting of the S&P 500 Index and a 40 percent weighting of the Shearson Lehman Hutton Government and Corporate Bond Index. The balanced index relates unmanaged market returns to a balanced portfolio more precisely than either a stock or a bond index would alone.

Balanced Mutual Fund: A mutual fund that includes two or more asset classes other than cash. In a typical balanced mutual fund, the asset classes are equities and fixed-income securities.

Basis Point: One-hundredth of a percentage point, or 0.01 percent. Basis points are often used to express changes or differences in yields, returns, or interest rates. Thus, if a portfolio has a total return of 10 percent versus 7 percent for the S&P 500, the portfolio is said to have outperformed the S&P 500 by 300 basis points.

Bear Market: A prolonged period of falling stock prices. There is no consensus on what constitutes a bear market or bear leg. SEI, one of the most widely used performance measurement services, normally defines a bear market or bear leg as a drop of at least 15 percent over two back-to-back quarters.

Beginning Value: The market value of a portfolio at the inception of the period being measured by the customer statement.

Benchmark: A standard by which investment performance or trading execution can be judged. The most widely used performance benchmark is the total return of the S&P 500.

Beneficiary: Similar to the beneficiary of a life insurance policy, the person who receives a death benefit when another party to the annuity contract dies prior to the date upon which the annuity begins paying out benefits.

Beta: The linear relationship between the return on the security and the return on the market. By definition, the market, usually measured by the S&P 500 Index, has beta of 1.00. Any stock or portfolio with a higher beta is generally more volatile than the market, while any with a lower beta is generally less volatile than the market.

Bond: Long-term, short-term, and high-yield. Debt instruments that pay lenders a regular return. Short-term bonds are 5 years or less. High-yield bonds pay lenders a higher rate of return because of perceived risk.

Bond Rating: Method of evaluating the possibility of default by a bond issuer. Standard & Poor's, Moody's Investors Service, and Fitch's Investors Service analyze the financial strength of each bond's issuer, whether a corporation or a government body. Their ratings range from AAA (highly unlikely to default) to D (in default). Bonds rated B or below are not investment grade—in other words, institutions that invest other people's money may not, under most state laws, buy them.

Book-to-Market Ratio: Size of company's book (net) value relative to the market price of the company.

Broker: An individual with a series 7 license entitled to buy and sell securities, especially stock, on behalf of clients and charge for that service.

Broker Dealer: A firm employing brokers among other financial professionals.

Bull Market: A prolonged period of rising stock prices. SEI, one of the most widely used performance measurement services, normally defines a bull market or bull leg as a rise of at least 15 percent over two back-to-back quarters.

Business Day: A day when the New York Stock Exchange is open for trading.

Call Option: An arrangement in which the investor has the right, but not an obligation, to buy a security at a preset price within a specified time. A put gives the investor the right to sell a security at a preset price within a specified time. Calls and puts are therefore essentially bets on whether the underlying security will rise or fall in price. The option holders gain or lose in proportion to changes in the values of the new indexes, which in turn reflect the net asset value performances of the funds that comprise the indexes.

Cap: Small cap, large cap. The stock market worth of an individual equity. Large-cap stocks can be found on the New York Stock Exchange. Small-cap stocks are often listed on the NASDAQ.

Capital Appreciation: The total return minus any income or dividends of the security.

Capital Appreciation or Depreciation: An increase or decrease in the value of a mutual fund or stock due to a change in the market price of the fund. For example, a stock that rises from $50 to $55 has a capital appreciation of 10 percent. Dividends are not included in appreciation. If the price of the stock fell to $45, it would have a depreciation of 10 percent.

Capital Preservation: Investment in a conservative manner so as not to put capital at risk.

Cash: Investment in any instrument (often short-term) that is easily liquidated.

Commission: A transaction fee commonly levied by brokers and other financial middlepeople.

Compound Annual Return: Geometric mean. The geometric mean is more appropriate when one is comparing the growth rate for an investment that is continually compounding.

Compounding: The reinvestment of dividends and/or interest and capital gains. This means that over time dividends, interest, and capital gains grow exponentially. For example, $100 earning compound interest at 10 percent per year accumulates to $110 at the end of the first year and $121 at the end of the second year, etc., based on this formula: compound sum=principal (1+ interest rate)(number of periods).

Conservative: A characteristic relating to a mutual fund, a stock, or an investment style. There is no precise definition of the term. Generally, the term is used when the mutual fund manager's emphasis is on the below-market betas.

Contract Anniversary: Any anniversary of the contract date.

Contract Date: The date of issue of this contract.

Contract Owner: The person or persons designated as the contract owner in the contract. The term shall also include any person named as joint owner. A joint owner shares ownership in all respects with the contract owner. Prior to the annuity date, the contract owner has the right to assign ownership, designate beneficiaries, make permitted withdrawals and exchanges among subaccounts, and guarantee rate options.

Contrarian: An investment approach characterized by buying securities that are out of favor.

Core Savings Strategy: The home of your safe dollars that provides you overall financial security. A long-term commitment of savings not to be touched except in an emergency.

Correction: A reversal in the price of a stock, or the stock market as a whole, within a larger trend. While corrections are most often thought of as declines within an overall market rise, a correction can also be a temporary rise in the midst of a longer-term decline.

Correlation: A statistical measure of the degree to which the movement of two variables is related.

Coupon: The periodic interest payment on a bond. When expressed as an annual percentage, it is called the *coupon rate*. When multiplied by the face value of the bond, the coupon rate gives the annual interest income.

CPI: Consumer price index, maintained by the Bureau of Labor Statistics, a measure of the changes in the cost of a specified group of consumer products relative to a base period. Because it represents the rate of inflation, the CPI can be used as a general benchmark for gauging the maintenance of purchasing power.

Currency: A nation's paper notes, once redeemable but not now.

Currency Risk: Possibility that foreign currency one holds may fall in value relative to the investor's home currency, thus devaluing overseas investments.

Current Return on Equity (ROE): A ratio that measures profitability as the return on common stockholders' equity. It is calculated by dividing the reported earnings per share for the latest 12-month period by the book value per share.

Current Yield: A bond's annual interest payment as a percentage of its current market price. The current yield is calculated by dividing the annual coupon interest for a bond by the current market price. The coupon rate and the current yield on a bond are equal when the bond is selling at par. Thus, a $1,000 bond with a coupon of 10 percent that is currently selling at $1,000 will have a current yield of 10.0 percent. However, if the bond's price drops to $800, the current yield becomes 12.5 percent.

Death Benefit: The greater of the contract's accumulated value on the date the company receives due proof of death of the annuitant or the adjusted death benefit. If any portion of the contract's accumulated value on the date that we receive proof of the annuitant's death is derived from the multiyear guaranteed rate option, that portion of the accumulated value will be adjusted by a positive market value adjustment factor, if applicable.

Deferred Annuity: An annuity whose contract provides that payments to the annuitant be postponed until a number of periods have elapsed, e.g., when the annuitant attains a certain age.

Deviation: Movement of instrument or asset class away from expected direction. In investment terminology it is most often associated with asset-class analysis.

Dissimilar Price Movement: The process whereby different asset classes and markets move in different directions.

Diversification: The way large sponsors reduce risk by using multiple mutual fund styles. In broad terms, a first time investor might diversify his or her investments among mutual funds, real estate, international investments, and money market instruments. A mutual fund might diversity by investing in many companies in many different industry groups.

Dividend: The payment from a company's earnings normally paid on common shares declared by a company's board of directors to be distributed pro rata among the shares outstanding.

Dollar Cost Averaging: A system of buying stock or mutual funds at regular intervals with a fixed dollar amount. Under this system an investor buys by the dollar's worth rather than by the number of shares.

Dow Jones Industrial Average (DJIA): A price-weighted average of 30 leading blue-chip industrial stocks, calculated by adding the prices of the 30 stocks and adjusting by a divisor, which reflects any stock dividends or splits. The Dow Jones Industrial Average is the most widely quoted index of the stock market, but it is not widely used as a benchmark for evaluating performance. The S&P 500 Index, which is more representative of the market, is the benchmark most widely used by performance measurement services.

Efficiency: The process of generating maximum reward from funds invested across a spectrum of asset classes.

Efficient Frontier: The point where the maximum amount of risk that an investor is willing to tolerate intersects the maximum amount of reward that can potentially be generated.

Emerging Growth Fund: New companies that may be relatively small in size with the potential to grow much larger.

Emerging Growth Mutual Fund: Mutual fund comprised of industries and companies whose growth rates are likely to be both rapid and independent of the overall stock market. *Emerging,* of course, means new. This implies such companies may be relatively small with the potential to grow much larger. Such stocks are generally much more volatile than the stock market in general and require constant, close attention to developments.

Emerging Markets: Countries beginning to build financial marketplaces with appropriate safeguards.

EPS (Earnings per Share) Growth: The annualized rate of growth in reported earnings per share of stock.

Equities: Stocks. Equity mutual funds are made up of many individual stocks. A stock is a right of ownership in a corporation. The shorthand name for stocks, bonds, and mutual funds is equities.

Excellent or Unexcellent Companies: Companies with either high (excellent) or low (unexcellent) stock market performances.

Exchange: One voluntary transfer from any subaccount or general account guaranteed option.

Exchange Privilege: A shareholder's right to switch from one mutual fund to another within one fund family. This is often done at no additional charge. This enables investors to put their money in an aggressive-growth stock fund, e.g., when they expect the market to turn up strongly, then switch to a money market fund when they anticipate a downturn.

Execution Price: The negotiated price at which a security is purchased or sold.

Expected Return: The expected amount to be received under an annuity contract, based on the periodic payment and the annuitant's life expectancy when the benefits begin. Calculated as the weighted average of its possible returns, where the weights are the corresponding probability for each return.

Expenses: Costs of maintaining an invested portfolio.

Fee-Based: Applies to a manager, advisor, or broker whose charges are based on a set amount rather than transaction charges.

Fee-Only: Applies to a manager, advisor, or broker who charges an investor a preset amount for services.

Financial Advisor or Planner: One who helps investors with a wide variety of financial and investing issues including retirement, estate planning, etc. Often licensed and working for a larger financial entity.

Fixed Annuities: The type of annuity referred to by the interest rate paid by the issuing insurance company on the fund's place in the annuity. The fixed annuity offers security in that the rate of return is certain. Typically, with a fixed annuity the insurance company declares a current interest rate and sets the interest rate.

Fixed-Income Mutual Funds: This term largely speaks for itself. Fixed-income mutual fund managers invest money in bonds, notes, and other debt instruments. They have a broad range of styles, involving market timing, swapping to gain quality or yield, setting up maturity ladders, etc. A typical division of the fixed-income market is between short (up to 3 years), intermediate (3 to 15 years), and long (15 to 30 years).

Forecasts: Predictions of analysts usually associated with stock picking and active money management.

Free Look: A 10-15 day period in most annuity contracts after contract delivery when the owner can return the annuity and receive a full refund of the premium.

Front-End Load: A fee charged when an investor buys a mutual fund or a variable annuity.

Fund Rating: Evaluation of the performance of invested money pools, often mutual funds by such entities as Chicago-based Morningstar.

Fund Shares: Shares in a mutual fund.

Fundamentals: The financial statistics that traditional analysts and many valuation models use. Fundamental data include stock, earnings, dividends, assets and liabilities, inventories, debt, etc. Fundamental data are in contrast to items used in technical analysis, such as price momentum, volume trends, and short-sales statistics.

General Account: The account which contains all our assets other than those held in our separate accounts.

Global Diversification: Investment of funds around the world in regions and markets with dissimilar price movements.

Guaranteed Interest Rate: In a fixed annuity, the minimum interest rate that is guaranteed by the insurance company to be credited each year to the cash value.

Guaranteed Rate Options: The 1-year guaranteed rate option and the multiyear guaranteed rate option.

Hot Tip: Slang for an individual investment, often a stock, that is apparently poised to rise (but may not).

Income Growth Mutual Fund: The primary purpose in security selection here is to achieve a current yield significantly higher than that of the S&P 500. The stability of the dividend and the rate of growth of the dividends are also of concern to the income buyer. These portfolios may own more utilities and less high technology and may own convertible preferreds and convertible bonds.

Index Fund: A passively managed portfolio designed and computer-controlled to track the performance of a certain index, such as the S&P 500. In general, such mutual funds have performance within a few basis points of the target index. The most popular index mutual funds are those that track the S&P 500, but special index funds, such as those based on the Russell 1000 or the Wilshire 5000, are also available.

Indexing: Disciplined investing in a specific group (asset class) of securities so as to benefit from its aggregate performance.

Individual Investor: Buyer or seller of securities for personal portfolio.

Investment objective: The money goals one wishes to reach.

Inflation: A monetary phenomenon generated by an overexpansion of credit which drives up prices of assets while diminishing the worth of paper currency.

Institutional Investor: Corporation or fund with market presence.

Interest: The rate a borrower pays a lender.

Interest Rate Guarantee: Guarantee that the renewal rate will never fall below a particular level. Typical policies today have a 4 to 5 percent guarantee.

Intrinsic Value: The theoretical valuation or price for a stock. The valuation is determined by using a valuation theory or model. The resulting value is compared with the current market price. If the intrinsic value is greater than the market price, the stock is considered undervalued.

Invest: Place, in a disciplined fashion, money in financial instruments so as to gain a return. Given the emergence of valid academic research regarding asset class investment methods, an individual who depends mostly on active management and stock picking may come to be considered a speculator rather than an investor.

Investment Advisor: See *Advisor.*

Investment Discipline: A specific money strategy one espouses.

Investor Discomfort: Realization that risk is not appropriate and reward is not predictable in a given portfolio.

Investment Guru: A money manager or analyst, often employed by Wall Street and commonly looked on as having special insight into the market. See *Noise.*

Investment Philosophy: Strategy justifying short- or long-term buying and selling of securities.

Investment Policy: An investment policy statement that forces the investor to confront risk tolerance, return objectives, time horizon, liquidity needs, the amount of funds available for investment, and the investment methodology to be followed.

Investment Policy Statement: Embodiment of the essence of the financial planning process. It includes (1) assessing where you are now, (2) detailing where you want to go, and (3) developing a strategy to get there.

Investment Wisdom: Process of understanding valid academic research concerning asset allocation.

IPOs: Initial public offerings. The sale of stock in a company going public for the first time.

Joint Owner: The person or persons designated as the contract owner in an annuity contract. A joint owner shares ownership in all respects with the contract owner.

Liquidity: Ability to generate cash on demand when necessary.

Load Fund: A mutual fund that is sold for a sales charge (load) by a brokerage firm or other sales representative. Such funds may be stock, bond, or commodity funds, with conservative or aggressive objectives. The stated advantage of a load fund is that the salesperson will explain the fund to the customer and advise him or her when it is appropriate to sell as well as when to buy more shares.

Lump-Sum Distribution: Single payment to a beneficiary covering the entire amount of an agreement. Participants in individual retirement accounts, pension plans, profit-sharing, and executive stock option plans generally can opt for a lump-sum distribution if the taxes are not too burdensome when the participants become eligible.

Management Fee: Charge against investor assets for managing the portfolio of an open- or closed-end mutual fund as well as for such services as shareholder relations or administration. The fee, as disclosed in the prospectus, is a fixed percentage of the fund's asset value, typically 1 percent or less per year.

Margin: A loan often offered to investors by broker dealers for the purpose of allowing the investor to purchase additional securities. In a down market, margin loans can be called and portfolios liquidated when the value of the loan threatens to exceed the value of the portfolio.

Market: In investing terms, a place where securities are traded. Formerly meant a physical location but now may refer to an electronic one as well.

Market Bottom: The date that the bear leg of a market cycle reaches its low, not identified until some time after the fact. In the peak-to-peak cycle ended September 30, 1987, the market bottom came on August 12, 1982, when the S&P 500 closed at 102.42, down 27.1 percent from its previous bull market peak. The most recent bear leg ended on December 4, 1987, when the S&P 500 closed at 223.9. Market bottoms can also be defined as the month or quarter end closest to the actual bottom date.

Market Capitalization: The current value of a company, determined by multiplying the latest available number of outstanding common shares by the current market price of a share. For example, on December 29, 1989, IBM had about 590 million shares outstanding, and the stock closed at $94.13. Thus, its market capitalization was $55 billion. Market cap is also an indication of the trading liquidity of a particular issue.

Market Timing: The attempt to base investment decisions on the expected direction of the market. If stocks are expected to decline, the timer may elect to hold a portion of the portfolio in cash equivalents or bonds. Timers may base their decisions on fundamentals (e.g., selling stocks when the market's price/book ratio reaches a certain level), on technical considerations (such as declining momentum or excessive investor optimism), or a combination of both.

Market Value: The market or liquidation value of a given security or of an entire pool of assets.

Matrix Pricing: As an example, an asset class fund that is limited to securities with maturities of 2 years or less. The manager will extend maturities when there is a reward for doing so (when the yield curve is steep), and will hold short maturities when longer maturities do not provide additional expected return (when the yield curve is flat or inverted).

Maturities: For bonds, the date at which a borrower must redeem the capital portion of the loan.

Model Portfolio: A theoretical construct of an investment or series of investments.

Modern Portfolio Theory: In 1950, Professor Harry Markowitz started to build an investment strategy that took more than 30 years to develop and be recognized as modern portfolio theory; he won the Nobel Prize for his work in 1990.

Money Market Fund: Fund of short-term fixed instruments and cash equivalents. These instruments make up the portfolio, and their objective is to maximize principal protection. Even though these accounts have short- term (one-day) liquidity, they typically pay more like 90- to 180-day CDs versus passbook or one-week CDs.

Municipal Bonds: Fixed-income securities issued by government agencies.

Mutual Fund: A pool of managed money, regulated by the Securities and Exchange Commission, in which investors can purchase shares. Funds are not managed individually as they might be by a private money manager.

Mutual Fund Families: A number of funds with different investment objectives within a family of funds. For example, a mutual fund family may include a money market fund, a government bond fund, a corporate bond fund, a blue-chip stock fund, and a more speculative stock fund. If an investor buys a fund in the family, she or he is allowed to exchange that fund for another in the same family. This is usually done with no additional sales charge.

National Association of Securities Dealers, Inc. (NASD): The principal association of over-the-counter (OTC) brokers and dealers that establishes legal and ethical standards of conduct for its members. NASD was established in 1939 to regulate the OTC market in much the same manner as organized exchanges monitor actions of their members.

Net Asset Value (NAV): The market value of each share of a mutual fund. This figure is derived by taking a fund's total assets (securities, cash, and receivables), deducting liabilities, and then dividing that total by the number of shares outstanding.

Net Trade: Generally, an over-the-counter trade involving no explicit commission. The investment advisor's compensation is in the spread between the cost of the security and the price paid by the customer. Also, a trade in which shares are exchanged directly with the issuer.

Noise: Information about investing that is not supported by valid academic research.

No-Load Fund: Mutual fund offered by an open-end investment company that imposes no sales charge (load) on its shareholders. Investors buy shares in no-load funds directly from the fund companies, rather than through a broker, as is done in load funds. Because no broker is used, no advice is given on when to buy or sell.

Nominal Return: The actual current dollar growth in an asset's value over a given period. See also *Total Return* and *Real Return.*

Nonqualified Contract: An annuity which is not used as part of or in connection with a qualified retirement plan.

Operating Expense: Cost associated with running a fund or portfolio.

Optimization: A process whereby a portfolio, invested using valid academic theory in various asset classes, is analyzed to ensure that risk/reward parameters have not drifted from stated goals.

Outperform: Exceed expectations or historical performance for any given market.

Over-the-Counter: A market made between securities dealers who act as either principal or broker for their clients. This is the principal market for U.S. government and municipal bonds.

Owner's Designated Beneficiary: The person to whom ownership of an annuity contract passes upon the contract owner's death, unless the contract owner was also the annuitant, in which case the annuitant's beneficiary is entitled to the death benefit. (*Note:* this transfer of ownership to the owner's designated beneficiary will generally not be subject to probate, but will be subject to estate and inheritance taxes. Consult with your tax and estate advisor to be sure which rules will apply to you.)

Packaged Products: Specific types of products underwritten and packaged by manufacturing companies that can be bought and sold directly through those companies. Packaged products are not required to go through a clearing process. Packaged products include mutual funds, unit investment trusts (UITs), limited partnership interests, and annuities.

Partial Liquidity: In most annuities, ability of policyholders to withdraw up to 10 percent per year of their account value without a penalty or surrender charge.

Payee: The contract owner, annuitant, annuitant's beneficiary, or any other person, estate, or legal entity to whom benefits are to be paid.

Percentage Points: Used to describe the difference between two readings that are percentages. For example, if a portfolio's performance was 18.2 percent versus the S&P 500's 14.65, it outperformed the S&P by 3.6 percentage points.

Portfolio: A separate investment series of the funds. Also used to refer to the subaccount that invests in the corresponding portfolio.

Portfolio Turnover: Removal of funds from one financial instrument to place in another. This process can be costly.

Price/Earnings (P/E) Ratio: The current price divided by reported earnings per share of stock for the latest 12-month period. For example, a stock with earnings per share during the trailing year of $5 and currently selling at $50 per share has a price/earnings ratio of 10.

Principal: The original dollar amount invested.

Prospectus: The document required by the Securities and Exchange Commission that accompanies the sale of a mutual fund or annuity, outlining risks associated with certain types of funds or securities, fees, and management. At the core of the prospectus is a description of the fund's investment objectives and the portfolio manager's philosophy.

Put: Right of the investor to sell a security at a preset price within a specified time.

Qualified Contract: An annuity contract that is part of an employee benefit plan and has met certain requirements under the Internal Revenue Code. The contributions made into a qualified contract are income tax-deductible to the employer making the contribution.

Quality Growth Mutual Fund: Long-term investment in high-quality growth stocks, some of which might be larger, emerging companies while others might be long-established household names. Such a portfolio might have volatility equal to or greater than that of the overall market, but less than that of an emerging growth portfolio.

Quartile: A ranking of comparative portfolio performance. The top 25 percent of mutual fund managers are in the first quartile, those ranking from 26 to 50 percent are in the second quartile, from 51 to 75 percent in the third quartile, and the lowest 25 percent in the fourth quartile.

Rate of Return: The profits earned by a security, measured as a percentage of earned interest and/or dividends and/or appreciation.

Ratings: Performance and creditworthiness measurement of funds and corporations generated by Lipper, Moody's, Morningstar, and others. These ratings, when used to evaluate active fund managers, may be misleading since past performance is no guarantee of future success.

Real Return: The inflation-adjusted return on an asset. Inflation adjusted returns are calculated by subtracting the rate of inflation from an asset's apparent, or nominal, return. For example, if common stocks earn a total return of 10.3 percent over a period of time, but inflation during that period is 3.1 percent, the real return is the difference, or 7.2 percent.

Rebalancing: A process whereby funds are shifted within asset classes and between asset class to ensure the maintenance of the efficient frontier. See *Optimization.*

Reinvested Dividends: Dividends paid by a particular mutual fund that are reinvested in that same mutual fund. Some mutual funds offer automatic dividend reinvestment programs. In the complex equation theoretically used to determine the performance of the S&P 500, each company's dividend is reinvested in the stock of that company.

REITs: Real estate investment trusts. Bundled, securitized real estate assets often traded on the New York Stock Exchange.

Relative Return: The return of a stock or a mutual fund portfolio compared with some index, usually the S&P 500. For example, in 1989, American Brands had a total return of 12.2 percent in *absolute* terms. In isolation, that sounds good. After all, the historical annualized return on common stocks has been 10.3 percent. But because the S&P 500 had a return of 31.7 percent in 1989, American Brands underperformed the index in *relative* terms by 19.5 percentage points. Thus, its relative return was –19.5 percentage points.

Renewal Rate History: A copy of bank renewal rates, to see how their rates have held after the initial rate guarantee period.

Risk: The uncertainty of future rates of return, which includes the possibility of loss. This variability or uncertainty causes "rational" investors to expect higher returns on investments where the actual timing or amount of payoffs is not guaranteed.

Risk-Free Rate of Return: The return on an asset that is considered virtually riskless. U.S. government Treasury bills are typically used as the risk-free asset because of their short time horizon and the low probability of default.

Risk, Systematic: Potential for predictable, quantifiable loss of funds through the application of valid academic research to the process of disciplined asset class investing.

Risk Tolerance: Investor's innate ability to deal with the potential of losing money without abandoning investment process.

Risk, Unsystematic: Associated with investment in an undiversified portfolio of individual instruments through active management.

ROI: Return on investment. The amount of money generated over time by placement of funds in specific financial instruments.

Rule of 72: Divide the number 72 by the compound interest rate you have chosen. The result is the number of years it takes your money to double.

Securities: Tradable financial instruments.

Securities and Exchange Commission (SEC): The keystone law in the regulation of securities markets. It governs exchanges, over-the-counter markets, broker-dealers, the conduct of secondary markets, extension of credit in securities transactions, the conduct of corporate insiders, and principally the prohibition of fraud and manipulation in securities transactions. It also outlines the powers of the Securities and Exchange Commission to interpret, supervise, and enforce the securities laws of the United States.

Securities Investor Protection Corporation (SIPC): A government-sponsored organization created in 1970 to insure investor accounts at brokerage firms in the event of the brokerage firm's insolvency and liquidation. The maximum insurance of $500,000, including a maximum of $100,000 in cash assets per account, covers customer losses due to brokerage house insolvency, not customer losses caused by security price fluctuations. SIPC coverage is conceptually similar to Federal Deposit Insurance Corporation coverage of customer accounts at commercial banks.

Security Selection: Process of picking securities, especially stocks for investment purposes.

Separate Account: An account independent of the general assets of the company. The separate account invests in the portfolios.

Shares: Specific portions of tradable equity, a share of stock. It generally refers to common or preferred stocks.

Single-Premium Deferred Annuity: An annuity purchased with a lump-sum premium payment which earns interest for a period of years before the payout period begins.

S&P Common Stock Rankings: Rankings that measure historical growth and stability of earnings and dividends. The system includes eight rankings:

A+, A, and A–	Above average
B+	Average
B, B–, and C	Below average
NR	Insufficient historical data or not amenable to ranking process.

As a matter of policy, S&P does not rank the stocks of foreign companies, investment companies, and certain finance-oriented companies.

S&P 500 Index: The performance benchmark most widely used by sponsors, managers, and performance measurement services. This index includes 400 industrial stocks, 20 transportation stocks, 40 financial stocks, and 40 public utilities. Performance is measured on a capitalization-weighted basis. The index is maintained by Standard & Poor's Corporation, a subsidiary of McGraw-Hill, Inc.

Speculator: One who uses an active management style to invest.

Standard Deviation: How far from the mean historic performance has been, either higher or lower. Volatility can be statistically measured using standard deviation. The mean is simply the middle point between the two historic extremes of the performance of the investment you are examining. The standard deviation measurement helps explain what the distribution of returns likely will be. The greater the range of returns, the greater the risk. Generally, the current price of a security reflects the expected total return of its investment and its perceived risk. The lower the risk, the lower the return expected.

Stock: A contract signifying ownership of a portion of a public or private company.

Stock Picker: Someone who is actively trying to select companies whose equity may rise in the short or long term. Valid academic research shows that this process is unworkable and results are no better than random.

Strategic Asset Allocation: Determination of an appropriate asset mix for a customer based on long-term capital market conditions, expected returns, and risks.

Subaccount: That portion of the variable annuities separate account that invests in shares of the funds' portfolios. Each subaccount will invest in only a single portfolio.

Surrender Charge: A charge made for a withdrawal from (in excess of 10 percent per year) or surrender of an annuity contract before the annuity starting date; often scales down over time.

Surrender Value: The accumulated value, adjusted to reflect any applicable market value adjustment for amounts allocated to the multiyear guaranteed rate option, less any early withdrawal charges for amounts allocated to the 1-year guaranteed rate option, less any amount allocated to the guaranteed equity option, less any premium taxes incurred but not yet deducted.

Systemic Withdrawal Plan: A program in which shareholders receive payments from their mutual fund investments at regular intervals. Typically, these payments are drawn first from the fund's dividends and capital gains distribution, if any, and then from principal as needed.

401(k) Section of the Internal Revenue Code: In simplest terms, a before-tax employee savings plan.

12b–1 Mutual Fund: Mutual fund that assesses shareholders for some of its promotion expenses. These funds are usually no-load, so no brokers are involved in the sale to the public. Instead, the funds normally rely on advertising and public relations to build their assets. The charge usually amounts to about 1 percent or less of a fund's assets. A 12b-1 fund must be specifically registered as such with the Securities and Exchange Commission, and the fact that such charges are levied must be disclosed.

Tactical Allocation: Investment strategy allocating assets according to investor expectations of directions of regional markets and asset classes.

Tax-Efficient Fund: Money pool which makes no taxable distributions to investors.

Technical Analysis: Any investment approach that judges the attractiveness of particular stocks or the market as a whole based on market data, such as price patterns, volume, momentum, or investor sentiment, as opposed to fundamental financial data, such as earnings dividends.

Time Horizon: The amount of time someone can wait to generate or take profits from an investment.

Time-Weighted Rate of Return: The rate at which $1 invested at the beginning of a period would grow if no additional capital were invested and no cash withdrawals were made. It provides an indication of value added by the investment manager and allows comparisons to the performance of other investment managers and market indexes.

Total Return: A standard measure of performance or return including both capital appreciation (or depreciation) and dividends or other income received. For example, a stock is priced at $60 at the start of a year and pays an annual dividend of $4. If the stock moves up to $70 in price, the appreciation component is 16.7 percent, the yield component is 6.7 percent, and the total return is 23.4 percent. That oversimplification does not take into account any earnings on the reinvested dividends.

Trading Costs: Fees or commissions paid to move money from one financial instrument to another.

Treasury Bills: A U.S. financial security issued by Federal Reserve banks for the Treasury as a means of borrowing money for short periods. The bills are sold at a discount from their maturity value, pay no coupons, and have maturities of up to 1 year. Because they are a direct obligation of the federal government, they are free of default risk. Most Treasury bills are purchased by commercial banks and held as part of their secondary reserves. Treasury bills regulate the liquidity base of the banking system in order to control the money supply. For example, if the authorities wish to expand the money supply, they can buy Treasury bills, which increase the reserves of the banking system and induce a multiple expansion of bank deposits.

Transaction Costs: Any fees or commissions generated and paid in the management of a portfolio. Another term for execution costs. Total transaction costs (or the cost of buying and selling stocks) have three components: (1) the actual dollars paid to the broker/advisor in commissions; (2) the market impact, i.e., the impact a manager's trade has on the market price for the stock (this varies with the size of the trade and the skill of the trader); and (3) the opportunity cost of the return (positive or negative) given up by not executing the trade instantaneously.

Turnover: The volume or percentage of buying or selling activity within a mutual fund portfolio relative to the mutual fund portfolio's size.

Underperform: Fail to meet expectations; applies to securities or markets.

Value Added: Value of returns over and above that of the stock market.

Value Mutual Fund: In this instance, the mutual fund manager uses various tests to determine an intrinsic value for a given security, and tries to purchase the security substantially below that value. The goal and hope are that the stock price in the fund will ultimately rise to the stock's fair value or greater. Price to earnings, price to sales, price to cash flow, price to book value, and price to breakup value (or true net asset value) are some of the ratios examined in such an approach.

Value Stocks: Stocks with high book-to-market valuations, i.e., companies doing poorly in the market that may have the potential to do better.

Variable Annuities: Insurance-based investment products which, like other forms of annuities, allow for growth of invested premiums to be free from taxation until withdrawals are made from the contract. Unique to variable annuities are several forms of investment alternatives that vary in potential for both reward and risk. Variable-annuity choices are broad enough that an investor can employ either an aggressive or a conservative approach, or a combination of both, while enjoying the benefits of tax-deferred growth. Guarantee of principal from loss upon death of the owner is covered by a death benefit provision.

Variable Annuity Accumulation and Distribution Phases: Two phases of the "life" of an annuity. The initial phase is the accumulation phase. This is the period in which contributions are made, either as a lump sum or in systematic payments. The contributions are invested in either a fixed or variable annuity. The assets compound tax-deferred until the contract owner makes the decision to distribute (second, distribution phase) the assets, either in a lump sum or systematically.

Volatility: The extent to which market values and investment returns are uncertain or fluctuate. Another word for *risk,* volatility is gauged by using such measures as beta, mean absolute deviation, and standard deviation.

Weighting: A term usually associated with proportions of assets invested in a particular region or securities index to generate a specific risk/reward profile.

Yield (Current Yield): For stocks, the percentage return paid in dividends on a common or preferred stock, calculated by dividing the indicated annual dividend by the market price of the stock. For example, if a stock sells for $40 and pays a dividend of $2 per share, it has a yield of 5 percent (or, $2 divided by $40).

For bonds, the coupon rate of interest divided by the market price is called current yield. For example, a bond selling for $1,000 with a 10 percent coupon offers a 10 percent current yield. If the same bond were selling for $500, it would offer a 20 percent yield to an investor who bought it for $500. (As a bond's price falls, its yield rises, and vice versa.)

Yield Curve: A chart or graph showing the price of securities (usually fixed income) through time. A flat or inverted yield curve of fixed-income instruments is thought by many to be an indicator of recession. This is because those who borrow at the far end of the curve usually pay more for their money than those who borrow for only a little while. When the yield curve is flat or inverted, there is little demand for long-term money, and this can be interpreted as a signal that there is little demand in the economy for the products that long-term borrowing would generate.

Yield to Maturity: The discount rate that equates the present value of the bond's cash flows (semiannual coupon payments, the redemption value) with the market price. The yield to maturity will actually be earned if (1) the investor holds the bond to maturity and (2) the investor is able to reinvest all coupon payments at a rate equal to the yield to maturity. When a bond is selling at par, the yield to maturity and the coupon rate are equal.

INDEX

About the Author

TODAY, LARRY CHAMBERS writes for some of the top national investment advisors representing over $3 billion in asset classes, as well as for one of the nation's leading CPA firms. Chambers has been published by major publishing houses, including Irwin, McGraw-Hill, Random House, Times Mirror, Dow Jones, and John Wiley & Sons, as well as featured in hundreds of national investment trade magazines.

The First Time Investor—Starting Out Safe and Smart, was a 1995 *Fortune* Book-of-the-Month Club selection; *The Wrap Advisor,* an Irwin best seller; and *Recondo,* published by Ballantine Books, a division of Random House, Inc., a specialty bestseller about the author's experiences in Vietnam during which he attended the U.S. Army Special Forces Reconnaissance School. (*Recondo* was the December 1995 main selection for the Military Book Club.)

After attending the University of Utah, where he received bachelor's and master's degrees and was elected to the Phi Kappa Phi honor society, Chambers joined E.F. Hutton. At E.F. Hutton, he gained experience in managed money consulting for over 500 private and institutional accounts, including pension and profit-sharing plans, foundations, state retirement funds, and university endowments. He achieved an outstanding track record, was named one of the top 20 brokers out of more than 5,000, and recieved numerous awards and acknowledgments.

Chambers is a member of the American Society of Journalists and Authors and the Society of American Business Editors and Writers, and he is on the advisory board for the *Journal of Investing,* an Institutional Investor publication.